Emissions Trading for Climate Policy

The 1997 Kyoto Conference introduced emissions trading as a new policy instrument for climate protection. Bringing together scholars in the fields of economics, political science, and law, this book provides a description, analysis, and evaluation of different aspects of emissions trading as an instrument to control greenhouse gases. The authors analyze theoretical aspects of regulatory instruments for climate policy, provide an overview of US experience with market-based instruments, draw lessons from existing trading schemes for the control of greenhouse gases, and discuss options for emissions trading in climate policy. They also highlight the background of climate policy and instrument choice in the US and Europe and of the emerging new systems in Europe, particularly the new EU directive for a CO_2 emissions trading system.

BERND HANSJÜRGENS is Professor of Economics at Martin Luther University Halle-Wittenberg. He is also the Head of the Department of Economics, UFZ Center for Environmental Research Leipzig-Halle.

Emissions Trading for Climate Policy

US and European Perspectives

Edited by

Bernd Hansjürgens

CAMBRIDGE
UNIVERSITY PRESS

CAMBRIDGE UNIVERSITY PRESS
Cambridge, New York, Melbourne, Madrid, Cape Town, Singapore,
São Paulo, Delhi, Dubai, Tokyo

Cambridge University Press
The Edinburgh Building, Cambridge CB2 8RU, UK

Published in the United States of America by Cambridge University Press, New York

www.cambridge.org
Information on this title: www.cambridge.org/9780521142045

First published 2005
This digitally printed version 2010

A catalogue record for this publication is available from the British Library

Library of Congress Cataloguing in Publication data

Emissions trading for climate policy: US and European perspectives/edited
by Bernd Hansjürgens.
   p. cm
Includes bibliographical references and index.
ISBN 0 521 84872 5
   1. Emissions trading. 2. Emissions trading–United States. 3. Emissions
trading–European Union countries. I. Hansjürgens, Bernd.
HC79.P55E515 2005 363.738′7–dc22 2005047003

ISBN 978-0-521-84872-5 Hardback
ISBN 978-0-521-14204-5 Paperback

Contents

Figures

Tables

Contributors

MIKAEL SKOU ANDERSEN NERI (Danish Environmental Institute)

SVEN BODE Hamburger Weltwirtschaftliches Institut

A. DENNY ELLERMAN Center for Energy and Environmental Policy Research, Massachusetts Institute of Technology

CAROLYN FISCHER Resources for the Future

HENRIK HAMMAR Department of Economics, Gothenburg University

BERND HANSJÜRGENS UFZ Center for Environmental Research Leipzig-Halle

CHARLES D. KOLSTAD Bren School of Environmental Science and Management, University of California at Santa Barbara

RICHARD D. MORGENSTERN Resources for the Future

MICHAEL RODI Law Faculty, University of Greifswald

REIMUND SCHWARZE Institute for Economics, Technical University Berlin

ROBERT N. STAVINS John F. Kennedy School of Government, Harvard University

THOMAS STERNER Department of Economics, Gothenburg University

GERT TINGGAARD SVENDSEN Department of Economics, The Aarhus School of Business

PETER ZAPFEL Environment Directorate-General, European Commission

Preface

Since the Kyoto Protocol was signed in 1997, emissions trading has become a widely discussed instrument for climate policy. One reason for the attention emissions trading has received is that it had already been the subject of intense debate in the United States owing to the introduction of several national US programs in the early 1980s and 1990s. However, the idea of using emissions trading as an instrument for climate policy has not yet received much attention in the literature.

The aim of this book is to help fill this gap by bringing together scholars in the fields of economics, political science, and law, and thereby providing a description, analysis, and evaluation of various aspects of emissions trading as an instrument for controlling greenhouse gases.

The chapters of this book were first presented and discussed at the "Climate Protection and Emissions Trading – US and European Perspectives" conference in Dresden (Germany) on October 20–22, 2002; the content was then revised for the purpose of this book. The conference was supported and financed by the Egon Sohmen Foundation. I would like to thank the Foundation for its strong support for the whole enterprise.

In the preparation of the conference and the book I received assistance from Dr. Frank Wätzold and Frank Gagelmann. I also owe thanks to Ms. Ogarit Uhlman, without whose outstanding organizational support the conference could not have taken place. In addition, two anonymous referees provided helpful comments on preliminary versions, which clearly improved the quality of the book.

Production of this book would not have been possible without Anton Georgiev's preparation of the index. Finally, I would like to thank Sabine Linke for her diligent efforts in assembling the text, tables, graphs, and references from the various authors into a coherent manuscript.

BERND HANSJÜRGENS

The Egon Sohmen Foundation

Egon Sohmen was born in Linz, Austria, on June 1, 1930 and died in Heidelberg, Federal Republic of Germany, on March 8, 1977. He was educated at the universities of Vienna, Kansas, and Tübingen, and at the Massachusetts Institute of Technology, from which he received a doctorate in economics in 1958. He taught economics at Yale University from 1958 to 1961, at the University of Saarland in Saarbrücken from 1961 to 1969, and at Heidelberg University from 1969 to his death. Sabbatical leave was spent at the University of Minnesota in 1963–64, and at the Smithsonian Institution in Washington, DC in the spring of 1975.

Sohmen played a significant part in the 1960s in making the case for flexible exchange rates respectable. He wrote widely on the subject, attacking the Bretton Woods system and insisting that free-floating would produce exchange rates that approached equilibrium continuously, as opposed to fixed-rate systems with their encouragement of speculation, wide departures from equilibrium, and ultimately the necessity of parity change. With the adoption of floating rates in 1973, he turned his attention to other problems in economic theory, with an emphasis on competitive markets.

The Egon Sohmen Foundation was founded in 1987 by Helmut Sohmen in memory of his brother. The Foundation is a private nonprofit organization. It promotes research in economics and wishes to contribute to the debate on important public policy issues. Since 1990, the Egon Sohmen Foundation has focused on holding regular international symposia, the Egon Sohmen Symposia, with distinguished scholars. It also organizes the yearly Egon Sohmen Lectures at those places where Egon Sohmen studied or taught.

Abbreviations

AAU	Assigned Amount Unit
ABT	averaging, banking, and trading
ACEA	European Automobile Manufacturers Association
AGO	Australian Greenhouse Office
BACT	Best Available Control Technology
BAT	Best Available Technology
CAFE	Corporate Average Fuel Economy
CCAP	Center for Clean Air Policy
CCLA	Cimate Change Levy Agreement
CDM	Clean Development Mechanism
CEPF	Confederation of European Forest Owners
CEPI	Confederation of European Paper Industries
DEA	Danish Energy Agency
ECJ	European Court of Justice
EPA	Environmental Protection Agency
EPRI	Electric Power Research Institute
ET	emissions trading
ETS	Emissions Trading Scheme
FCCC	Framework Convention on Climate Change
GHG	greenhouse gas
IEA	International Energy Agency
IETA	International Emissions Trading Association
IPCC	Intergovernmental Panel on Climate Change
IPPC	Integrated Pollution Prevention and Control
JAMA	Japan Automobile Manufacturers Association
JI	Joint Implementation
KAMA	Korea Automobile Manufacturers Association
OECD	Organization for Economic Cooperation and Development
RACT	Reasonable Available Control Technology
RECLAIM	Regional Clean Air Incentives Market
RTC	RECLAIM Trading Credit

SIP   State Implementation Plan
TRI   Toxic Release Inventory
UCTE   Union for the Co-ordination of Transmission
               of Electricity
UNCTAD   United Nations Conference on Trade and
               Development
WBCSD   World Business Council for Sustainable
               Development

1 Introduction

Bernd Hansjürgens

Climate policy and emissions trading after Kyoto

The 1997 Kyoto Conference ushered in a new direction in the discussion of climate protection. Its final document, the Kyoto Protocol to the Framework Convention on Climate Change, assigned in 1997, established "quantified emission limitation and reduction commitments" to OECD countries and some economies in transition ("Annex I countries"). This heralded a completely new tack in climate policy: whereas the need to cut greenhouse gas emissions[1] had already been acknowledged at the United Nations World Summit in Rio de Janeiro in 1992, it was only at the Kyoto Conference that specific reduction targets for signatory countries were laid down for the first time.

Another fresh direction brought about by the Kyoto Protocol was the introduction of new policy instruments for climate protection, namely the Clean Development Mechanism, Joint Implementation, and emissions trading (ET). Since then emissions trading, in particular, has become a widely discussed instrument for climate policy. One reason for the attention emissions trading has received is that it had already been the subject of intense debate in the United States owing to the introduction of several national US programs in the early 1980s and 1990s (see below).

Ever since the Kyoto Protocol was signed, intensive discussion has raged over the need to comply with the Protocol, strategies for doing so, and the details of these new instruments for climate protection. Recent developments have revealed interesting features in US and European climate policy. On the one hand, great differences persist in terms of the goals of climate protection. The United States sets great store by present growth and high flexibility, while Europe focuses more on early action to limit the future costs of climate change. On the other hand, US and European positions have started to converge regarding the choice of instrument, especially on the usefulness of emissions trading as an instrument for climate policy. This is apparent from the new EU proposal for a

1

CO_2 emissions trading system in Europe, which was published in October 2003. The European CO_2 Emissions Trading Scheme (ETS) will be the largest emissions trading system worldwide and constitutes thus the real "grand policy experiment."[2] Its success or failure will be decisive not only for the direction of future climate policy, but also for the design of future systems in emissions trading in many regions of the world. It is too early to say whether the proposed design options of the European system will indeed succeed. However, as the analysis in this book demonstrates, the European ETS draws on the experience of the United States and thus employs the successful design of the US trading schemes.

The idea of using emissions trading as an instrument for climate policy is relatively new, and so far has not received much attention in the literature. The aim of this book is to help fill this gap by bringing together scholars in the fields of economics, political science, and law, and provide a description, analysis, and evaluation of different aspects of emissions trading as an instrument to control greenhouse gases. The authors analyze theoretical aspects of regulatory instruments for climate policy, provide an overview of US experience with market-based instruments, draw lessons from existing emissions trading schemes for the control of greenhouse gases, and discuss options for emissions trading in the field of climate policy. They also highlight the background of climate policy and instrument choice in the United States and Europe and of the emerging new systems in Europe. Particular attention is devoted to the new EU directive for a CO_2 emissions trading system since this constitutes a major shift in European environmental policy.

The remainder of this introductory chapter briefly introduces emissions trading as a regulatory instrument for environmental protection. It includes a short history of its major applications in environmental policy and provides an overview of the rest of the book.

Emissions trading as a market-based instrument

The idea behind emissions trading is to assign permits (similar to property rights) governing the limited use of the environment, with the sources subject to the trading scheme being required to surrender an allowance for every unit of a pollutant they emit. The total number of permits issued guarantees that the overall environmental target will be met. The permits are allocated to polluters who can either use them to cover their own emissions or exchange them with other polluters. The permits are allocated to firms either by selling them, i.e. by auctions, or free of charge, i.e. by a "grandfathering mechanism." Polluters who have excess permits can sell emissions rights on the permit market, whereas polluters who need additional permits can purchase them on the market. Firms make their abatement decisions by comparing the cost of additional abatement measures and the price of emissions rights on the permit market. Polluters with higher marginal abatement costs purchase permits, while polluters with lower marginal abatement costs carry out abatement measures and sell their surplus permits on the market. Thus emissions are reduced wherever abatement costs are lowest. This leads to an environmental policy at lowest cost for society.

Once the overall emissions target has been set and the permits have been allocated to the polluters, the government can step back and let the permit market work. Governmental action is limited to supervising the market, monitoring adequately, and applying sanctions in the case of non-compliance. Ensuring the polluters' emissions are covered by permits is the government's major responsibility.

Of course, the goal of cost-effective environmental regulation can also be achieved by command-and-control measures, i.e. by using emissions standards at every single source. The way to achieve the cost savings would be to set different standards according to firms' abatement costs. However, such adjustments would be controversial for at least two reasons (Ellerman *et al.*, 2003, p. 2):

1 The use of facility-specific standards would lead to unequal treatment of firms in the economy. This would result in political resistance, especially where the firms are in competition.
2 Setting facility-specific targets would require an enormous amount of information on the part of the regulatory authorities. Since the information about abatement costs is not in the hands of the regulators but instead held by the firms operating the facilities, it would be almost impossible for cost-minimizing emissions reduction to be achieved through differentiated emissions standards.

Emissions trading provides a way of achieving cost savings without the need for the regulator to collect information about abatement costs. Instead, the market mechanism provides the necessary information and leads to cost-effective decisions about abatement measures. This is one reason why economists prefer market-based instruments (like emissions trading schemes) to command-and-control measures.

When economists talk about the cost savings that can be achieved through emissions trading, they are not referring to very small amounts. Early analysis suggested that cost savings could be as high as 90 percent compared to command-and-control policies (Tietenberg, 1985). In the US Acid Rain Program, however, these high cost savings could not be reached but were still estimated to be in the order of 50 percent of the total compliance costs.[3] These cost savings were in the beginning mainly realized by internal "trading" within firms and to a lesser degree by "external" trading among firms on the allowance market; this picture changed when the trading market developed (Ellerman, 2000). The estimated cost savings in the upcoming European emissions trading market are also considerable. A recently published study carried out on behalf of the European Commission estimated that cost savings of about 30 percent could be achieved through emissions trading compared to command-and-control instruments for climate protection.[4]

In addition to its cost savings, emissions trading is often promoted because of its perceived ability to stimulate innovation. Although our knowledge in this respect is somewhat limited, there is some research indicating a significant potential for emissions trading to encourage innovation and technological change.[5] The argument of promoting innovation is of special importance in the field of climate change policy. If technological progress and innovation are a key engine of growth, then green technology and green innovations could be an engine of sustainable, "climate-friendly" growth. And if instruments can be introduced which create a higher incentive to use innovative technological solutions, much of society's resources can be saved.

There are two distinct fundamental forms of emission trading systems: credit-based systems and cap-and-trade systems (Ellerman *et al.*, 2003, p. v, Tietenberg, 2003, p. 408). In credit-based systems, only the amount of emissions representing over-compliance above a specific standard can be traded. Each "trade" must be pre-certified relative to an emissions standard by the relevant governmental agency. Hence, the command-and-control background is still rather strong in these systems and the added market-based elements are rudimentary. In a cap-and-trade system, the entire amount of emissions can be traded and the trades do not have to be pre-certified by a government authority. An overall environmental objective is set (the cap), the emission permits are distributed among the business community, and the sources subject to the cap are required to surrender an allowance for every unit they emit. This second type can be introduced irrespective of any command-and-control measures represented by specific emissions standards for the firms. Whereas credit-based systems are a way of introducing more flexibility into an existing command-and-control world, cap-and-trade systems represent a transition to market-based instruments which rely totally on market forces to create the necessary information and incentives. These two fundamental forms of emissions trading can also be found in practice.

Emissions trading in practice

The idea of emissions trading can be traced back to Herman Dales (1968), who elaborated the idea on the basis of Ronald Coase's (1960) seminal paper.[6] However, it was a long time before the notion of market-based instruments and emissions trading became widely accepted in practice on either side of the Atlantic. Environmental policy was clearly dominated by a regulatory framework based on command-and-control measures. These measures allow for environmental goods to be utilized by defining and prescribing certain performance standards (technical solutions) such as the Best Available Control Technology (BACT) or the Reasonable Available Control Technology (RACT) on the one hand, and the concentration of pollutants in the environment on the other. The success of command-and-control instruments has been mixed. Some policies have been very effective in reducing emissions (e.g. in Germany in the 1980s; see Wätzold, 2004), while others have performed poorly, being exorbitantly expensive yet still failing to achieve environmental targets (Ellerman *et al.*, 2000, p. 3).

In the 1960s and 1970s market-based instruments drew skepticism and sometimes even hostility from non-economists. Whenever they were none the less employed, Europeans preferred environmental taxation while emissions trading was chosen in the United States. The introduction of emissions trading took place step by step, initially arousing little interest among the public. In the 1970s several forms of credit-based emissions trading schemes evolved in US air quality policy: bubble, netting, offset, and banking policies.[7] Very similar to the air quality programs of the 1970s was the Lead Trading Program for gasoline that was implemented in the 1980s. It differed mainly in allowing for trading without pre-certification (Kerr and Newell, 2001, Ellerman *et al.*, 2003). However, as mentioned above, these "first-generation" emissions trading systems were an instrument designed to achieve more flexibility in a command-and-control environment, rather than a market instrument with strong incentives.

This all changed at the beginning of the 1990s when the amendment of Title IV of the US Clean Air Act in 1990 introduced a cap-and-trade system as the "second generation" of emissions trading systems. This allowance market, which came into effect in 1995, was aimed at reducing sulfur dioxide, the main precursor of acid rain.[8] Other trading schemes followed, such as the Regional Clean Air Incentives Market (RECLAIM) in Southern California to combat SO_X and NO_X, two of the main substances responsible for high ozone concentrations in the

Southern California Basin.[9] The RECLAIM program spawned legislation in 1993 and came into effect in 1994. Another cap-and-trade program which was implemented was the Northeast NO_X Budget Trading Program, a multi-jurisdictional partnership between federal and state governments which went into operation in nine northeastern states in 1999. In 2004, it was expanded to include nineteen states and the District of Columbia (Burtraw and Evans, 2003). These new emissions trading experiments attracted plenty of attention from the academic and the business community.

All these developments took place in the United States. Before the Kyoto Protocol was signed, Europe had almost no experience of emissions trading. In Europe the instruments for climate protection in general and the idea of emissions trading in particular received little attention for a long time. Instead, the focus was on taxes and other forms of public charge, especially in the Nordic countries (Norway, Sweden, Finland, and Denmark) and in Germany.

It was the Kyoto Conference which finally brought about a change in instrument choice in some European countries and which led to several programs and pilot studies in emissions trading. The best-known emissions trading programs in existence in Europe are those at the national level in the UK and Denmark. However, the suggestion which has recently received the most attention is the Directive for a CO_2 ETS put forward by the European Commission in October 2003.[10] Since this scheme includes some 10,000–12,000 sources on the trading market, it is a second major experiment in emissions trading following the SO_2 markets and other experiments in the United States. "The unprecedented scope of these [European, B. H.] programmes breaks new ground in terms of geographic coverage, the number of participants, and the types of polluting gases covered" (Tietenberg, 2003, p. 402).

In Figure 1.1 the milestones in the development of emissions trading systems are described.

As the new European ETS is the cornerstone for further climate policy, it deserves deeper analysis. Particular attention must be devoted to the question of whether emissions trading, which was originally geared to pollutants other than greenhouse gases, could be a promising instrument for climate policy. To what extent does emissions trading lead to cost savings and innovation? What can we learn from the US experiences about emissions trading systems for greenhouse gases? What design options should be chosen? Is the new European ETS destined to be a success? These are some of the questions this book addresses and seeks to answer.

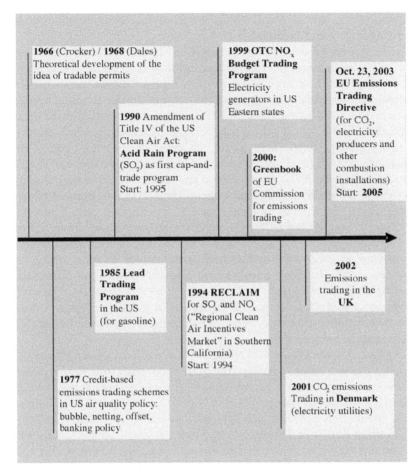

Figure 1.1. Milestones in the development of emissions trading schemes.

Overview of the book

The book has three parts. Part I deals with regulatory instruments for climate protection and emissions trading in the abstract.

In chapter 2 (Thomas Sterner and Henrik Hammar, "Designing instruments for climate policy"), the range of policy options for climate protection is analyzed, concentrating on the special design options market-based instruments must have if they are to be chosen as candidates for climate policy. The chapter illustrates that the design options in climate policy are somewhat different from textbook design options developed for other pollutants.

With respect to instrument choice in climate policy, one aspect requires closer analysis: the role of innovation and technological change. In the long run these are the decisive factors for the abatement costs of greenhouse gas emissions. This is all the more important as in the field of climate policy we are talking about a time-frame of decades or even centuries. If we succeed in implementing instruments which induce innovations we will be able to cut the costs of reducing greenhouse emissions considerably and thus reduce the burden on society. Therefore the influence of ET on innovation and technological change is a key factor for the success of climate policies. However, our current knowledge about the effects of environmental instruments and emissions trading on innovations and technological change is rather limited. For this reason two contributions deal with the effects of regulatory instruments on innovation and technological change in more detail. In chapter 3 "Technical innovation and design choices for emissions trading and other climate policies" are analyzed (Carolyn Fischer), while in chapter 4 this analysis is deepened in "Incentives to adopt new abatement technology and US–European regulatory cultures" (Reimund Schwarze).

Against this background of the theory of market-based instruments and emissions trading, Part II of the book then turns to US experiences of emissions trading as a market-based instrument and the general US approach to climate policy.

As mentioned above, most experience in emissions trading has been acquired in the United States over the past ten years. However, this was in connection with various environmental issues, such as acid rain and regional air quality management problems. The question is: what does US experience tell us about climate protection? What are the lessons we should bear in mind when designing an emissions trading scheme for CO_2? Chapter 5 (Robert N. Stavins, "Implications of the US experience with market-based environmental strategies for future climate policy") highlights the experience of US domestic market-based instruments. Some normative implications for the design of emissions trading schemes for climate policy are drawn. The experiences with US market-based instruments are also the topic of chapter 6 (A. Denny Ellerman, "US experience with emissions trading: lessons for CO_2 emissions trading"). However, this chapter refers exclusively to the SO_2 allowance trading program which was implemented in the early 1990s when Title IV of the Clean Air Act was amended to combat acid rain. As the SO_2 allowance trading program is the largest existing program in the US, and is clearly a precursor for other programs (e.g. the RECLAIM program in Southern California), it represents the most important experience in emissions trading. The lessons learned from this program could also be extremely useful for a CO_2 emissions trading system. The chapter presents some important conclusions for CO_2 emissions trading in general and the European ETS in particular.

However, the analysis of the US approach to pollution control goes beyond examining existing policy instruments such as SO_2 allowance trading. As the United States is far from reaching the Kyoto commitment of reducing CO_2 emissions by 7 percent by 2008–2012, relative targets in the form of greenhouse gas intensities could be a way to bring the United States back to future summits on climate policy. The advantages of intensity targets, which are often overlooked, are analyzed in chapter 7 (Charles D. Kolstad, "Climate change policy viewed from the USA and the role of intensity targets"). They are also one decisive element of President Bush's climate initiative which was presented in his Valentine's Day announcement in February 2002.

In addition to the topic of relative climate objectives, another interesting feature of current US climate policy can be identified. The recent withdrawal of the United States from the agreements of the Kyoto Protocol opens up opportunities for different domestic actions to mitigate emissions. As these domestic actions could serve as potentially powerful models for other countries, it is highly relevant which instrument and which policy design will be chosen at the US domestic level. It is relatively clear that such a policy will also rely on the instrument of emissions trading. However, the design options are different from those of the SO_2 Acid Rain Program. In chapter 8 (Richard D. Morgenstern, "Design issues of a domestic carbon emissions trading system in the USA") some important design issues of a domestic CO_2 emissions trading system are discussed (i.e. upstream or downstream systems, allocation of permits, safety valves, etc.). The considerations in this chapter do not only concern a possible domestic system in the United States, but were also discussed in Europe when the European trading schemes were designed. They are also relevant for further developments on the international level.

On the basis of the experience of emissions trading in the United States and the directions of US climate policy, part III of the book then deals with the new developments in climate policy in Europe, addressing in particular the European initiatives for CO_2 emissions trading. In fact, the recent efforts to control greenhouse gases in Europe show a remarkable development, and many new lessons can be learnt from the recent European advances.

Europe's recent climate policy is all the more surprising as Europe consists of sovereign countries, each with its own approach to climate policy and instrument choice. Therefore, certain forces in European climate policy can be observed which are seeking merely loose cooperation of independent states. At the same time there is a demand for stronger centralization and harmonized climate policy. Chapters 9 and 10 deal with these developments in European climate policy and thus serve as a background to the understanding of the European emissions trading systems. In chapter 9 (Mikael Skou Andersen, "Regulation or coordination: European climate policy between Scylla and Charybdis") the history of European climate policy is described, focusing in particular on the development toward EU "Burden-Sharing" in 1998 and the path to emissions trading in the following years. Clearly, the outcome of the European ETS is the result of the political process that drove its design, especially the influence of politicians, the EU member states, and selected industrial interest groups.[11] A closer look at the role of lobbying and rent-seeking is therefore undertaken in chapter 10 (Gert Tinggaard Svendsen, "Lobbying and CO_2 trade in the EU") where the influence of lobbying is assessed. On the basis of a public-choice approach, the difference in the proposed design of the European ETS between the Green Paper (before lobbying) and the final Directive Proposal (after lobbying) is evaluated.

In chapter 11, the new directive of the European Commission is then discussed (Peter Zapfel, "Greenhouse gas emissions trading in the EU: building the world's largest cap-and-trade scheme"), with an in-depth analysis of its design elements. Attention is paid to the debate before the directive was passed so that an understanding of the role of different design options is obtained. As one of the most difficult aspects of this ETS is its integration with existing regulations, the legal aspects of such an enterprise play a dominant role for its implementation in practice. These aspects are analyzed in chapter 12 (Michael Rodi, "Legal aspects of the European Emissions Trading Scheme"). As mentioned above, it is not only the question of whether emissions trading fits within EU law that has to be taken into account, but also the legislative requirements of the member states.

A characteristic feature of the EU ETS is – as demonstrated in chapter 11 – its openness to other pollutants and regulatory systems. If the idea of pricing the environment is understood as a process rather than a final state, ways and means have to be found, in the long run, to combine the EU ETS with other national and international schemes. In this respect, linking up different emissions trading schemes is a challenge which is extremely important and which has not been tackled before.

The first step is to analyze the possibilities and limits of linking up existing schemes. In chapter 13 (Sven Bode, "Emissions trading schemes in Europe: linking the EU Emissions Trading Scheme with national programs"), domestic emissions trading schemes in Europe are analyzed, namely those in Denmark and the UK (the two countries where national CO_2 emissions trading systems were employed before the EU ETS cames into force). It is then discussed whether and how these trading systems at the national level of two member states can be linked up with the EU ETS.

In the last chapter of the book (Bernd Hansjürgens, "Concluding observations"), the most important findings of the previous chapters are brought together. The chapter focuses on global warming as a natural case for the use of emissions trading, the design options of the EU ETS, and some lessons for emissions trading in general.

Notes

1 While carbon dioxide (CO_2) is the major human-made greenhouse gas, the Kyoto Protocol also covers methane (CH_4), nitrous oxide (N_2O), hydro-fluorocarbons (HFCs), perfluorocarbons (PFCs) and sulfur hexafluoride (SF_6). The conversion rates between these gases are called global warming equivalents. They allow each pollutant's contribution to global warming to be expressed as units of carbon dioxide equivalents.

2 Stavins (1998) spoke of the US SO_2 trading scheme as a "grand policy experiment." As the EU CO_2 trading comprises 10,000–12,000 sources, it will exceed the SO_2 trading by a factor of five in terms of covered installations. See also Kruger and Pizer (2004).

3 See Burtraw (1996), Burtraw and Swift (1996), and Ellerman *et al.* (2000).

4 See "Economic analysis of EU-wide emissions trading," http://europa.eu.int/comm/environment/enveco/studies2.htm; see also Zapfel (2001).

5 With respect to the national Acid Rain Program, see Burtraw (2000). See also Kerr and Newell (2001), and chapters 3 and 4 in this book.

6 Another important early contribution was that of Crocker (1966).

7 For a discussion of these various forms of ET schemes, see for example, Montgomery (1972), Hahn and Noll (1982), Tietenberg (1985), Baumol and Oates (1988), Hahn (1989), and Hahn and Hester (1989a, 1989b).

8 For a comprehensive analysis of Title IV of the Acid Rain Program, see the careful study by Ellerman *et al.* (2000); see also Tietenberg (1998), Hansjür-gens (1998), and the books edited by Sorrell and Skea (1999) and Kosobud (2000). The term "second-generation" instrument can be found in Fromm and Hansjürgens (1996, 1998) or Stavins and Whitehead (1997). For the lessons learned from the SO_2 allowance trading in the Acid Rain Program, see also part III of this book.

9 See South Coast Air Management District (1993), Fromm and Hansjürgens (1996), and Lent (2000).

12   *Bernd Hansjürgens*

10 See European Union (2003). For a first evaluation of the EU proposal, see Gagelmann and Hansjürgens (2002); see also chapters 11 and 12 of this book.

11 As in the US SO$_2$ market there was also a strong political influence from regional stakeholders; the introduction of the EU ETS is, at least in this respect, very similar to the introduction of the US SO$_2$ allowance trading. For the history of the Acid Rain Program, see Kete (1993). For the political economy, see Joskow and Schmalensee (1998) or Ellerman *et al.* (2000, ch. 3).

References

Baumol, W. J., and Oates, W. E. 1988. *The Theory of Environmental Policy.* New York: Cambridge University Press.

Burtraw, D. 1996. "The SO$_2$ allowance trading program: cost savings without allowance trades," *Contemporary Economic Policy* 14: 79–94.

2000. "Innovation under the tradable sulphur dioxide emission permits programme in the US electricity sector," in OECD (ed.). *Innovation and the Environment.* Paris: OECD, pp. 63–84.

Burtraw, D., and Evans, D. 2003. *The Evolution of NO$_X$ Control for Coal-Fired Power Plants in the United States.* Discussion Paper 03–23, Washington, DC: Resources for the Future.

Burtraw, D., and Swift, B. 1996. "A new standard of performance: an analysis of the Clean Air Act's acid rain program," *Environmental Law Review News and Analyses* 26: 10411–23.

Coase, R. 1960. "The problem of social cost," *Journal of Law and Economics* 3: 1–44.

Crocker, T. 1966. "The structuring of atmospheric pollution control systems," in H.Wolozin, (ed.). *The Economics of Air Pollution.* New York: W. W. Norton & Co., pp. 61–86.

Dales, J. H. 1968. *Pollution, property and prices.* Toronto: University of Toronto Press.

Ellerman, A. D. 2000. "From autarkic to market-based compliance," in Kosobud (ed.), pp. 190–203.

Ellerman, A. D., Joskow, P., and Harrison, D., Jr. 2003. *Emissions Trading in the US: Experience, Lessons, and Considerations for Greenhouse Gases.* Washington, DC: PEW Center on Global Climate Change.

Ellerman, A. D., Joskow, P. L., Schmalensee, R., Montero, J.-P., and Bailey, E. 2000. *Markets for Clean Air. The US Acid Rain Program.* Cambridge: Cambridge University Press.

European Union 2003. "Directive 2003/87/EC of the European Parliament and of the Council of 13. October 2003 establishing a system for greenhouse gas emissions trading within the European Community and amending Council Directive 96/61/EC." ABL 275. Brussels, October 25, 2003.

Fromm, O., and Hansjürgens, B. 1996. "Emissions trading in theory and practice. An analysis of RECLAIM in Southern California," *Environment and Planning C: Government and Policy* 14: 367–84.

1998. "Zertifikatemärkte der 'zweiten Generation' – Die amerikanischen Erfahrungen mit dem Acid Rain- und dem RECLAIM-Programm" ("Second-
generation emissions trading – the US experience with the acid rain- and the
RECLAIM programs"), in H. Bonus (ed.). *Umweltzertifikate – Der steinige
Weg zur Marktwirtschaft*. Berlin: Analytica, pp. 150–65.

Gagelmann, F., and Hansjürgens, B. 2002. "Climate protection through
tradable permits: the EU proposal for a CO_2 emissions trading system in
Europe," *European Environment* 12: 185–202.

Hahn, R. W. 1989. "Economic prescriptions for environmental problems: how
the patient followed the doctor's order," *Journal of Economic Perspectives* 3:
95–114.

Hahn, R. W., and Hester, G. L. 1989a. "Marketable permits: lessons for theory
and practice," *Ecology Law Quarterly* 16: 361–406.

1989b. "Where did all the markets go? An analysis of EPA's emissions trading
program," *Yale Journal on Regulation* 6: 109–53.

Hahn, R., and Noll, R. 1982. "Designing a market for tradable permits," in
W. Magat (ed.). *Reform of Environmental Regulation*. Cambridge: Cambridge
University Press, pp. 119–46.

Hansjürgens, B. 1998. "The sulfur dioxide allowance trading market: recent
developments and lessons to be learned," *Environment and Planning C:
Government and Policy* 16: 341–61.

Joskow, P. L., and Schmalensee, R. 1998. "The political economy of market-
based environmental policy: the US acid rain program," *Journal of Law and
Economics* 41: 37–83.

Kerr, S., and Newell, R. 2001. *Policy-Induced Technology Adoption: Evidence from
the US Lead Phasedown*. Discussion Paper 01–14, Washington, DC:
Resources for the Future.

Kete, N. 1993. "The politics of markets: the acid rain control policy in the 1990
Clean Air Act Amendments." Unpublished Ph.D. dissertation, Johns
Hopkins University.

Kosobud, R. F. 2000 (ed.). *Emissions Trading. Environmental Policy's New
Approach*. New York: John Wiley & Sons.

Kruger, J., and Pizer, W. A. 2004. *The EU Emissions Trading Directive: Opportunities and Potential Pitfalls*. Discussion Paper 04–24, Washington, DC:
Resources for the Future.

Lent, J. M. 2000. "The RECLAIM program (Los Angeles' market-based emissions reduction program) at three years," in Kosobud (ed.), pp. 219–40.

Montgomery, W. D. 1972. "Markets in licenses and efficient pollution control
programs," *Journal of Economic Theory* 3: 395–418.

Sorrell, S., and Skea, J. (eds.) 1999. *Pollution for Sale. Emissions Trading and Joint
Implementation*. Cheltenham: Edward Elgar.

South Coast Air Quality Management District 1993. *RECLAIM*, vol. I: *Development Report and Proposed Rules*. Riverside, CA.

Stavins, R. N. 1998. "What can we learn from the grand policy experiment?
Lessons from SO_2 allowance trading," *Journal of Economic Perspectives* 12:
69–88.

Stavins, R. N., and Whitehead, B. W. 1997. "Market-based environmental
policies," in M. Chertow and D. Esty (eds.). *Thinking Ecologically: The*

Next Generation of Environmental Policy. New Haven: Yale University Press, pp. 105–17.

Tietenberg, T. 1985. *Emissions Trading: An Exercise in Reforming Pollution Policy.* Washington, DC: Resources for the Future.

1998. "Tradable permits and the control of air pollution," in H. Bonus (ed.). *Umweltzertifikate – Der steinige Weg zur Marktwirtschaft.* Berlin: Analytica, pp. 11–31.

2003. "The tradable-permit approach to protecting the commons: Lessons for climate change," *Oxford Review of Economic Policy* 19: 400–19.

Wätzold, F. 2004. "SO$_2$ emissions in Germany: regulations to fight *Waldsterben*," in W. Harrington, R. D. Morgenstern, and T. Sterner (eds.). *Choosing Environmental Policy: Comparing Instruments and Outcomes in the United States and Europe.* Washington, DC: Resources for the Future, pp. 23–40.

Zapfel, P. 2001. "Handel mit den Treibhausgas-Emissionen in der EU – Grünbuch und andere Aktivitäten" ("Trade with greenhouse gas emissions in the EU – greenbook and other activities"), in Arbeitsgemeinschaft für Umweltfragen (AGU) (ed.). *Umweltlizenzen und Umweltzertifikate (Environmental Licenses and Environmental Certificates).* Bonn: AGU, pp. 53–66.

Part 1

Regulatory instruments for climate policy: theoretical aspects

2   Designing instruments for climate policy

Thomas Sterner and Henrik Hammar

Introduction

The purpose of this chapter is to discuss the design of environmental policy instruments with a particular focus on climate change. Economics holds some vital keys to the *implementation* in society of the technical or biological methods that natural scientists and engineers devise. There are already environmentally sound ways of supplying energy for buildings, transport, etc. These technical solutions provide the *possibility* of production with less carbon emission, less risk of nuclear accidents, less air pollution, etc. However, whether these techniques are adopted in the real world will depend on social "rules" the design of which can be improved by good economic analysis.[1]

There are more options than just tradable permits. Among the policies highlighted are: the creation of well-defined property rights, subsidies, charges (of different kinds – emission, input, output), user fees, tariff construction, deposit refunds, imposition of technical standards, technology standards, emission standards, bans, quotas, the provision of information, labeling, and the provision of infrastructure or other public goods. We believe that there is much theoretical and empirical work, relevant for successful policy-making, which remains to be done on how these various instruments can be used and how they can be combined.

The need for policy instruments for combating climate change

To reach the Kyoto greenhouse gas (GHG) emissions target of an overall reduction of 5 percent (from 1990 levels) among developed countries is just a first step toward stabilizing the atmospheric carbon content at much lower levels. The long-run goal is a much larger reduction of global emissions, a formidable and very probably quite expensive task. It is therefore crucial to search for cost-effective policies.

The costs and success of the first wave of policies addressing climate change are likely to be of crucial importance in terms of support for more stringent future policies. One of the frustrations for many environmentalists is that even simple solutions to serious environmental problems do not get implemented. If today's existing and suggested policies – primarily carbon (and energy) taxes and the Kyoto Protocol's flexible mechanisms – can reduce emissions at acceptable costs, one can expect increasing support for more stringent climate policies. Large increases in carbon (or energy) taxes on gasoline and diesel are not popular, but the more generous the allocation of carbon permits to the trading sectors, the larger the tax increases that are needed in the non-trading sectors.

The structure of this chapter is as follows. First the need for environmental policy instruments is discussed in terms of market and policy failures. Market failures – external effects, public goods, non-competitive markets, and imperfect information – have to be analyzed on a basis of a solid understanding of property rights. It is the exact definition of these rights that defines the characteristics of the market and of market failures. We then discuss the range of policy options and the selection and design of policies based on various criteria.

Property is often described as a collection of rights such as the right to use the property for productive purposes, the rights to sell, lease, and inherit the property, and the right to exclude others. There are important legal, cultural, and psychological aspects to ownership. Historically, property rights have evolved to include more types of rights. An economist would see this as a response to our need to minimize uncertainty and transaction costs as well as a reflection of increased scarcity as population grows in a finite space. The history of property rights is clearest for land. After this, rights have been gradually extended to more complex issues, leading to rights to water, subterranean rights, and various forms of common property. Understanding these developments is important since it provides the underpinning for understanding the rights to other natural and environmental resources including less tangible objects such as biodiversity, clean air, and the right to emit greenhouse gases.

Externalities are unintended "side-effects" of production or consumption. This is well illustrated by carbon emission from the burning of energy in the form of fossil fuels. Energy is in this context not a "bad"; it is the emissions from combustion that create negative externalities. These are real costs but typically they are not fully borne by the emitters. The same applies to the health effects of air pollution from industry and traffic and numerous other activities. The very existence of externalities can be thought of as a consequence of incomplete property rights, and significant transaction costs (Coase, 1960).

Public goods are "goods" or services that are enjoyed in common, such as public defense and law and order; one could even say that different attributes or properties of the atmosphere, such as its oxygen or carbon content, are a form of public good or resource. The market tends not to supply these goods sufficiently, since, once the good is provided, it is hard to exclude those who do not pay, which means that no one will pay – at least not in the ordinary sense of market transactions. Instead, political processes are needed (such as the election of a government which collects taxes and finances public goods). *Common pool resources* are akin to public goods but, as the term suggests, they are not goods but rather resources used for production or consumption and not easily amenable to private ownership. The resource may be mobile or the costs of fencing may be too high. Instead, the resource may be managed cooperatively by a village, or by the world as is the case for the climate system. Just as public goods may be undersupplied by the market, so common pool resources may be overutilized if the sense of communal ownership control is not strong enough to limit access by the users.

Non-competitive markets such as monopolies or oligopolies imply that supply is distorted. Typically too little produce will be sold at too high a price. This is bad since it implies a loss to the economy. In some particular cases, however, it may have some advantages from an environmental viewpoint. If the market is monopolized for a good like coal or oil with negative environmental effects, the profit-maximizing behavior of the monopolist will actually decrease the size of the negative environmental externality as long as a lower level of production and higher price are associated with lower emissions. The occurrence of monopolies in the economy is partly related to underlying cost structures such as decreasing costs of large-scale production. When monopolies are deemed harmful, policy-makers typically regulate them.

Asymmetric information is perhaps the most pervasive of the market failures. Economists know there are no "free lunches" yet still assume "perfect information." Understanding the characteristics of information asymmetry not only helps in the design of policy instruments to deal with monitoring difficulties, but it also goes to the heart of the essential dilemma of how to promote social goals such as equity while preserving the incentives for work and efficiency. Both imperfect markets and imperfect information cause the simple laws of welfare economics to break down. In the simplest market models the efficient solution also maximizes welfare but in more realistic models it is impossible to separate efficiency from equity issues.

Looking back a few decades, the energy crisis of the 1970s led to research into energy-saving technologies for and into "alternative" technologies for energy production. Later the prospect of resource depletion subsided, but local and global pollution problems such as global climate change have continued to put pressure on this kind of research, which has met with some success. Many good technologies exist for reducing energy use, such as fluorescent lighting, heat pumps, "hyper-cars", and tyristors, or for generating energy, such as wind power, solar power, and bio-fuels. Nevertheless they are not widely used because the consumer price of energy is still too low and many technologies are not commercially viable. Present prices do not include the external costs of local and global environmental problems. The costs of children and adults getting asthma and bronchitis in the large urban areas are real costs (health and productivity loss) just like the costs associated with the risks of climate-induced rise in the sea level. These costs, however, do not appear on our electricity bills or in the price of gasoline. Taxes, permits, or other policies are needed to internalize these costs so that the consumer faces the real total cost of energy use, which will automatically encourage the adoption of energy-efficient techniques.

The range of policy options

It is often said that the main dividing line in environmental policy-making is between regulation and market-based instruments, but, in practice, there is a much more subtle spectrum of choices. Economic policy in general is not simply a choice between old-fashioned planning and *laissez-faire* capitalism. Society needs intermediate policies with a good deal of fine-tuning. With several goals such as efficiency and distribution, one would expect to find that different combinations of policy instrument are needed for different tasks. Similarly, it is sometimes alleged that economic policy instruments are basically unrealistic, and thus hardly ever used. This has by now been shown to be wrong. There is quite a large number of market-based instruments like taxes, charges, and deposit refunds in northern Europe, including formerly planned economies such as Poland, and various developing countries. Tradable permit schemes[2] are used for pollution control in the United States, and outside the United States notably in fishery management. Information provision, eco-labeling, liability, and many other schemes show that, in practice, a menu of policies is being used.

There are also more "inadvertent" – but very important – economic policies, such as energy taxes and subsidies, which have not always been formulated primarily with environmental goals in mind but which certainly do provide ample illustrations of the way environmental charges work. Many other forms of policy-making, such as physical licensing and other control instruments, are, nevertheless, still predominant. This should, however, not upset economists since, according to economic theory, there are many cases when it is appropriate to use physical regulations. Having said this, it still seems that market-based policies get somewhat less credit than they deserve, which is a reason to mention a number of such schemes here.

Table 2.1 gives an overview of policy options and makes some attempt at organizing them into a policy matrix. The rows of the matrix are policies and there are two columns, one for abatement of carbon and other climate gas emissions and the other for land management policies which are intended to either reduce emissions, increase absorption, or facilitate adaptation to climate change.

In the first row we have property rights and these rights may be private, public, or collective. Kyoto defines emission reduction obligations that are also a form of rights at the level of nation states, which will most likely also be expressed as rights at the level of industries. In the case of forests, property rights may be important for averting the deforestation that may follow from open access.

Rows 2–5 and 15 are fees and taxes. These may be applied to the emission directly as a carbon tax. When this is not possible, taxes may be on an input, as a coal or oil tax, or on the use of an output, such as electricity. One of the most effective instruments has been gasoline tax and other fuel taxes. The experience of applying differing fuel taxes in various countries provides an important lesson. Although these were rarely if ever instituted to deal with climate change, they have actually been very effective for that purpose: among both developing and industrialized countries, we find that the countries that (for some reason) have higher fuel taxes also have considerably lower fuel demand and thus carbon emissions. The broad picture is that most European countries have fuel prices that are twice as high as in the United States and the result is fuel consumption which is half as much; this has had very large effects on global carbon emissions. A closer analysis shows, however, that the political economy of setting fuel taxes is quite complex; see Hammar *et al.*, (2004).

In row 6 we have deposit refund systems, which act somewhat like a tax if the product is thrown away and not returned. It has been suggested that similar mechanisms could be used in other areas as a form of "presumptive tax" which can be refunded if the industry concerned can prove abatement (for instance, by capturing and storing carbon dioxide in underground aquifers). Fee-bate systems (fees for "bad"

Table 2.1. *A policy matrix for management of climate change issues*

		Policies for abatement of climate gases	Land management, forest agriculture and Adaptation policies
1	Property rights	National commitments under Kyoto	Forest rights
2	Emission taxes	Carbon taxes	
3	Input charges	Coal or oil taxes; fuel taxes	Taxes on fertilizers
4	Output charges	Electricity or heat taxes	Timber taxes
5	User fees/tariff schemes	Tariffs for district heating or electricity	
6	Deposit refund systems	Taxes on CO_2 refunded on proof of abatement	
7	Subsidies	Subsidies for energy-saving insulation of buildings etc.	Reforestation landscape subsidies
8	Tradable rights	Trade in carbon rights	Credits for afforestation in JI or CDM
9	Technology standards	Prohibition on flaring of gas	Rules for sustainable use of forests or wetlands, etc.
10	Emission limits	CAFE standards	
11	Bans	Prohibition of CFCs	Prohibited deforestation
12	Liability		
13	Information disclosure	Information on energy efficiency of appliances	Forest certification
14	Public participation	Voluntary agreements	Community-based forestry
15	International fines	Economic sanctions if ratified national commitments are not met	Economic sanctions if deforestation of JI or CDM projects
16	Provision of public goods	Research on new technologies	Public forest reserves; dykes against sea rise

choices and rebates for "good" choices) can also be seen in this context. One could imagine revenue-neutral taxes or charges that refund the revenues to the agents that buy the most energy-efficient equipment (e.g. car, furnace, boiler, etc.). Row 7 is subsidies, a very popular instrument with polluters and often used in natural resource management too – for instance, subsidies for reforestation.

Row 8 shows the creation of new markets through "quasi-rights," such as tradable emission permits which are likely to be the main instrument for carbon reduction. If emission reduction credits can be gained through afforestation or even averted deforestation (the latter not currently allowed under Kyoto) then land management can be brought in and used for instance within the context of Joint Implementation or the Clean Development Mechanism.

The next category of instruments (rows 9–11) is the more traditional kind of control through standards and (non-tradable) permits or bans and other regulations. Standards for energy efficiency such as the US CAFE standards are a relevant example. Row 12 is liability, which may be relevant for health damage from occupational exposure. In principle the case might be made that fossil fuel users are liable for the drowning of parts of Bangladesh but we do not (yet) know of any relevant cases where this concept is accepted or developed.

A fairly recent concept in policy-making is summarized in rows 13–14. These are instruments based on the provision of information and through this the fostering of public participation in various forms. In the USA, the Toxic Release Inventory (TRI) is the most striking example. Other examples of involving the public through information provision include the eco-labeling that is fairly common in (northern) Europe. The possibilities of the market (consumers, retailers, and producers) procuring energy-efficient equipment can also be effectively enhanced through laws and regulations on the energy efficiency characteristics of equipment. One good example of this is the European Parliament and Council Directive 1999/94/EC relating to the availability of consumer information on fuel economy and CO_2 emissions in respect of the marketing of new passenger cars. The mere provision of information can generate significant processes in product, labor, and financial markets. In addition, various forms of voluntary agreements or similar mechanisms may be added, as in row 14. The voluntary agreement between the European, Korean, and Japanese automobile manufacturers (ACEA, KAMA, and JAMA) and the European Commission to reduce average CO_2 emissions from passenger cars (European Commission 1999) is one example of this.

The use of fines in different forms (row 15) can be very effective in increasing the likelihood of regulatory compliance at the national level. Finally, row 16 ends with the perhaps most direct and obvious "instrument," namely the provision of public goods. This is, of course, the main instrument when it comes to areas such as municipal waste management or the provision of public parks. When it comes to climate change the most obvious examples may be the funding of research and possibly public funding or provision of forests.

Designing policy instruments

The most important criterion is undoubtedly welfare maximization but in practical politics this may be too abstract and it is common to have a number of separate sub-goals. The most important include efficiency, incentive compatibility, and equity, or at least some consideration of the distribution of cost burdens. These goals are not perfectly clear nor separable and the political process is often a struggle in which different groups place differing emphases on them and have different interpretations of them.

Efficiency means that if the instrument operates as planned, it would achieve the environmental goals at least cost. Incentive compatibility means that the agents involved, particularly the polluters, but also regulators, victims, and others, have an incentive to provide information and undertake abatement as intended. Distributional and equity concerns imply that the distribution of costs should be perceived as "fair." Naturally these criteria interact; for example, polluters who think a particular distribution of costs is grossly unfair will try to resist and stop implementation. They will not have an incentive to collaborate and, particularly if there are asymmetries of information or power, this will ultimately lead to inefficiency.

This implies a focus on the *criteria and conditions* that are most important for policy selection. Typically it is the combination of certain criteria and conditions that is decisive. The *criteria* also turn out to be of varying importance depending on the *conditions* that characterize a particular issue. When dealing with environmental problems with moderate abatement costs in an economy with an even distribution of income, equity may be less important. Conversely when dealing with issues that affect health and ultimately life in countries with large income disparities, distributional concerns may be the most important. When dealing with markets characterized by powerful monopolies or serious information asymmetries the issues of incentive compatibility may well dominate. In other cases it may be the complexity of the ecosystem that is the most prominent factor deciding the design of the appropriate instrument. If there is a risk of serious and irreversible damage then caution may dictate the use of some very powerful instruments like prohibitions.

Environmental regulators face many different combinations of instruments and criteria but a few examples may illustrate the type of issues at hand. If abatement costs vary considerably then efficiency dictates that market mechanisms such as taxes or tradable permits be used. These instruments lead to the equalization of marginal abatement costs, which implies that the environmental goal is reached at the least cost. If, on the other hand, the damage costs are sufficiently heterogeneous, then more physical, quantitative instruments may be required, for such as zoning or differentiated regulations, individual licenses, etc. If there are important information asymmetries, then policy instruments need to be designed to be self-revealing, as is the case of deposit refund schemes. In many situations, the distribution of costs is important as well as the power of the polluters and the relative weakness of the environmental protection agencies. This typically means that instruments such as taxes are impossible. However, tradable permits allow the planner to fine-tune the distribution of costs to make a policy politically acceptable. Similarly, charges that are refunded or paid into environmental funds may be used to "buy acceptance" from important polluters and at the same time to strengthen the public agencies themselves.

Climate policies are at work, but seem not to be sufficiently stringent to meet emission goals. When discussing climate policies one should also bear in mind that there are numerous other policies and taxes that are not *motivated* by an aim to reduce CO_2 emissions, but are equally or more important in controlling greenhouse emissions, the energy tax being one of the most important by raising the price of fossil fuels (as well as other energy sources). This fact has many implications for climate policy. In the case of fuels used for transport it means that in terms of achieving fossil CO_2 emissions reductions the *total* level of fuel taxation is more important than the level of carbon tax. In the longer term this might change, if non-fossil alternative fuels become more important, but as long as gasoline and diesel are the major transport fuels the level of fuel taxation will determine emissions, with the level of carbon taxation affecting them to a lesser extent. This should not be interpreted that we believe that the carbon tax share in gasoline tax is wrong. Environmental taxes, and environmental policies in general, should if possible be based upon the problem at hand. In this perspective the carbon tax and energy tax are theoretically a world apart although their effects on carbon emissions are comparable.

Efficiency with heterogeneous abatement costs

When abatement costs vary widely, considerable cost savings can be made by letting low-cost firms do most of the required clean-up. This provides a very strong case in favor of market-based instruments such as taxes and tradable permits, although this could conceivably also include deposit refund schemes, subsidies, and others. This is an example of the usual "specialization" which is one of the strongest arguments for the market mechanism. Good examples can be found in the area of energy economics or global climate change. The marginal cost of decreasing the atmospheric concentration of greenhouse gases will vary enormously among, say, the transport sector, industry and the forestry or agricultural sectors, as well as among countries. This makes fossil carbon taxes potentially interesting.

When focusing on reductions of greenhouse gas emissions with a fossil origin, one might forget that energy efficiency is *generally* important for other reasons too. Energy efficiency in non-fossil alternatives, as long as these are not in abundance, will most likely become *increasingly* important since most other forms of energy imply some type of environmental problem.

Difficulty in monitoring emissions

It is not uncommon to find that emissions are hard to monitor. This may be because there are many small, dispersed or mobile polluters, as is the case with the consumers of fossil carbon (from oil etc.), that contribute to global climate change. In those cases where there is a strong one-to-one relationship between the consumption or production of one particular product and the emission concerned, then input, output, or product taxes are good proxy instruments. Taxes on fossil carbon are a relatively good example when it comes to dealing with global warming while taxes on gasoline are a relatively inefficient instrument to deal with local emissions. The emissions from a car and the health impact of those emissions are not just proportional to gasoline used but depend in a complex way on many other factors. Some other external effects of driving are, however, roughly proportional to consumption of gasoline (risks, wear and tear on roads, carbon emissions, etc.). Gasoline is therefore often selected as a product that can be taxed in lieu of taxing emissions.

There is an increasing interest in the European Union regarding distance-based charging of the external costs associated with heavy goods vehicles (see, for example the discussion on the so-called Euro-vignette directive (1999/62/EC)). If distance-based charging systems are implemented, fuel taxes for those vehicles included in the systems can more accurately be described as carbon emission taxes owing to the direct proportionality between carbon content and carbon dioxide emissions.

Uncertainty over damage costs and efficiency

With perfect certainty it is quite easy to show the symmetry between price- and quantity-type instruments. Thus a tax of t dollars per ton of effluent will essentially have the same effect as requiring a mandatory limit equal to x tons if the marginal cost of abatement is t at the level x. When there is uncertainty about the abatement costs, however, the symmetry breaks down and it can be shown that if the marginal damage costs are very steep, and/or taxes are hard to adjust, quantitative permits are preferred to taxes or fees. The prohibition of certain highly poisonous pesticides is an example. In the climate change case, the damage functions are very hard to assess. However, there is some evidence on the potentially dramatic changes in the climate system when emissions increase, i.e. threshold effects, that is highly politically and economically relevant. We face both the expected disappearance of island states (e.g. the Maldives) and an increased prevalence of heavy storms. The large risks and the uncertainty of their temporal and geographic distribution that characterize the expected damage from climate change pose difficult questions for policy-makers.

In cases where there are dramatic thresholds, a regulation that sets a limit to emissions at "secure" levels can be justified since it may not be desirable to experiment in the search for the optimal tax level. Instead an absolute standard is needed (such as absolute prohibition of certain very toxic chemicals). The costs of a small mistake in the "target dose" can be terribly high and the precision of the quantitative instrument in this case is higher. An interesting political aspect of uncertainty in reaching emission targets with taxes is what happens if Kyoto targets are not met? If an emissions goal is politically important to fulfill, a tradable permit system has obvious advantages. The EU CO_2 emissions trading scheme caps a significant proportion of CO_2 but far from all greenhouse gas emissions. The ambition to include more sectors and not only CO_2 should in this light be a priority issue. Conversely, however, when the cost of abatement rises steeply and the marginal cost of damage is relatively flat a price-type instrument such as a tax is to be preferred. In this case it is the tax that has greater precision with respect to avoiding what could be excessive economic costs (maybe of bankruptcy and unemployment) if a standard is set that happens to be too stringent. It is sometimes argued that damage costs for greenhouse gas emissions are relatively flat. Even though this is certainly true for some broad ranges in carbon emissions, it can be of utmost importance to acknowledge the potential and expected non-linearities in how the climate responds to increasing carbon emissions. This fact is one good reason for the ambition to cap the emissions in a tradable permit system. To cap a larger proportion of the emissions by including more sectors would in any case make marginal abatement costs for reducing greenhouse gas emissions converge across sectors.

*Intertemporal efficiency with technical change, inflation,
or economic growth*

If abatement technology develops rapidly over time so that costs fall, then a tax and a standard will again have very different effects. The tax will continue to provide a very strong incentive for more abatement while a standard will tend to become non-binding and have little effect. Typically, environmentalists would prefer the standard but the actual optimal outcome again depends on the relative slopes of the abatement and damage curves. If the damage curve is flat (as with many stock pollutants), then certainly the continued pressure for abatement provided by the price-type instrument will tend to be preferable. If the damage curve is very steep then once you are safely under the threshold, the value of continued abatement is not so great and a standard would be preferable, to avoid unnecessary abatement costs! A related (but opposite) effect occurs in economies with rapid inflation. Unless the charge is adjusted it falls in real value and may thus become inappropriately low. Clearly this can be a disadvantage compared to quantitative standards in this case.

One obvious relationship is that between economic growth and carbon emissions. There is considerable evidence that this relation will, in the absence of strong policies, continue in the foreseeable future, in spite of the increasing use of biomass and other climate-neutral energy. This implies that, all else equal, it will be increasingly difficult to reach carbon emission goals as we get richer. Hence one natural suggestion would be that carbon (and energy) taxes should be adjusted for GDP growth. This would be particularly relevant for the sectors/users that are not included in the trading system. Such an adjustment would also be very promising in trying to break the historical relationship between economic growth and fossil carbon emissions. From a legal perspective it would probably be quite easy to add a "GDP-adjusting paragraph" in the EU directives on minimum tax rates on energy. This would also secure important tax revenues and *at the same time* ease the fear of undesired effects on competition between countries when trying to combat climate change. It remains to be seen whether the political obstacles of achieving this on the European level are insurmountable. If carbon-related taxes are not linked to economic growth, it will most likely be harder to meet Kyoto emission targets, both in the short and in the longer term.

Measurability and technical and ecological complexity

When the environmental conditions to be monitored are sufficiently complex, as maybe the case with many different chemicals in large industrial plants, then it is hard to see how a tax can be designed in a sufficiently detailed way, and individual licensing may be the best option. One reason for this is that a tax has to be very precise. Preferably one would want a straightforward quantitative measure such as kilos of sulfur. If the goal is fuzzier, such as avoiding eutrophication or acidification, then it might be conceivable to construct an index or set of weights so that a tax schedule could be used. With complex ecosystems the difficulties increase. Not only would a vector of different "prices" be needed for different chemicals but the regulator might also want to differentiate between emissions at different points, etc. Although this type of tax instrument has actually been designed and used it was primarily in the former Soviet Union and the interpretation of taxes in a planned economy is quite different from that in a market economy. It would generally be thought of as difficult to pass this type of tax law in a market economy. Not only is the level of detail daunting but the risk of choosing the wrong levels is also problematic. The regulator loses direct control over the quantities emitted. If the tax level is "too low" a company might decide to emit a large amount of some toxic chemical in the middle of a city and the regulator would lack the instruments to stop this. This is clearly a risk that can be thought of in terms of a steep damage curve, which, as mentioned, favors individual regulation.

The design of a trading system also hinges on measurability: the buyers and sellers of permits need to know that the permit is valid for the right amount, time-period, etc. The design choice between upstream and downstream trading systems can be understood in this perspective. Put differently, this choice depends on the expected size and nature of transaction costs associated with a CO_2 trading system. Even though it is theoretically possible to suggest that *individuals* should have a permit when, for instance, filling their car with gasoline, this has so far never been a viable policy option. From an environmental viewpoint, demanding that all carbon emissions from fossil fuel burning (and emissions of other greenhouse gases) should be capped is very attractive. But, from a transaction costs perspective, capping all emissions could hardly be achieved by a downstream design. Hence, making oil companies liable for holding carbon permits for the fuel (for transport purposes) they are selling would be the natural solution from a transaction costs perspective.

Other instruments that may be very appropriate include the labeling, informational, and liability instruments. An example of a promising labeling scheme is the development of greenhouse gas indicators to monitor and to disclose greenhouse gas emissions by industry. Such a system makes information more visible in companies' balance sheets and thereby strengthens the incentive to seek cheap abatement options such as investment in energy-efficient technology, alternative energy sources, new production processes, etc. Most likely, the incentives for this type of information disclosure will be stronger when there are complementary market-based policies, such as a trading system, at work, not least via the financial sector.

Burden of cost and issues of political feasibility

The fact that congestion and overuse of commons (e.g. an excessive amount of greenhouse gas emissions that will jeopardize the welfare of future generations) can be technically rectified by a tax has been mentioned. While the number of users or the congestion may easily be brought down to an optimal level, the users may, as a collective, be worse off in welfare terms than they were before the tax. There is an important class of problems where the users are thought to have historical rights to their level of activity. They will clearly resist the notion of a state taking the entire surplus even if it did bring down emissions to sustainable levels. In other cases the polluter may simply be so powerful that he has the ability to avoid or stop taxes. In both these situations a tax is impossible, but it does not mean that there are no other policies available. Rights can be created, either full property rights or at least pollution permits that are allocated freely. Also price-type instruments such as charges can be used as long as the proceeds are (at least partially) refunded or used in some way that is a benefit to (and decided by) the community concerned. In the case of a suggested trading system for carbon permits, the regulated operators also feel a historical right to emit. This is no less relevant when discussing whether to lift carbon taxes or not when the new trading system comes into place. If previous carbon taxes (or, in some cases, energy taxes) are not lifted, there will be an additional regulation, which is well motivated from a climate change perspective. From the regulated interests perspective, sometimes exposed to international competition, the argument of fair competition tends to be heavily used. In the USA, road charges are earmarked for road funds, and in many developing or transitional countries environmental fees are earmarked for environmental funds. These earmarkings do entail the risk of inefficient use of public funds but in some cases this may be the price one has to pay to get sufficient political acceptability.[3]

The choice of allocation mechanism for a CO_2 emissions trading system has been much discussed. From an efficiency perspective the permits should be auctioned, allowing for an efficient use of revenues. The EU trading scheme is based mainly on the free allocation of permits (that are either grandfathered or benchmarked permits allocated according to historical emissions). The main reason for this is that it is a way of getting acceptance from the regulated interests. However, a generous allocation might imply problems for other sectors in achieving their goals in a low-cost way. Typically, marginal CO_2 emissions reductions in the transport sector are more costly than emission abatements in large parts of the energy and industrial sectors. If the opt-in option for the transport sector is used, it will most likely buy carbon rights from the "original" trading sectors. In Kyoto jargon, the EU CO_2 emissions trading scheme, with the generous allocation of permit rights to the trading sector, is almost analogous to the creation of "hot air." (The term "hot air" refers to an abundance of rights. It is generally used to describe the situation in Russia, and some neighbouring countries, that were given emission rights in proportion to industrial production in an earlier period. The collapse of heavy industry in these countries created emisssion " reductions" that had nothing to do with abatement but could still be sold.)

Judging from the design of the trading scheme, the operators in the scheme appear to have significant lobbying capacity. The principal method of allocation (grandfathering, i.e. operators obtain carbon rights according to historical emissions) is perhaps the most obvious expression of this. However, this also implies higher costs for other sectors. Although political support is important, it should still be an obvious goal to keep abatement and mitigation costs down. If the current European emissions trading system is too lenient in terms of stricter emissions requirements, this will imply higher abatement costs for the non-trading sectors, *as long as the Kyoto agreement on emissions reductions is strictly met.*

Missing markets in insurance and banking

Insurance is generally not fully supplied by the market. Information asymmetry implies a market failure through adverse selection of clients (it is the high-risk people who buy the insurance policies) and moral hazard (once people have a policy they may start to be reckless). These factors will lead to an undersupply of insurance. People with little income who are very dependent on natural resources typically operate at high levels of risk and typically cannot get the insurance they would need. Nor (for similar reasons) do they have access to regular banking or saving services. The result may be extreme vulnerability to climate variation such as a rise in the sea level rise, storms, etc. The missing markets in insurance and banking actually is likely to increase the expected damage of climate change and *increase the desirability of abatement and of outside efforts to contain or prevent damage.*

The number of polluters

The number of polluters and the structure of markets are other conditions that may have profound effects on the choice and design of policy instruments. If there is only one polluter – a monopoly – a tax will get passed on; moreover, it will have perverse incentives since monopolies already are characterized by too low a level of output – an effect which will be worsened by a tax. Furthermore, if there is just one polluter, the decision-makers would generally be loath to go through the whole general process of writing a tax law and would tend rather to use individual negotiation. If, on the other hand, the number of agents is very large a system of tradable permits might be hard to administer and a system of taxes might be preferable.

In fact, collecting revenues from energy taxes (e.g. on gasoline) is generally associated with transaction costs which are low compared to the size of the tax revenues. If all agents who emitted carbon dioxide were included in a tradable permit system where permits were auctioned, transaction costs would probably be quite high (at least with today's techniques). This is an argument for continuing to use taxes and leaving a number of sectors (such as private transport, heating, etc.) outside the trading system, although the emissions from these sectors could also be capped with an upstream solution of the trading system.

Rent-seeking and political economy

It is well known that public policies are decided not just by abstract considerations of optimality but by lobbying and the interplay of more or less powerful groups in policy-making. Naturally the policy-maker should anticipate this and avoid certain instruments that are particularly prone to this type of problem. Subsidies are one obvious candidate: they are not only expensive in direct terms but even more so in terms of the wasted energy spent on lobbying (and corruption). Even the allocation of permits or mechanisms for refunding will typically be the subject of considerable lobbying and this needs to be taken into account. These issues are particularly likely to be important if the targeted polluters have any of a number of characteristics. If they are a small subgroup with regional or ethnic characteristics they are likely to feel discriminated against; similarly if they are poor, in which case welfare considerations become particularly prominent. On the other hand, if they are rich and powerful they may have the capacity to stop or stall implementation for that reason. If they are a small homogeneous group they can more easily organize. For each of these cases, allocation, refunding, or compensation mechanisms may have to considered separately.

Economy-wide effects

Most analysis of policy instruments is carried out as partial analysis and typically this will suffice. There are, however, cases when the repercussions throughout the economy need to be taken into account. A tax, for instance, raises revenues that can be used for public spending on damage mitigation or on other environmental issues or for reducing the burden of other taxes. In fact, the way they are used will affect the cost of the instrument under discussion. Refunding lump sums, lowering other taxes, or earmarking for some purpose are all different methods and they have to be compared not only with an optimal tax system in the absence of the environmental tax, but also with the situation where the environmental problem is solved by some other method, such as physical regulation. Environmental taxes have revenue recycling effects which are good since they imply that the state benefits from not having to raise other taxes. However, there are also tax interaction effects that imply a welfare loss, because the cost of taxation rises when consumer choice is distorted. This latter effect is, however, inevitable and operates even if a regulatory instrument is used for environmental clean-up – in which case, however, the positive revenue recycling effect is absent. In the case of climate policies, the revenue recycling effects are potentially very large and taking advantage of them will imply much lower overall costs for climate policy. This argues in favor of auctioning or selling permits (or of using taxes).

Concluding comments

Constructing policy instruments for sustainable development is a complex task and there is no reason to expect any easy answers. There is no single method for deciding on macroeconomic policies or even on health and defense priorities. In the case of environmental and resource policies, there are several layers of complexity and the policy instruments have to be specially tailored to fit a number of very different situations. Often several goals are pursued simultaneously and a whole array of instruments may have to be used together. One of the challenges is to overcome market failures without incurring policy failures that are worse.

In the case of climate change the technical and ecological conditions are so complex and exist at so many levels that we are bound to see complex policy packages with many instruments chosen. This may carry a risk of "regulatory capture" if polluters dominate (and maybe corrupt) the regulators. The polluting firms often have more information and typically greater resources at their disposal. The regulators are faced not just with the dilemma of designing policy instruments but, first and foremost, with the need to construct their own agencies. The US EPA (Environmental Protection Agency) has, together with state and local inspectorates, many tens of thousands of employees. Most in developing countries agencies have only a handful of staff and sometimes these staff have little technical training and equipment, as well as only vague legal ground to stand on.

In these circumstances, voluntary and informational policy instruments may be important first steps. By collecting and disseminating information, an agency, like the environmental ministry in Indonesia, can achieve several important goals. It creates a baseline for future action. It encourages transparency in that individual inspectors can, at least not secretly agree to unreasonable emissions. It can build relationships with the polluting industries which are not purely adversarial and it opens the way for pressure from customers, workers, investors, neighbors, and other groups concerned. Many (though far from all) problems can be greatly diminished by very simple means and it is of considerable importance to build positive partnerships in which the agency assumes not only the role of a policeman but perhaps more that of a facilitator and teacher. One important task is to help local industries acquire a reasonable perspective on the range of abatement technologies and the requirements posed by customers in the national and international markets. Also access to technology and credit are important features. Local agencies cannot fulfill this task well if they are understaffed and underfunded. Small fees on appropriately selected pollutants can help to provide required finance. A certain degree of pragmatism is important here. Finding the exact "Pigouvian" level may not be very important in an economy where this level is likely to change by several orders of magnitude on account of rapid industrialization, migration, technical progress in abatement, and other factors. Establishing the principle that pollution is a cost to be internalized and securing some finance for the local EPA may, however, both be very crucial goals. Thus a low fee that gets passed, and leads to payments (and some incentive effects for abatement) is clearly much better than a fee that has no chance of getting implemented and which would not stand the test of time anyway. An important lesson can, as mentioned, be learned from fuel taxes for the transport sector. For various reasons, these are in some countries either more or less politically feasible than other instruments, but in those countries where they have been used, they certainly have been very effective in reducing carbon emissions, and in some cases may help meet other objectives too.

Notes

1 There is a considerable literature on the design of policy instruments; see, for instance, Baumol and Oates (1988), Tietenberg (1990), Xepapadeas (1997) or Sterner(2002).
2 The vital characteristic of tradable permits is that they are a form of property. The fact that they are valuable creates incentives for conservation. For discussion of their background, function, and properties see Coase (1960), Dales (1968), Stavins (1998), or Sterner (2002).
3 There are some well-known examples in Poland, as well as in China and Colombia; see the New Ideas on Pollution Regulation database, http://www.worldbank.org/NIPR.

References

Baumol, W. J., and Oates, W. E. 1988. *The Theory of Environmental Policy*. New York: Cambridge University Press.
Coase, R. 1960. "The problem of social cost," *Journal of Law and Economics* 3: 1–44.
Dales, J. H. 1968. *Pollution, Property and Prices*. Toronto: University of Toronto Press.
European Commission 1999. "Commission recommendation of 5 February 1999 on the Reduction of CO_2 emissions from passenger cars." Brussels, 5.2.99 (1999/125/EC), *Official Journal of the European Communities* 13.2.1999. L 40/49.
"European Parliament and Council Directive 1999/62/EC of 17 June 1999 on the charging of heavy goods vehicles for the use of certain infrastructures," *Official Journal of the European Communities* 20.7.1999. L 187/42.
"European Parliament and Council Directive 1999/94/EC of 13 December 1999 relating to the availability of consumer information on fuel economy and CO_2 emissions in respect of the marketing of new passenger cars," *Official Journal of the European Communities* 18.1.2000. L 12/16.

Hammar, H., Löfgren, Å., and Sterner, T. 2004. "Political economy obstacles to fuel taxation," *Energy Journal* 25: 1–17.

Stavins, R. 1998. "What have we learnt from the grand policy experiment? Lessons from SO_2 allowance trading," *Journal of Economic Perspectives* 12: 69–88.

Sterner, T. 2002. *Designing Instruments for Resource and Environmental Policy.* Washington, DC: Resources for the Future.

Tietenberg, T. H. 1990. "Economic instruments for environmental regulation," *Oxford Review of Economic Policy* 6: 17–33.

Xepapadeas, A. 1997. *Advanced Principles in Environmental Policy.* Cheltenham: Edward Elgar.

3 Technical innovation and design choices for emissions trading and other climate policies

Carolyn Fischer

Introduction

Climate change is a serious public policy issue because it may impose costs on society, including adverse human health impacts, productivity losses, and degradation of valued natural resources. On the other hand, policies to reduce greenhouse gases can have serious economic consequences, such as higher costs of production and increased energy expenses for households. This trade-off is the classic problem for policymakers trying to strike a balance between the costs and benefits of environmental regulation.

The political balancing act would become much easier if policy could generate a "win–win" scenario with both environmental and economic benefits. Thus, much attention has been given to the "Porter hypothesis" that environmental regulation can actually increase the profits of firms, chiefly by encouraging them to look for more efficient production technologies that ultimately lower their costs (Porter and van der Linde, 1995). Economists traditionally doubt the concept of a free lunch: if such gains in efficiency were worthwhile in the first place, why would firms not take advantage of them without regulation? What appears to be cost savings due to regulation can often be negated by proper accounting of management time and other human resource costs, for example (Palmer *et al.*, 1995).

Some theories have been developed to explain how "win–win" situations might arise (Sinclair-Desgagné, 1999). For example, when companies have difficulties monitoring all aspects of employee and firm performance – like reducing environmental risks – incomplete information can lead to insufficient incentives for managers to devote attention to environmental performance relative to more obvious indicators.

This chapter is based on Resources for the Future's Climate Issues Brief 20, *Climate Change Policy Choices and Technical Innovation*.

Public policies that help firms improve incentives or that provide information that also helps overcome coordination failures can then indeed improve both environmental and financial outcomes. However, it is still unclear how widespread these opportunities would be.

Technology is increasingly being touted as the answer to the economy–environment trade-off. If technological progress is the engine of growth, then green technologies could be the engine of sustainable, climate-friendly growth. But beyond just looking for low-cost greenhouse gas abatement policies, some advocates propose that we can use clean technologies to take care of the environment without economic costs and without imposing environmental regulations. The search for such "win–win–win" scenarios is illustrated by a White House press release, in which President Clinton looked to promote bio-based energy technologies to "help grow the economy, enhance US energy security, and meet environmental challenges like global warming" (White House, 1999). Similarly, the Bush administration's National Energy Policy relies heavily on promoting new technologies to pursue the multiple goals of reliable, affordable, and environmentally sound energy. In particular, with respect to energy efficiency and the use of renewable resources, it touts a variety of public–private partnership programs that "save energy, cut energy bills, enhance economic growth, and reduce emissions of conventional air pollutants as well as greenhouse gases" (National Energy Policy, 2001, ch. 3, p. 11).

Can technology really allow us to have our free lunch and eat it too? Unfortunately, if it sounds too good to be true, it probably is. Good incentives for developing climate-friendly technologies depend critically on whether good climate policies are in place. Furthermore, the usefulness of public investment in green technology also depends on the incentives created by climate policies. Thus, while cases can be made for both greenhouse gas regulation and promotion of innovation, pursuit of these goals will involve hard choices and real resource costs, not the least of which is the opportunity cost of research and development expenditures.

The European Union has now implemented a program that caps carbon emissions and provides for trading of the emission allowances. By making carbon costly to emit, such a program can go far in creating incentives for innovation in technologies that reduce carbon dependence. However, the cap-and-trade program only applies to certain sectors, not all fossil fuel use. Meeting the Kyoto target will require a variety of other policies that target energy efficiency and innovation at the same time that member countries seek to mitigate impacts on consumer prices and on industrial competitiveness.

In this chapter, we present some of the economics of innovation as it relates to climate policy and explain how the two are fundamentally linked. Since climate policy will feature a broad portfolio of policy instruments, we discuss both traditional forms of regulation and market-based instruments for environmental management. In particular, we focus on the impact of an emissions trading program, including its scope, rules for allocating allowances, and interactions with other policies. We then discuss the appropriate role of the government in promoting research and development (R&D) and greenhouse gas abatement.

Private incentives to develop cleaner technologies

Economists note that the driving force behind the development of new and improved technologies is the profit motive. Firms realize greater profits if they can produce more and better products for the same cost, or if they can make the same products with less. Thus, they are willing to spend resources on research and development if the results will be lower costs and higher productivity.

Even without any explicit climate policies, this drive for more, better, and cheaper can lead to lower-emitting techniques. Energy is costly, so firms will want production processes that use less energy. For the same reason, consumers will demand products that use energy more efficiently as well. However, market forces will provide insufficient incentives to develop climate-friendly technologies if the market prices of energy inputs do not fully reflect their social cost (inclusive of environmental consequences). This incentive problem is magnified if energy prices do not even cover the costs of production (Fischer and Toman, 1998).

Even if energy prices reflect all production costs, without an explicit greenhouse gas policy, firms have no incentive to reduce their greenhouse gas emissions *per se* beyond the motivation to economize on energy costs. For example, a utility would happily find a way to generate the same amount of electricity with less fuel, but without a policy that makes carbon dioxide emissions costly, it would not care specifically about the carbon content of its fuel mix in choosing between, say, coal and natural gas. For firms to have the desire to innovate cheaper and better ways to reduce emissions (and not merely inputs), they must bear additional financial costs for emissions.

By imposing requirements that reflect these social trade-offs, policies designed to abate greenhouse gases also can have significant impacts on incentives for innovation. However, the incentives can differ greatly across the range of possible measures.

Command-and-control policies that dictate what specific technologies or processes a firm must use by design give firms little leeway. As a result, the firm has little or no incentive to employ a more cost-effective way to achieve the same emissions reduction, since it is not allowed to deviate from the specified technology. A policy mandating the "*best available technology*" might allow the firm to update or retrofit its production process with a more cost-effective technology. However, the firm would not want to develop a better technology that would achieve more abatement if that switch entailed higher total costs – even if from a social standpoint the extra reductions in pollution would justify the added costs.

The *threat* of future regulation can indeed induce innovation to develop the technology necessary for compliance; however, that threat must be credible. To the extent that governments express a second industrial policy goal, such as a preference for domestic technology, their credibility for implementing the environmental regulation is compromised, and the development of such a technology becomes less likely (Cadot and Sinclair-Desgangé, 1996).

Performance standards, which dictate a certain level of abatement but leave the methods up to the firm, give the firm an incentive to develop a cheaper method of attaining the standard. A problem with performance standards, however, is that firms have no incentive to perform beyond the standard, even if lower abatement costs make more abatement desirable from a social perspective.

Market-based instruments, such as emissions taxes or permits, create a price for emissions. Firms then reduce their emissions as long as the cost of an additional amount of abatement is less than the tax (or permit) cost of additional emissions. For the remainder of their emissions, they pay the tax, buy permits, or use permits that they could otherwise sell. This system ensures that marginal abatement costs are equalized across firms, meaning that total abatement costs cannot be lowered by shifting some abatement from one firm to another (see the seminal work by Kneese and Schultz [1975]). By developing a more cost-effective way to reduce pollution, an innovating firm can then save in two ways: on its costs for achieving its current level of abatement, and on its tax or emissions permit payments by performing additional abatement at the new, lower cost.

Thus far, the incentives discussed have been restricted to the firm's own gains from lower pollution abatement costs. Looking at this single-firm context, earlier analyses of environmental policy and innovation showed that emissions taxes and emissions permits generally provide more incentives for technological innovation than command-and-control policies like technology mandates and performance standards (Zerbe, 1970,

Magat, 1978, Downing and White, 1986). In a multiple-firm context, firms collectively pursuing their own innovations can have a significant impact on the overall cost of supplying abatement, creating important differences among market-based policies in equilibrium. With an emissions tax, all firms expand their abatement as innovation reduces costs; with a fixed quantity of emissions permits, however, widespread cost reductions cause the permit price to fall, which feeds back into lower innovation incentives.

Not only may multiple firms be involved in R&D, but new technologies or processes may also be useful for more than just the one firm performing the R&D. When innovations are more widely applicable, the effects on the market equilibrium will prove even more important in comparing both the policy incentives for innovation and their impacts on social welfare.

Incentives from licensing innovations

A technology developed to reduce one firm's costs of abating emissions may also help other firms do the same. As a result, the social gain from this technology consists of the cost reductions to all firms (and, potentially, gains from additional abatement once it is less costly to implement). Furthermore, if adopting the new technology helps these other firms' bottom lines, they will be willing to pay to obtain a license for it. Thus, with a well-functioning patent protection system, for example, the innovator can sell the fruits of its R&D to the potential adopters and reap the full social gains from the invention.

However, reaping those gains may be difficult. New knowledge can create "spillover benefits" for other parties for which the innovator is not compensated. Not every advance may receive a patent: basic research may not have specific, patentable applications. Still, broadening the overall knowledge base can make future valuable applications possible. Even if a new technology or process does receive a patent or copyright, it may be hard to enforce. For example, other firms may have the opportunity to imitate the innovation despite the patent, such as through reverse-engineering. Studies for commercial (or non-environmental) innovations suggest that appropriation rates vary considerably over different types of innovation, with an average rate of around 50 percent (Griliches, 1980, Griliches, 1992, Nadiri, 1993). The easier it is for other firms to imitate the innovation on their own, the less they will be willing to pay for a license, and the lower the gains the original innovator will be able to appropriate. As a result, the innovator will have less incentive to conduct R&D than would be best from a societal perspective.

On the other hand, the market for R&D might also encourage too much research. For example, several innovating firms competing for the rewards of a patent can collectively spend too much on redundant research. Thus, these "patent races" can lead to too much R&D. The consensus view, however, is that the private rate of return to R&D is well below the social rate of return (Mansfield *et al.*, 1977, Griliches, 1980, Bernstein and Nadiri, 1988). Thus, positive spillover effects prevail, and markets will tend to provide too little R&D.

Comparing policies with respect to innovation and adoption

When we take into account interactions among innovating firms and other firms potentially adopting the new technology (at a price), the analysis of how different abatement policies affect innovation becomes more complex and ambiguous. Table 3.1 summarizes the various incentives for innovation and gives an idea of their relative importance.

Command-and-control policies that specify a technology allow other adopters no more leeway than the innovator. Therefore, little or no

Table 3.1. *Incentives for innovation created by environmental policies*

Policy	Direct gains to innovating firm	Potential rents from adoption
Command-and-control	None	None
Best available technology	Negative: new standard raises overall compliance costs	Positive: tighter standard raises incentive to adopt
Performance standards	Positive, less than tax: limited to existing abatement costs	Positive, less than tax: limited to existing abatement costs
Emission tax	Positive: lowers abatement costs and taxed emissions	Positive: lowers abatement costs and taxed emissions
Auctioned emission permits	Positive, more than tax: lowers abatement costs and costs of all permits purchased	Positive, less than tax: buying permits becomes cheaper alternative
Grandfathered emission permits	Positive, less than tax: lowers abatement costs	Positive, less than tax: buying permits becomes cheaper alternative
Tradable performance standards/output-allocated permits	Positive, may be less than tax: initial abatement costs higher but lowers output subsidy	Positive, less than tax: initial abatement costs higher but permits become cheaper

incentive remains to employ more cost-effective pollution reduction techniques. However, a policy mandating the *"best available technology"* offers the possibility that the innovator's new technology would be made the standard. Then the other firms in the industry would have to pay to adopt it, if they could not come up with their own equivalent technology. Therefore, although the innovating firm's own pollution reduction costs could rise because of the new, stricter technology standard, the gains from other firms acquiring licenses for the technology could be large.

Under *performance standards*, adopting firms receive the same gains from abatement cost reduction as the innovator. They are willing to pay for a cheaper way to abate their emissions up to the standard, but they will not want to push reductions beyond the standard.

With *market-based mechanisms*, the development and industry-wide adoption of an innovation can affect not only individual firms' costs, but also the prices and quantities prevailing in the industry's market. Because different market-based mechanisms allow for different changes in prices and quantities of emissions, they have different implications for innovation (Fischer *et al.*, 2003). Taxes set the price of emissions, allowing total abatement to vary, while permits set the total amount of emissions, allowing the marginal cost of abatement to vary. Therefore, while one can choose a tax and an emissions cap that would generate the same outcome before innovation, product and technology markets will adjust differently after innovation, depending on the policy.

Under an *emissions tax*, as innovation makes abatement cheaper, the total amount of abatement will rise because it will be less expensive to reduce emissions some more than to pay taxes on all current emissions. With *emissions permits*, on the other hand, firms as a group will not abate more after the innovation, since the total amount is set by the cap. Therefore, the total abatement cost savings are less than under the tax, where more abatement was performed after innovation. Furthermore, as innovation lowers abatement costs, the price of emissions permits will fall.

From the point of view of the adopting firms, their individual decision on whether to acquire a license for the technology does not affect the permit price; however, they will attempt to anticipate the fall in the permit price caused by collective adoption of the innovation. The lower permit price means that they now have the less costly option of forgoing the new technology and buying cheaper permits instead. Thus, adopting firms will not be willing to pay as much for the innovation under permits as under the tax. This "adoption price effect" lowers the maximum royalty the innovating firm can charge to license the technology.

However, the price fall can benefit the innovator directly, if permits are auctioned. Then, a lower permit price means the innovator will not have to pay as much for the rest of its emissions. This "emissions payment effect" raises the gains to innovation. If permits are freely distributed, on the other hand, the price fall lowers the value of the innovator's allocated permits, which counteracts the emissions payment effect. Thus, free permits give less incentive to innovate than auctioned permits and less than taxes because of the smaller abatement cost savings and the adoption price effect.

It is harder to say whether auctioned permits or taxes generate more innovation, since the incentives depend critically on the adopting firms' ability to imitate the innovation. In general, with little imitation, unless the emissions payment effect is very large, taxes provide more innovation incentive. However, if imitation is substantial, preventing the innovator from recouping most gains, if any, from the adopters, auctioned permits provide more incentive.

With respect to climate policy, the more compartmentalized the emission permit programs, the larger will be the impact of a single innovation on permit prices. If a major fuel-saving invention is adopted by the trucking industry, it might have a small effect on permit prices in a broad-based cap-and-trade program, but it would have a large effect on a permit program limited to the trucking sector. Thus, in a broad-based carbon trading program, innovation incentives in a specific sector are going to resemble more closely those of a carbon tax.

Thus far we have discussed how the lump-sum allocation of permit rents affects innovation incentives. Another form of permit distribution, *output-based allocation* or rate-based allocation (also known as "updating"), creates still different incentives for innovation by changing the basic trade-off between production or conservation and emissions intensity. Rate-based allocations have featured prominently in early proposals for climate policies. For example, most of the over forty Climate Change Levy agreements negotiated in the United Kingdom specify energy per unit of output targets for the next ten years. Since emissions factors are defined for each energy form, these are equivalent to rate-based allocations. Other countries, like Canada, have been considering the use of output-based allocation as a means of limiting the adverse impacts on industries that compete in export markets with firms from countries that will not have a national greenhouse gas emissions limitation commitment. Output-allocated permits are also similar to *tradable performance standards*. In the USA, the latter form was used to phase out lead from gasoline, while the former has been proposed for allocation of NO_X emission allowances under the State Implementation Plan Call in some states and in the EPA's Federal Implementation Plan. The Bush climate plan also focuses on an emissions intensity standard. Portfolio standards for generation with renewable energy technologies are another similar form of rate-based policy.

Both output-allocated permits and tradable performance standards require firms to hold permits to cover their emissions, while they are allocated permits according to their output times an average emissions rate. Thus, above-average emitters must buy permits, while below-average emitters can sell them. This permit allocation method creates an implicit subsidy for output, since the more a firm produces, the more permits it gets.

This implicit subsidy affects innovation incentives in a number of ways that are not so obvious. First, it discourages firms from cutting back output, placing more of the abatement burden on lowering emission rates. As a result, for a given target level, total abatement costs are actually higher (Fischer, 2001). This inefficiency then raises the potential gains to innovation, although in a costly way. Second, while it may seem that an innovator would want to push costs even lower in order to gain market share and more subsidies, widespread adoption eliminates any such market share advantage. Furthermore, the subsidy lowers output prices across the industry compared to the other permit or tax schemes, meaning that the extra subsidy gains from expanding market share are largely negated by lower revenue gains. Thus, the output subsidy seems more likely to reduce innovation incentives for producers.

On the consumer side, the output subsidy implies lower prices and thereby less incentive to develop and use technologies that conserve energy or to offer products that may substitute for goods that require energy-intensive production. Of course, if consumers are not sensitive to prices, the conservation incentive is less significant and the distributional impacts potentially more important. The greater worry is the question of competitiveness and emissions leakage: if consumers can easily switch to products imported from countries without climate policies, conservation incentives are also lacking, while production-related emissions are diverted abroad. In this case, some support for output may be justified (Bernard *et al.*, 2001); however, tying this support to the value of the sector's average permit allocation can have counterintuitive effects on industry behavior, including innovation.

Innovation and social welfare

Although we have focused on innovation incentives, it is important to look beyond the question of which environmental policy generates the most R&D and think about overall impacts on societal well-being. Ultimately, the benefits from the environmental policy are generated by abatement; innovation is an important way to assist that goal, but it is an indirect measure. Furthermore, promoting innovation entails its own costs in terms of resources invested in environmentally oriented R&D that could be used elsewhere in the economy.

Policy-makers must choose environmental policies to balance the twin goals of targeting the appropriate level of emissions reductions and offering appropriate inducements for innovation. As we have seen, greenhouse gas abatement policies determine not only the price signals (or regulatory requirements) for emission abatement, but also the signals for innovation. Although a strong consensus has developed that market-based instruments tend to provide better incentives for both, the choice of particular instrument should depend on the context in which it is implemented. Just as the amount of innovation depends on those price signals, getting the right price signals depends on the amount of innov-ation, and both change over time as progress is made and information arrives.

Ideally, policy would take into account future innovation and the evolving costs and benefits of regulation in setting current and future emissions taxes or quotas. For "stock" pollutants, which build up over time, like greenhouse gases, current and future costs and benefits are particularly linked. To the extent that innovation reduces future abate-ment costs, it makes sense to postpone some emissions reductions until the future (Toman *et al.*, 1999). In other words, future innovation can have a significant impact on the emissions rate, both now and in the future. Of course, in reality, the results of R&D investments are highly uncertain, and predicting such a path may be difficult. Furthermore, frequent adjustments to policies may be difficult and involve significant administrative costs. In this case, policy-makers need to weigh the bene-fits and costs of inducing more or less innovation against those of too much or too little abatement.

A fixed tax policy does not allow emission prices to adjust, thus creating a risk of too much abatement if costs fall (assuming the tax starts out reflecting the initial damage costs of emissions, which then decline as emissions fall). However, taxes do allow the amount of abate-ment to fluctuate according to cost conditions. On the other hand, a permit policy does not allow an adjustment of the quantity of abatement, meaning that too little will be done if costs fall (and, conversely, too much effort will be put into abatement if costs rise). In general, with uncertain benefits and costs, quantity standards perform better when the marginal damages of emissions are relatively steep, whereas price policies (like a fixed tax) perform better when they are relatively flat compared to the costs (Weitzman, 1974). R&D, however, with its own uncertain prospects of success, can contribute to larger potential over- and undershooting with a tax, implying a certain bias in favour of quantity policies when innovation is important (Mendelsohn 1984). Still, in the case of greenhouse gas emissions, their potential damage is relatively insensitive to the rate of emissions at any particular time (although the total cost will likely rise as greenhouse gases accumulate in the atmosphere). These fairly constant benefits to abatement mean that the presence of uncertainty in abatement costs due to unpredictable innovation ultimately favors a tax-based approach over a quantity-based permits approach. The reason is that in these circumstances uncertainty about the volume of abatement imposes less of a burden on society than does abatement cost uncertainty (Pizer, 1999).

This intertemporal balancing act is further complicated by R&D spillovers. In essence, spillover effects and global warming pollution are two separate problems. Ideally, to correct for both requires two separate policy tools, one to provide good incentives for emissions control, the other to supplement for unappropriated gains to R&D. However, when R&D shortfalls cannot be ameliorated directly by available policies, such as research grants or tax credits, abatement policy is then forced to balance its impacts on the two problems. Some environmental policies may help offset imperfections in the market for innovation. But the cost may be wasted expenses on abatement (such as with a high tax) or wasted opportunities for abatement once costs fall (such as with auctioned permits). As with any good thing, one can have too much of innovation or of abatement, since those resources could be used elsewhere. Therefore, an overly strict environmental policy to compensate for shortcomings in R&D gives rise to its own costs; likewise, an overly generous R&D subsidy to make up for inadequately low emissions pricing can be wasteful.

Diffusion of technologies

The incentives to adopt a cleaner technology mirror those for creating it for oneself, namely the cost savings. Higher energy prices raise the returns to adopting energy-efficient technologies and thus encourage their diffusion. (For more discussion and empirical evidence regarding diffusion of energy-saving products, see Jaffe *et al.* [1999].)

However, even when potential cost savings are substantial, a techno- logical advance is not often adopted completely and immediately. Diffu- sion may lag because of adjustment costs (such as training personnel in a new production process that reduces energy use), information costs (like educating consumers about energy efficiency), or irreversible investments (like building a whole new plant with new-generation technology), or because an even better technology might be on the way, making the wait worthwhile. As these cases all represent real resource costs for the firm, avoiding or postponing adoption can be quite rational. Furthermore, in the absence of market failures or important returns to scale, delay or non-adoption can also be an appropriate allocation of resources from the point of view of society.

On the other hand, the innovator may choose to limit diffusion. A patent is essentially a temporary monopoly, and unless the innovator can charge higher prices to firms valuing the technology more (i.e. discriminate on price), royalties may be maximized by restricting licenses. A tension can then exist between the gains from spreading new technology today and those from promoting future innovation. Society would benefit most from the widest worthwhile diffusion of an existing innovation. For example, to convert as many vehicles on the road as possible, one might want to distribute freely the design of an engine modification that cost-effectively raises fuel efficiency. However, if automobile companies expected that to happen, they would have had little motivation to develop the modification in the first place. Therefore, when society values more immediate and complete distribution, such a policy must be done in a way that maintains the proper incentives for future innovation. In other words, the policy precedent should involve compensation (e.g. buying the patent rights) rather than expropriation or forced distribution (see also Blackman [1997], for a discussion of international diffusion policies).

In many cases, however, government can aid diffusion without compromising R&D incentives. Support for high-spillover advances, such as in basic knowledge from fundamental research, offers such an opportunity. Reducing adjustment costs can aid diffusion as well as incentives for innovation. Public institutions, with their existing infrastructure of regulatory expertise and contacts, can take advantage of returns to scale in gathering and distributing information. Public policy toward the environment could include the dissemination of best business practices and the subsidization of training in environmental management, thus helping firms to take advantage of any "win–win" opportunities that might otherwise be ignored (DeCanio, 1994, DeCanio and Watkins, 1998, Sinclair-Desgangé, 1999). However, the need for such subsidies depends on the extent to which there are internal management failures in firms, and on the extent to which these problems can be distinguished from the pursuit of unnecessary subsidies by firms. These issues remain controversial. Similarly, investment subsidies can reduce the barriers created by capital market problems (like impediments to borrowing), but they do come at the cost of scarce public funds and offer windfalls to those who would adopt anyway.

A policy mandating the best available technology is a type of forced diffusion. How the policy is designed greatly affects the pay-offs to innovation. Requiring all firms to buy the new technology puts few limits on what the innovator can charge, possibly resulting in too much incentive to innovate. If costs are a consideration in imposing a new standard, some limit will be put on such opportunities. If other firms can use alternative means to achieve the new standard, then pay-offs will be more in line with actual net benefits, unless imitation is an option. Finally, if the innovator is required to disseminate freely the advance, little incentive will exist for innovation. Thus, in situations where market-based instruments are not feasible and technology standards are used, policy design must also take innovation incentives into account.

The role of government in R&D

Economists generally agree that the main role of the government is to stick to the basics: first, to create the proper private incentives for environmental protection and for innovation; second, to supplement the socially useful R&D that the private sector does not tend to provide sufficiently.

For the first part, the government can provide institutions like a strong system of patents and copyrights to ensure inventors can reap the fruits of their efforts. To aid diffusion, the government can take cost-effective measures to lessen informational costs and other barriers that create transaction costs. If fast, low-cost distribution of new research and technologies is a priority, its implementation should remain consistent with preserving the long-run incentives for R&D, as discussed above.

With respect to climate change, the government should ensure producers face financial costs for their emissions that bear some resemblance to the expected future environmental costs, however inadequately these costs are currently measured. Market-based instruments not only promote cost-effective pollution reduction but also provide the most efficient incentives for investing in the development of environmentally friendly technologies.

Even with strong patents and emissions pricing, private firms may not invest in the right kinds or the right amounts of R&D. Basic research is a good example: one can rarely foresee all the useful applications that may arise from the expansion of the general knowledge base. Therefore, government has a central role in funding high-spillover research. One way to achieve this goal in a decentralized manner is through a system of competitive grants.

With respect to R&D for specific applications (such as particular manufacturing technologies or electricity generation), governments are notoriously bad at picking winners. (For an example involving a breeder reactor, see Cohen and Noll [1991].) The selection of these projects is best left to private markets, while the government ensures those markets face the socially correct price signals. One exception may be specific technologies that would aid in the implementation of more efficient greenhouse gas policies; for example, better emissions monitoring devices could reduce compliance and enforcement costs and enable the transition to market-based mechanisms for emissions control. In this case, in a sense, the government is the relevant market for the innovation. But for most cases, to the extent that markets still tend to provide insufficient R&D, broad rather than project-specific R&D subsidies are in order. (Wright [1983] discusses the efficiency of alternative research policy instruments in the context of stimulating commercial innovation.)

Above all, policy-makers concerned about climate change must recognize that incentives for abatement and innovation are inexorably linked. If failures in the market for R&D exist, and available policies cannot correct them, the choice of climate policy will be affected. If innovation incentives are lacking, the best climate policy response is likely to be looser regulation, reflecting the higher expected abatement costs, not stricter regulation to promote innovation. Similarly, if emissions are underpriced and too little abatement is performed, less investment in R&D may actually be warranted, since the new climate-friendly technologies will not be sufficiently exploited. Since greenhouse gases accumulate over time, incentives for their abatement and innovation are further intertwined, since current and future abatement can depend on each other as well as innovation, which in turn depends on abatement.

Thus, a technology policy is no substitute for environmental policy. The primary gains to environmental protection always come from reducing environmental damages in the most cost-effective manner, regardless of innovation. Innovation then has the potential to increase those gains, but the benefits of emissions-reducing innovations are by definition limited to the potential environmental gains (Parry *et al.*, 2003).

More than other policy instruments, market-based mechanisms offer the incentives both to protect the environment efficiently and to develop better methods of protection. Put simply, rather than looking for a free lunch, perhaps we should make a nutritious lunch.

References

Bernard, A., Fischer, C., and Vielle, M. 2001. *Is There a Rationale for Rebating Environmental Levies?* RFF Discussion Paper 01–31, Washington, DC: Resources for the Future.

Bernstein, J. L., and Nadiri, I. 1988. "Rates of return on physical and R&D capital and structure of the production process: cross section and time series evidence." Working Paper 2570, National Bureau of Economic Research, Cambridge, MA.

Blackman, A. 1997. *The Economics of Technology Diffusion: Implications for Greenhouse Gas Mitigation in Developing Countries.* Climate Issues Brief 5, Washington, DC: Resources for the Future.

Cadot, O., and Sinclair-Desgangé, B. 1996. "Innovation under the threat of stricter environmental standards," in C. Carraro, Y. Katsoulacos, and A. Xepapadeas (eds.). *Environmental Policy and Market Structure.* Dordrecht: Kluwer Academic Publishers.

Cohen, L., and Noll, R. 1991. *The Technology Pork Barrel.* Washington, DC: Brookings Institution.

DeCanio, S. J. 1994. "Agency and control problems in US corporations: the case of energy-efficient investment projects," *Journal of the Economics of Business* 1: 105–23.

DeCanio, S. J., and Watkins, W. E. 1998. "Investment in energy efficiency: do the characteristics of firms matter?" *Review of Economics and Statistics* 80: 95–107.

Downing, P. G., and White, L. J. 1986. "Innovation in pollution control," *Journal of Environmental Economics and Management* 13: 18–29.

Fischer, C. 2001. *Rebating Environmental Policy Revenues: Output Based Allocations and Tradable Performance Standards.* RFF Discussion Paper 01–22, Washington, DC: Resources for the Future.

Fischer, C., Parry, I. W. H., and Pizer, W. A. 2003. "Instrument choice for environmental protection when technological innovation is endogenous," *Journal of Environmental Economics and Management* 45: 523–45.

Fischer, C., and Toman, M. 1998. *Environmentally and Economically Damaging Subsidies: Concepts and Illustrations.* Climate Issues Brief 14, Washington, DC: Resources for the Future.

Griliches, Z. 1980. "Returns to research and development expenditures in the private sector", in J. W. Kendrick and B. Vaccara (eds.). *New Developments in Productivity Measurement.* NBER Studies in Income and Wealth 44, Chicago: University of Chicago Press.

1992. "The search for R&D spillovers," *Scandinavian Journal of Economics* 94 (supplement): S29–S47.

Jaffe, A. B., Newell, R. G., and Stavins, R. N. 1999. *Energy-Efficient Technologies and Climate Change Policies: Issues and Evidence.* Climate Issues Brief 19, Washington, DC: Resources for the Future.

Kneese, A., and Schultz, C. 1975. *Pollution, Prices, and Public Policy.* Washington, DC: Brookings Institution.

Magat, W. A. 1978. "Pollution control and technological advance: a dynamic model of the firm," *Journal of Environmental Economics and Management* 5: 1–25.

Mansfield, E., Rapoport, J., Romeo, A., Wagner, S., and Beardsley, G. 1977. "Social and private rates of return from industrial innovations," *Quarterly Journal of Economics* 41: 221–40.

Mendelsohn, R. 1984. "Endogenous technical change and environmental regulation," *Journal of Environmental Economics and Management* 11: 202–07.

Nadiri, M. I. 1993. "Innovations and technological spillovers." Working Paper 4423, National Bureau of Economic Research, Cambridge, MA.

National Energy Policy 2001. "Reliable, affordable, and environmentally sound energy for America's future," report of the National Energy Policy Development Group, May 2001 (http://www.whitehouse.gov/energy/National-Energy-Policy.pdf).

Palmer, K., Oates, W., and Portney, P. 1995. "Tightening environmental standards: the benefit-cost or the no-cost paradigm?" *Journal of Economic Perspectives* 9: 119–32.

Parry, I. W. H., Pizer, W. A., and Fischer, C. 2003. "How important is technological innovation in protecting the environment," *Journal of Regulatory Economics* 23: 237–55.

Pizer, W. 1999. *Choosing Price or Quantity Controls for Greenhouse Gases.* Climate Issues Brief 17, Washington, DC: Resources for the Future.

Porter, M. E., and van der Linde, C. 1995. "Toward a new conception of the environment–competitiveness relationship," *Journal of Economic Perspectives* 9: 97–118.

Sinclair-Desgagné, B. 1999. *Remarks on Environmental Regulation, Firm Behavior and Innovation.* Working Paper 99s–20, Montreal: Centre interuniversitaire de recherche en analyse des organisations (CIRANO).

Toman, M. A., Morgenstern, R. D., and Anderson, J. 1999. *The Economics of "When" Flexibility in the Design of Greenhouse Gas Abatement Policies.* Discussion Paper 99–38–REV, Washington, DC: Resources for the Future.

Weitzman, M. L. 1974. "Prices vs. quantities," *Review of Economic Studies* 41: 477–91.

White House 1999. "President Clinton and Vice-President Gore: Growing clean energy for the 21st century." The White House, Office of the Press Secretary, August 12, 1999 (http://clinton3.nara.gov/WH/Work/081299.html).

Wright, B. D. 1983. "The economics of invention incentives: patents, prizes and research contracts," *American Economic Review* 73: 691–707.

Zerbe, R. O. 1970. "Theoretical efficiency in pollution control," *Western Economic Journal* 8: 364–76.

4 Incentives to adopt new abatement technology and US–European regulatory cultures

Reimund Schwarze

Introduction

There is a debate in the environmental economics literature on the firm's incentive to develop and adopt new abatement technologies under different policy instruments. While many economists would agree that incentive-based instruments such as environmental taxes and tradable permits provide superior incentives to invest in cost–saving abatement technologies compared to command-and-control type policies, some authors have challenged this view either by looking at specific groups of emitters (Malueg, 1989) or at different stages along the innovation chain (Fischer, this volume, ch. 3). Another debate concerns the relative ranking of economic instruments. In a series of papers several authors have claimed that economic instruments can be ranked from highest-incentive to lowest-incentive in the following order: (i) auctioned permits, (ii) emission taxes, (iii) grandfathered permits (Milliman and Prince, 1989, Jung *et al.*, 1996). This view has occasionally been challenged (Buchholz, 1993, Schwarze, 2001, Requate and Unold, 2003) because it contradicts the fundamental equivalence theorem of auctioned and free permits in a setting that is not considering the use of public funds. Similarly, Laffont and Tirole (1994) have argued that permits could induce underinvestment in abatement R&D because of falling permit prices and perceived government racheting.

This chapter demonstrates that this debate reflects a general trade-off between the goal of stimulating new technology and the goal of dynamic efficiency. High incentives to adopt new environmental technology are in many cases not dynamically efficient, while dynamically efficient policies are in many cases not providing the highest incentive for the diffusion of new abatement technologies. Emission taxes and Best Available Technology (BAT) approaches provide higher incentives for the diffusion of new abatement technologies than tradable permits of either sort, auctioned (A-permits) or grandfathered (G-permits). But only tradable permits are dynamically efficient with regard to the underlying approach of standards and prices.

Taxes versus tradable permits

Our current understanding of the incentives to develop and adopt new environmentally friendly technology is driven by a very simple model that goes back to Zerbe's (1970) seminal work on "Theoretical efficiency in pollution control." The essential logic of this model can be explained by a simple graph (Figure 4.1). Let MAC_0 represent the existing abatement technology and MAC_1 the relatively advanced technology. Furthermore, assume an environmental policy that is characterized by a pollution standard E_0. E_0 can be implemented by a pollution tax t_0 or an equivalent permit market that generates a permit price z_0.

The claimed superiority of auctioned tradable permits (Milliman and Prince, 1989, Jung *et al.*, 1996) derives from the fact that prices in fixed quantity markets are going to fall to a level below z_0, presumably z_1. If this price reduction is factored in by users as a benefit of applying the new technology, tradable permits would provide by far the greatest incentive for innovation and early adoption. But as one can easily see by comparing the cost of abatement when using the new technology as an early mover ($E,A,z_1,0$ *plus* fixed costs of adoption) to not using the technology at all as a wait-and-see type ($E,D,z_1,0$) it pays to "free-ride" on the price effect if fixed costs are substantial, i.e. higher than EAD.

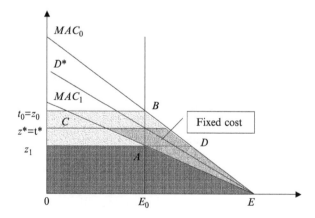

Figure 4.1. Taxes versus permits.

Fischer (this volume, ch. 3) has labeled this the "adoption price effect". However, the "adoption price effect" is not simply a dilution of incentives to adopt; it poses a much more serious problem. If the roles of innovators and adopters are not predetermined and if the time span between the introduction and the complete diffusion of the new technology is not large, it does not pay to assume the role of an innovator because "innovation free-riding" would be much more rewarding! On the other hand, innovation free-riding cannot be an equilibrium for the industry, because if everybody waits to reap the benefit of pecuniary spillovers, nobody would move to adopt the technology and everybody would be disappointed. The equilibrium is a mixed strategy where some parties adopt the new technology and others do not (Buchholz, 1993, Schwarze, 2001). This would lead to a demand curve ($D^\star$) on the permit market that lies somewhere between MAC_0 and MAC_1. Given $D^\star$, tradable permits provide much weaker incentives to adopt new abatement technology than environmental taxes. In the case of taxes, MAC_1 would always lead to a complete diffusion of the new technology, whereas in the case of tradable permits the new technology would only be partially adopted. In other words, the diffusion of new technologies under permits is incomplete. Surprisingly, this result also holds if the environmental tax is lower than z_0, e.g. $t^\star$. If we assume that the fixed costs of innovation are substantial (area indicated as "Fixed cost" in Figure 4.1) for both tradable permits and environmental taxes, a tax of $t^\star$ would suffice for complete diffusion while a similar permit price ($z^\star$) would not! Bottom line: taxes provide superior incentives for a broad-based adoption of new environmental technologies compared to tradable permits.

But is this incentive efficient? The answer to this question depends on the policy target. If E_0 were our abatement target with and without the new technology, only permits would be dynamically efficient. A complete diffusion of the abatement technology would not be cost-minimizing given a standard-price approach! Bottom line: while tradable permits provide weaker incentives to adopt new technologies than taxes, they are dynamically efficient.

Best Available Technology

Let me now touch upon the issue of BAT incentives. It is well established in the literature that there are much stronger incentives for late adopters of new technology than for early adopters or single innovators (Malueg, 1989). This fact can be explained by a simple graph (Figure 4.2).

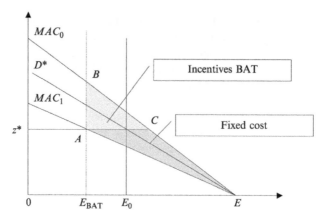

Figure 4.2. Best Available Technology.

In this diagram we assume a high-cost old technology (indicated by MAC_0) and a low-cost new technology (indicated by MAC_1). Given an emission standard of E_0 and relevant fixed cost of adoption (as indicated), a tradable permit market would equilibrate at $z^\star$, as explained earlier. This equilibrium is characterized by a partial adoption of the new technology. Now assume that policy-makers would orientate to the Best Available Technology (BAT). Adoption of MAC_1 by some emitters would then indicate that E_{BAT} is "feasible" at the firm level. A BAT policy would consequently prescribe E_{BAT} for *all* emitters, including the users of MAC_0 technology. Comparing the incentive to adopt MAC_1 technology in complying with E_{BAT} for the late adopters with the incentive to use the new technology for the early adopters on the permit market we find that the latter is considerably smaller. The early users of MAC_1 technology barely covered their fixed costs of adoption in the permit market whereas the late adopters of MAC_1 technology have an additional cost saving of ABC in complying with E_{BAT} under command-and-control.

But again: is this stronger incentive for the followers under the BAT approach efficient? Clearly not. If E_0 were our emissions standard, E_{BAT} for *all* emitters would imply overcompliance with our emission standard. Shifting to E_{BAT} can thus be interpreted as implicitly shifting the emission standard to a higher level than E_0. But raising the standard will always increase the incentive to adopt new cost-saving technology, regardless of the instrument applied. Comparing tradable permits and BAT policy according to the same standard – as is needed for a "fair" comparison! – would, however, indicate that BAT approaches are providing stronger incentives for late adopters at excessive cost. In other words, they are dynamically inefficient!

To sum up: high incentives to adopt new environmental technology are in many cases not dynamically efficient, and many dynamically efficient policies are not providing the greatest incentive for the diffusion of new abatement technologies. If we want maximal incentives for the adoption of new technologies (regardless of cost), we should go for taxes or BAT approaches. If, however, we strive for dynamic efficiency, we would achieve better results with tradable permits of either sort, A-permits or G-permits.

US and European regulatory cultures

This result leads to speculation on whether the current dominance of taxes and BAT approaches – in most fields of environmental policy other than climate change – in the EU could be driven by an implicit calculus to "force" technological progress, whereas the US reliance on tradable permits may be driven by a desire for static and dynamic efficiency.

Table 4.1 compares the targeted SO_2 reductions for Phase I and Phase II units in the United States (in terms of specific emissions) with the targets of similar programs in Germany and the EU. The figures demonstrate that the current targets for US utilities are far less demanding than those which German utilities have faced since 1988. The new EU Directive for power plants sets even more ambitious targets.

There is an obvious link between ambitious goals and the choice of instruments. Given 90 percent reduction targets in the EU, there is simply not enough to trade despite extreme costs. Indeed, the demanding BAT approach of European environmental policy is blamed for many failed attempts to have sulfur trading at the EU level or within some member states (Sorell, 1999).

Table 4.1. *SO_2 targets in the USA and Europe*

Plant size	United States Clean Air Act (1990)	German Large Scale Combustion Act (1988)	European Large Scale Combustion Directive (1999)
Large	2800 mg SO_2/m^3 (Phase I: 1995–2000)	400 mg SO_2/m^3 (> 300 MW)	200 mg SO_2/m^3 (> 300 MW)
Small	1400 mg SO_2/m^3 (Phase II: 2000–2010)	1000 mg SO_2/m^3 (< 300 MW)	400 mg SO_2/m^3 (< 300 MW)

While it is clearly "unfair" to compare policies of different countries with differing targets, the figures in Table 4.1 evidently demonstrate that BAT approaches *can* deliver better in terms of advanced technology than tradable permits. The basic truth is that far-reaching goals such as in the EU provide stronger incentives to develop and adopt new technology than less demanding policies like those in the USA, irrespective of the instruments applied. Of course, such greater incentives come at higher costs (Wätzold, 2004).

But why did the European Union chose tradable permits in the case of climate change policy? My best answer is this: the Europeans selected carbon trading by contract with the USA and some other countries, known as the Umbrella Group, as part of the UNFCCC negotiating process of the early nineties. Indeed, the Umbrella Group's proposal for international carbon trading initially met with many objections from the EU. Remnants of this attitude can still be found in the so-called supplementary requirement of Art. 17 of the Kyoto Protocol, which essentially caps carbon trading to 50 percent of the assigned amounts of carbon rights. This requirement was included in the Protocol largely at the insistence of the EU. Figuratively speaking, the European Union was the hesitant bride. Now, with the father lost, we are at an advanced stage in expecting his baby, and hopefully we will end up with this baby like another "surrogate mother" in a recent US court case. She fell so much in love with her baby that she refused to deliver her "product" to her contract partners.

References

Buchholz, W. 1993. "Der Standard-Preis-Ansatz bei Vermeidungstechnologien mit positiven Fixkosten." Unpublished manuscript; available from the author: wolfgang.buchholz@uni-regensburg.de.
Jung, C., Krutilla, K., and Boyd, R. 1996. "Incentives for advanced pollution abatement technology at the industry level: an evaluation of policy alternatives," *Journal of Environmental Economics and Management* 30: 95–111.
Laffont, J. J., and Tirole, J. 1994. "Environmental policy, compliance and innovation," *European Economic Review* 38: 555–62.
Malueg, D. A., 1989. "Emission credit trading and the incentive to adopt new pollution abatement technology," *Journal of Environmental Economics and Management* 16: 52–57.
Milliman, S. R., and Prince, R. 1989. "Firm incentives to promote technological change in pollution control," *Journal of Environmental Economics and Management* 17: 247–65.
Requate, T., and Unold, W. 2003. "Environmental policy incentives to adopt advanced abatement technology: will the true ranking please stand up?" *European Economic Review* 47: 125–46.

Schwarze, R., 2001. "Zur dynamischen Anreizwirkung von Umweltzertifikaten," *Zeitschrift für Umweltpolitik und Umweltrecht* 20: 519–36.

Sorell, S. 1999. "Why sulfur trading failed in the U.K.," in S. Sorell and J. Skea (eds.). *Pollution for Sale*. Cheltenham: Edward Elgar, pp. 170–207.

Wätzold, F. 2004. "SO_2 emissions in Germany: regulations to fight *waldsterben*," in W. Harrington, R. D. Morgenstern, and T. Sterner (eds.). *Choosing Environmental Policy: Comparing Instruments and Outcomes in the United States and Europe*. Washington, DC: Resources for the Future, pp. 23–40

Zerbe, R. O., 1970. "Theoretical efficiency in pollution control," *Western Economic Journal* 8: 364–76.

Part 2

The US approach to pollution control:
lessons for climate policy

5 Implications of the US experience with market-based environment strategies for future climate policy

Robert N. Stavins

Introduction

Perspectives in the United States regarding potential public policies to address the threat of global climate change have developed over time within the context of domestic US environmental policies and public and private attitudes toward those policies. Over the past two decades, as market-based environmental policy instruments have been proposed and implemented in the United States, the concept of harnessing market forces to protect the environment has evolved from political anathema to being politically correct. In this chapter, I reflect on these experiences, and assess their implications for current considerations of potential domestic climate policies.[1]

Environmental policies typically combine the identification of a goal with some means to achieve that goal. Although these two components are often linked within the political process, I focus here exclusively on the second component, the means – the "instruments" – of environmental policy. Market-based instruments are regulations that encourage behavior through market signals rather than through explicit directives regarding pollution control levels or methods. These policy instruments, such as tradable permits or pollution charges, can reasonably be described as "harnessing market forces,"[2] because if they are well designed and implemented, they encourage firms or individuals to undertake pollution control efforts that are in their own interests and that collectively meet policy goals.

By way of contrast, conventional approaches to regulating the environment are often referred to as "command-and-control" regulations, since they allow relatively little flexibility in the means of achieving goals. Such regulations tend to force firms to take on similar shares of the

This chapter draws, in part, upon Stavins (2000, 2002, 2003). The author is responsible for any errors.

pollution-control burden, regardless of the cost. Command-and-control regulations do this by setting uniform standards for firms, the most prevalent of which are technology- and performance-based standards. Technology-based standards specify the method, and sometimes the actual equipment, that firms must use to comply with a particular regulation. A performance standard sets a uniform control target for firms, while allowing some latitude in how this target is met.

Holding all firms to the same target can be expensive and, in some circumstances, counterproductive. While standards may effectively limit emissions of pollutants, they typically exact relatively high costs in the process, by forcing some firms to resort to unduly expensive means of controlling pollution. Because the costs of controlling emissions may vary greatly among firms, and even among sources within the same firm, the appropriate technology in one situation may not be appropriate (cost-effective) in another. Thus, control costs can vary enormously on account of a firm's production design, physical configuration, the age of its assets, or other factors. One frequently cited survey of eight empirical studies of air pollution control found that the ratio of actual aggregate costs of the conventional, command-and-control approach to the aggregate costs of least-cost benchmarks ranged from 1.07 for sulfate emissions in the Los Angeles area to 22.0 for hydrocarbon emissions at all domestic DuPont plants (Tietenberg, 1985).[3]

Furthermore, command-and-control regulations tend to freeze the development of technologies that might otherwise result in greater levels of control. Little or no financial incentive exists for businesses to exceed their control targets, and both technology-based and performance-based standards discourage adoption of new technologies. A business that adopts a new technology may be "rewarded" by being held to a higher standard of performance and not given the opportunity to benefit financially from its investment, except to the extent that its competitors have even more difficulty reaching the new standard.[4]

In theory, if properly designed and implemented, market-based instruments allow any desired level of pollution clean-up to be realized at the lowest overall cost to society, by providing incentives for the greatest reductions in pollution by those firms that can achieve these reductions most cheaply.[5] Rather than equalizing pollution levels among firms (as with uniform emission standards), market-based instruments equalize the incremental amount that firms spend to reduce pollution – their marginal cost (Montgomery, 1972, Baumol and Oates, 1988, Tietenberg, 1995). Command-and-control approaches could – in theory – achieve this cost-effective solution, but this would require that different standards be set for each pollution source, and, consequently, that policy-makers obtain detailed information about the compliance costs each firm faces. Such information is simply not available to government. By contrast, market-based instruments provide for a cost-effective allocation of the pollution control burden among sources without requiring the government to have this information.

In contrast to command-and-control regulations, market-based instruments have the potential to provide powerful incentives for companies to adopt cheaper and better pollution-control technologies. This is because with market-based instruments, particularly emission taxes, it always pays firms to clean-up a bit more if a sufficiently low-cost method (technology or process) of doing so can be identified and adopted (Downing and White, 1986, Malueg, 1989, Milliman and Prince, 1989, Jaffe and Stavins, 1995, Jung et al., 1996, Jaffe et al., 2002).

In the next section of the chapter, I examine the normative implications of US experience with market-based environmental policies over the past thirty years.[6] And in the final section, I offer some critical caveats and tentative conclusions.

Implications

Although there has been considerable experience in the United States with market-based instruments for environmental protection, this relatively new set of policy approaches has not replaced nor come anywhere close to replacing conventional, command-and-control approaches. Further, even when and where these approaches have been used in their purest form and with some success, they have not always performed as anticipated. Therefore, I ask what implications arise from our experiences. In particular, I consider normative implications for design and implementation of market-based instruments, analysis of prospective and adopted systems, and identification of new applications.[7]

Implications for design and implementation

The performance to date of market-based instruments for environmental protection provides compelling evidence for environmentalists and others that these approaches can achieve major cost savings while accomplishing their environmental objectives. The performance of these systems also offers lessons about the importance of flexibility, simplicity, the role of monitoring and enforcement, and the capabilities of the private sector to make markets of this sort work.

In regard to flexibility, it is important that market-based instruments should be designed to allow for a broad set of compliance alternatives, in terms of both timing and technological options. For example, allowing flexible timing and intertemporal trading of permits – that is, banking allowances for future use – played an important role in the SO_2 allowance trading program's performance (Ellerman *et al.*, 1997), much as it did in the US lead rights trading program a decade earlier (Kerr and Maré, 1997). One of the most significant benefits of using market-based instruments is simply that technology standards are thereby avoided. Less flexible systems would not have led to the technological change that may have been induced by market-based instruments (Burtraw, 1996, Ellerman and Montero, 1998, Bohi and Burtraw, 1997, Keohane, 2001), nor the induced process innovations that have resulted (Doucet and Strauss, 1994).

With regard to simplicity, transparent formulae – whether for permit allocation or tax computation – are difficult to contest or manipulate. Rules should be clearly defined up front, without ambiguity. For example, requiring prior government approval of individual trades may increase uncertainty and transaction costs, thereby discouraging trading; these negative effects should be balanced against any anticipated benefits due to requiring prior government approval. Such requirements hampered EPA's Emissions Trading Program in the 1970s, while the lack of such requirements was an important factor in the success of lead trading (Hahn and Hester, 1989). In the case of SO_2 trading, the absence of requirements for prior approval reduced uncertainty for utilities and administrative costs for government, and contributed to low transaction costs (Rico, 1995).

While some problematic program design elements reflect miscalculations of market reactions, others were known to be problematic at the time the programs were enacted, but nevertheless were incorporated into programs to ensure adoption by the political process. One striking example is the "20 percent rule" under EPA's Emissions Trading Program. This rule, adopted at the insistence of the environmental community, stipulates that each time a permit is traded, the amount of pollution authorized thereunder must be reduced by 20 percent. Since permits that are not traded retain their full quantity value, this regulation discourages permit trading and thereby increases regulatory costs (Hahn, 1990).

Experience also argues for using absolute baselines, not relative ones, as the point of departure for credit programs. The problem is that without a specified baseline, reductions must be credited relative to an unobservable hypothetical one – what the source would have emitted in the absence of the regulation. A combined system – where a cap-and-trade program is combined with voluntary "opt-in provisions" – creates the possibility for "paper trades," where a regulated source is credited for an emissions reduction (by an unregulated source) that would have taken place in any event (Montero, 1999). The result is a decrease in aggregate costs among regulated sources, but this is partly due to an unintentional increase in the total emissions cap. As was experienced with EPA's Emissions Trading Program, relative baselines create significant transaction costs by essentially requiring prior approval of trades as the authority investigates the claimed counterfactual from which reductions are calculated and credits generated (Nichols *et al.*, 1996).

Experiences with market-based instruments also provide a powerful reminder of the importance of monitoring and enforcement. These instruments, whether price- or quantity-based, do not eliminate the need for such activities, although they may change their character. In the many programs reviewed in this chapter where monitoring and/or enforcement have been deficient, the results have been ineffective policies. One counterexample is provided by the US SO_2 allowance trading program, which includes (costly) continuous emissions monitoring of all sources. On the enforcement side, the Act's stiff penalties (much greater than the marginal cost of abatement) have provided sufficient incentives for the very high degree of compliance that has been achieved (Schmalensee *et al.*, 1998, Stavins, 1998).

In nearly every case of implemented cap-and-trade programs, permits have been allocated without charge to participants. The same characteristic that makes such allocation attractive in positive political economy terms – the conveyance of scarcity rents to the private sector – makes allocation without charge problematic in normative, efficiency terms (Fullerton and Metcalf, 1997). It has been estimated that the costs of SO_2 allowance trading would be 25 percent less if permits were auctioned rather than allocated without charge, because revenues can be used to finance reductions in pre-existing distortionary taxes (Goulder *et al.*, 1997). Furthermore, in the presence of some forms of transaction costs, the post-trading equilibrium – and hence aggregate abatement costs – are sensitive to the initial permit allocation (Stavins, 1995). For both reasons, a successful attempt to establish a politically viable program through a specific initial permit allocation can result in a program that is significantly more costly than anticipated.

Improvements in instrument design will not solve all problems. One potentially important cause of the mixed performance of implemented market-based instruments is that many firms are simply not well equipped to make the decisions necessary to utilize these instruments fully. Since market-based instruments have been used on a limited basis only, and firms are not certain that these instruments will be a lasting component on the regulatory landscape, most companies have chosen not to reorganize their internal structure to exploit fully the cost savings these instruments offer. Rather, most firms continue to have organizations that are experienced in minimizing the costs of complying with command-and-control regulations, not in making the strategic decisions allowed by market-based instruments.[8]

The focus of environmental, health, and safety departments in private firms has been primarily on problem avoidance and risk management, rather than on the creation of opportunities made possible by market-based instruments. This focus has developed because of the strict rules companies have faced under command-and-control regulation, in response to which companies have built skills and developed processes that comply with regulations, but do not help them benefit competitively from environmental decisions (Reinhardt, 2000). Where significant changes in structure and personnel are absent, the full potential of market-based instruments will not be realized.

Implications for analysis

When assessing market-based environmental programs, economists need to employ some measure by which the gains of moving from conventional standards to an economic-incentive scheme can be estimated. When comparing policies with the same anticipated environmental outcomes, aggregate cost savings may be the best yardstick for measuring the success of individual instruments. The challenge for analysts is to make fair comparisons among policy instruments: either idealized versions of both market-based systems and likely alternatives; or realistic versions of both (Hahn and Stavins, 1992).

It is not enough to analyze static cost savings. For example, the savings due to banking allowances should also be modeled (unless this is not permitted in practice). It can likewise be important to allow for the effects of alternative instruments on technology innovation and diffusion (Milliman and Prince, 1989, Doucet and Strauss, 1994, Jaffe and Stavins, 1995), especially when programs impose significant costs over long time horizons (Newell *et al.*, 1999). More generally, it is important to consider the effects of the pre-existing regulatory environment. For example, the level of pre-existing factor taxes can affect the total costs of regulation (Goulder *et al.*, 1997), as indicated above.

Implications for identifying new applications

Market-based policy instruments are considered today for nearly every environmental problem that is raised, ranging from endangered species preservation to what may be the greatest of environmental problems, the greenhouse effect and global climate change.[9] Experiences with market-based instruments offer some guidance to the conditions under which such approaches are likely to work well, and when they may face greater difficulties.

First, where the cost of abating pollution differs widely among sources, a market-based system is likely to have greater gains, relative to conventional, command-and-control regulations (Newell and Stavins, 2002). For example, it was clear early on that SO_2 abatement cost heterogeneity was great, because of differences in ages of plants and their proximity to sources of low-sulfur coal. But where abatement costs are more uniform across sources, the political costs of enacting an allowance trading approach are less likely to be justifiable. Given the exceptional diversity of anthropogenic sources of greenhouse gas emissions, this first implication argues strongly for the use of market-based instruments for addressing global climate change.

Second, the greater is the degree of mixing of pollutants in the receiving airshed or watershed, the more attractive will a market-based system be, relative to a conventional uniform standard. This is because taxes or tradable permits, for example, can lead to localized "hot spots" with relatively high levels of ambient pollution. This is a significant distributional issue, and it can also become an efficiency issue if damages are non-linearly related to pollutant concentrations. In cases where this is a reasonable concern, the problem can be addressed, in theory, through the use of "ambient permits" or through charge systems that are keyed to changes in ambient conditions at specified locations (Revesz, 1996). But despite the extensive theoretical literature on such ambient systems going back to Montgomery (1972), they have never been implemented, with the partial exception of a two-zone trading system under Los Angeles' RECLAIM program. Because greenhouse gases are uniformly-mixed pollutants, this second implication also recommends the use of market-based instruments in the climate change context.

Third, the efficiency of price-based (tax) systems compared with quantity-based (tradable permit) systems depends on the pattern of costs and benefits. If uncertainty about marginal abatement costs is significant, and if marginal abatement costs are quite flat and marginal benefits of abatement fall relatively quickly, then a quantity instrument will be more efficient than a price instrument (Weitzman, 1974). Furthermore, when there is also uncertainty about marginal benefits, and marginal benefits are positively correlated with marginal costs (which, it turns out, is not uncommon), then there is an additional argument in favor of the relative efficiency of quantity instruments (Stavins, 1996).

On the other hand, the regulation of stock pollutants will often favor price instruments when the optimal stock level rises over time (Newell and Pizer, 2000). It should also be recognized that despite the theoretical efficiency advantages of hybrid systems – non-linear taxes, or quotas combined with taxes – in the presence of uncertainty (Roberts and Spence, 1976, Kaplow and Shavell, 1997),[10] virtually no such hybrid systems have been adopted. The stock pollutant nature of greenhouse gases argues in favor of price-based mechanisms.

Fourth, the long-term cost-effectiveness of taxes versus tradable permit systems is affected by their relative responsiveness to change. This arises in at least three dimensions. In the presence of rapid rates of economic growth, a fixed tax leads to an increase in aggregate emissions, whereas with a fixed supply of permits there is no change in aggregate emissions (but an increase in permit prices). In the context of general price inflation, a unit (but not an *ad valorem*) tax decreases in real terms, and so emissions levels increase; whereas with a permit system, there is no change in aggregate emissions. In the presence of exogenous technological change in pollution abatement, a tax system leads to an increase in control levels, i.e. a decrease in aggregate emissions, while a permit system maintains emissions, with a fall in permit prices (Stavins and Whitehead, 1992). These implications regarding responsiveness to change suggest that a national preference between taxes and tradable permits will reasonably depend upon specific domestic circumstances.

Fifth, tradable permits will work best when transaction costs are low, and experience demonstrates that if properly designed, private markets will tend to render transaction costs minimal. Sixth, a potential advantage of tradable permit systems in which allocation is without charge, relative to other policy instruments, is associated with the incentive thereby provided for pollution sources to identify themselves and report their emissions (in order to claim their permits).

Seventh, it is important to keep in mind that in the absence of decreasing marginal transaction costs (essentially volume discounts), the equilibrium allocation and hence aggregate abatement costs of a tradable permit system are independent of initial allocations (Stavins 1995). Hence, an important attribute of a tradable permit system is that the allocation decision can be left to politicians, with limited normative concerns about the potential effects of the chosen allocation on overall cost-effectiveness. In other words, cost-effectiveness or efficiency can be achieved, while distributional equity is simultaneously addressed with the same policy instrument. This is one of the reasons why an international tradable permit mechanism is particularly attractive in the context of concerns about global climate change. Allocation mechanisms can be developed that address legitimate equity concerns of developing countries, and thus increase the political base for support, without jeopardizing the overall cost-effectiveness of the system.[11]

Eighth and finally, considerations of political feasibility point to the wisdom (more likely success) of proposing market-based instruments when they can be used to facilitate a cost-effective, aggregate emissions reduction (as in the case of the SO_2 allowance trading program in 1990), as opposed to a cost-effective reallocation of the status quo burden. Policy instruments that appear impeccable from the vantage point of research institutions, but consistently prove infeasible in real-world political institutions, can hardly be considered "optimal."

Caveats and conclusions

Some eighty years ago, economists first proposed the use of corrective taxes to internalize environmental (and other) externalities (Pigou 1920). But it was a little more than a decade ago that the portfolio of potential economic-incentive instruments was expanded to include quantity-based mechanisms – tradable permits – and these incentive-based approaches to environmental protection began to emerge as prominent features of the US policy landscape.

Given that most experience with market-based instruments has been generated quite recently, one should be cautious about drawing conclusions from these experiences. Important questions remain. For example, relatively little is known empirically about the impact of these instruments on technological change. Also, much more empirical research is needed on how the pre-existing regulatory environment affects performance, including costs. Moreover, the great successes with tradable permits have involved air pollution: acid rain, leaded gasoline, and chlorofluorocarbons. Experience (and success) with water pollution is much more limited, and in other areas there has been no experience at all. Even for air pollution problems, the differences between SO_2 and acid rain, on the one hand, and the combustion of fossil fuels and global climate change, on the other, suggest that a rush to judgment regarding global climate policy instruments is unwarranted.

Furthermore, the experiences reviewed in this chapter are of *domestic* US policies, and to whatever degree they offer implications for potential future climate policies such implications would be for *domestic* policies (and primarily for the United States). But climate change is fundamentally a global problem, and successful policies to address it will need to feature international, if not fully global, dimensions. Unfortunately, international versions of domestic policy instruments, such as tradable permit systems, cannot be based upon simple extrapolations to the multinational realm. When economists consider domestic environmental problems, they ordinarily put aside participation and compliance issues, because the existence of an effective government vested with effective coercive powers is assumed. In the international domain, however, full national sovereignty for individual nations means that free-rider problems make it unlikely that adequate participation and compliance will be achieved (Barrett and Stavins, 2002).[12]

There are sound reasons why the political world has been slow to embrace the use of market-based instruments for environmental protection, including the ways economists have packaged and promoted their ideas in the past: failing to separate means (cost-effective instruments) from ends (efficiency); and treating environmental problems as little more than "externalities calling for corrective taxes." Much of the resistance has also been due, of course, to the very nature of the political process and the incentives it provides to both politicians and interest groups to favor command-and-control methods instead of market-based approaches.

But, despite this history, market-based instruments have moved center stage, and policy debates look very different from the time when these ideas were characterized as "licenses to pollute" or dismissed as completely impractical. Market-based instruments are considered seriously for each and every environmental problem that is tackled, ranging from endangered species preservation to regional smog to global climate change. Market-based instruments – and, in particular, tradable permit systems – will enjoy increasing acceptance in the years ahead.

No particular form of government intervention, no individual policy instrument – whether market-based or conventional – is appropriate for all environmental problems. Which instrument is best in any given situation depends upon a variety of characteristics of the environmental problem, and the social, political, and economic context in which it is being regulated. There is clearly no policy panacea. Indeed, the real challenge for bureaucrats, elected officials, and other participants in the environmental policy process comes in analyzing and then selecting the best instrument for each situation that arises.

Notes

1 Note that I consider the potential implications of US experiences with market-based environmental strategies for possible future *domestic* climate policies. The normative and positive lessons that can be drawn for the *international* dimensions of climate policies (for example, for the architecture

or specific policies employed in current or future international agreements) are much more tenuous and are outside the scope of this analysis. I comment on this in the concluding section of the chapter.

2 See Organization for Economic Cooperation and Development (1989, 1991, 1998), Stavins (1988, 1991), and US Environmental Protection Agency (1991, 1992, 2001). Another strain of literature – known as "free market environmentalism" – focuses on the role of private property rights in achieving environmental protection.

3 These numbers are subject to misinterpretation. *Actual* command-and-control instruments are being compared with *theoretical* benchmarks of cost-effectiveness, i.e. what a perfectly functioning market-based instrument would achieve in theory. A fair comparison among policy instruments would involve either idealized versions of both market-based systems and likely alternatives; or realistic versions of both (Hahn and Stavins, 1992).

4 When more stringent standards are put in place for new sources relative to existing ones, a common practice in US environmental law (under so-called "new source review"), the result is a particularly perverse set of incentives that act to retard technological change (Gruenspecht and Stavins, 2002).

5 In this chapter, I focus on market-based policy instruments in the environmental realm, chiefly those instruments that reduce concentrations of pollution, as opposed to those that operate in the natural resources realm. This means, for example, that tradable development rights, wetlands mitigation banking, and tradable permit systems used to govern the allocation of fishing rights are not reviewed. The distinction between environmental and natural resource policies is somewhat arbitrary. Some policy instruments which are seen to bridge the environmental and natural resource realm, such as removing barriers to water markets, are considered.

6 Experiences in the United States with market-based environmental policy instruments have been both numerous and diverse, and can be considered within four major categories: pollution charges; tradable permits; market friction reductions; and government subsidy reductions. For a comprehensive survey, see Stavins (2003).

7 For an examination of positive political economy implications, see Keohane *et al.* (1998).

8 There are some interesting exceptions. See Hockenstein *et al.* (1997).

9 See, for example, Goldstein (1991) and Bean (1997) on species protection, and Fisher *et al.* (1996), Hahn and Stavins (1995), Schmalensee (1996), and Stavins (1997) on applications to global climate change. More broadly, see Ayres (2000).

10 In addition to the efficiency advantages of non-linear taxes, they also have the attribute of reducing the total (although not the marginal) tax burden of the regulated sector, relative to an ordinary linear tax, which is potentially important in a political economy context.

11 See, for example, the proposal for "growth targets" by Frankel (1999).

12 There are also a host of other, more specific problems that arise in the international domain. For example, the theory of tradable permits assumes the existence of profit-maximizing or cost-minimizing agents who have

knowledge of their own marginal abatement cost functions. Such a simple objective function cannot be assumed in the case of national governments, nor can satisfaction of the related information requirement. This is examined in detail by Hahn and Stavins (1999).

References

Ayres, R. E. 2000. "Expanding the use of environmental trading programs into new areas of environmental regulation," *Pace Environmental Law Review* 18: 87–118.

Barrett, S., and Stavins, R. N. 2002. "Increasing participation and compliance in international climate change agreements" Working Paper, John F. Kennedy School of Government, Harvard University.

Baumol, W. J., and Oates, W. E. 1988. *The Theory of Environmental Policy*. New York: Cambridge University Press.

Bean, M. J. 1997. "Shelter from the storm: endangered species and landowners alike deserve a safe harbor," *The New Democrat* (March/April): 20–21.

Bohi, D., and Burtraw, D. 1997. "SO_2 allowance trading: how do expectations and experience measure up?" *Electricity Journal* 10: 67–75.

Burtraw, D. 1996. "The SO_2 emissions trading program: cost savings without allowance trades," *Contemporary Economic Policy* 14: 79–94.

Doucet, J., and Strauss, T. 1994. "On the bundling of coal and sulphur dioxide emissions allowances," *Energy Policy* 22: 764–70.

Downing, P. B., and White, L. J. 1986. "Innovation in pollution control," *Journal of Environmental Economics and Management* 13: 18–27.

Ellerman, D., and Montero, J. 1998. "The declining trend in sulfur dioxide emissions: implications for allowance prices," *Journal of Environmental Economics and Management* 36: 26–45.

Ellerman, D., Schmalensee, R., Joskow, P., Montero, J., and Bailey, E. 1997. *Emissions Trading Under the US Acid Rain Program: Evaluation of Compliance Costs and Allowance Market Performance*. Cambridge, MA: MIT Center for Energy and Environmental Policy Research.

Fisher, B., Barrett, S., Bohm, P., Kuroda, M., Mubazi, J., Shah, A., and Stavins, R. 1996. "Policy instruments to combat climate change," in J. P. Bruce, H. Lee and E. F. Haites (eds.). *Climate Change 1995: Economic and Social Dimensions of Climate Change*. New York: Cambridge University Press, pp. 397–439.

Frankel, J. A. 1999. "*Greenhouse gas emissions.*" Policy Brief No. 52, The Brookings Institution, Washington, DC.

Fullerton, D., and Metcalf, G. 1997. "Environmental controls, scarcity rents, and pre-existing distortions." Working Paper 6091, National Bureau of Economic Research, Cambridge, MA.

Goldstein, J. B. 1991. "The prospects for using market incentives to conserve biological diversity," *Environmental Law* 21: 985–1014.

Goulder, L., Parry, I., and Burtraw, D. 1997. "Revenue-raising vs. other approaches to environmental protection: the critical significance of pre-existing tax distortions," *RAND Journal of Economics* 28: 708–31.

Gruenspecht, H. K., and Stavins, R. N. 2002. "New source review under the Clean Air Act: ripe for reform," *Resources* 147: 19–23.

Hahn, R. W. 1990. "Regulatory constraints on environmental markets," *Journal of Public Economics* 42: 149–75.

Hahn, R. W., and Hester, G. L. 1989. "Marketable permits: lessons for theory and practice," *Ecology Law Quarterly* 16: 361–406.

Hahn, R. W., and Stavins, R. N. 1992. "Economic incentives for environmental protection: integrating theory and practice," *American Economic Review* 82: 464–68.

    1995. "Trading in greenhouse permits: a critical examination of design and implementation issues," in H. Lee (ed.). *Shaping National Responses to Climate Change: A Post-Rio Policy Guide*. Cambridge, MA: Island Press, pp. 177–217.

    1999. *What Has the Kyoto Protocol Wrought? The Real Architecture of International Tradable Permit Markets*. Washington, DC: AEI Press.

Hockenstein, J. B., Stavins, R. N., and Whitehead, B. W. 1997. "Creating the next generation of market-based environmental tools," *Environment* 39: 12–20, 30–33.

Jaffe, A. B., Newell, R. N., and Stavins, R. N. 2002. "Environmental policy and technological change," *Environment and Resource Economics* 22: 41–69.

Jaffe, A. B., and Stavins, R. N. 1995. "Dynamic incentives of environmental regulation: the effects of alternative policy instruments on technology diffusion," *Journal of Environmental Economics and Management* 29: S43–S63.

Jung, C., Krutilla, K., and Boyd, R. 1996. "Incentives for advanced pollution abatement technology at the industry level: an evaluation of policy alternatives," *Journal of Environmental Economics and Management* 30: 95–111.

Kaplow, L., and Shavell, S. 1997. "On the superiority of corrective taxes to quantity regulation." NBER Working Paper 6251, National Bureau of Economic Research, Cambridge, MA.

Keohane, N. O. 2001. "Essays in the economics of environmental policy." Unpublished Ph.D. thesis, Harvard University.

Keohane, N. O., Revesz, R. L., and Stavins, R. N. 1998. "The choice of regulatory instruments in environmental policy," *Harvard Environmental Law Review* 22: 313–67.

Kerr, S., and Maré, D. 1997. "Efficient regulation through tradeable permit markets: the United States lead phasedown." Working Paper 96–06, Department of Agricultural and Resource Economics, University of Maryland, College Park.

Malueg, D. A. 1989. "Emission credit trading and the incentive to adopt new pollution abatement technology," *Journal of Environmental Economics and Management* 16: 52–57.

Milliman, S. R., and Prince, R. 1989. "Firm incentives to promote technological change in pollution control," *Journal of Environmental Economics and Management* 17: 247–65.

Montero, J. P. 1999. "Voluntary compliance with market-based environmental policy: evidence from the US acid rain program," *Journal of Political Economy* 107: 998–1033.

Montgomery, D. 1972. "Markets in licenses and efficient pollution control programs," *Journal of Economic Theory* 5: 395–418.

Newell, R. G., Jaffe, A. B., and Stavins, R. N. 1999. "The induced innovation hypothesis and energy-saving technological change," *Quarterly Journal of Economics* 114: 941–75.

Newell, R. G., and Pizer, W. 2000. *Regulating Stock Externalities Under Uncertainty*. Discussion Paper 98–02 (revised), Washington, DC: Resources for the Future.

Newell, R., and Stavins, R. N. 2002. "Cost heterogeneity and the potential savings from market-based policies," *Journal of Regulatory Economics* 23: 43–59.

Nichols, A., Farr, J., and Hester, G. 1996. *Trading and the Timing of Emissions: Evidence from the Ozone Transport Region*. Cambridge, MA: National Economic Research Associates.

Organization for Economic Cooperation and Development 1989. "Economic instruments for environmental protection." Paris.
  1991. "Environmental policy: how to apply economic instruments." Paris.
  1998. "Applying market-based instruments to environmental policies in China and OECD countries." Paris.

Pigou, A. C. 1920. *The Economics of Welfare*. London: Macmillan.

Reinhardt, F. L. 2000. *Down to Earth: Applying Business Principles to Environmental Management*. Boston: Harvard Business School Press.

Revesz, R. L. 1996. "Federalism and interstate environmental externalities," *University of Pennsylvania Law Review* 144: 2341–416.

Rico, R. 1995. "The U.S. allowance trading system for sulfur dioxide: an update of market experience," *Environmental and Resource Economics* 5: 115–29.

Roberts, M. J., and Spence, M. 1976. "Effluent charges and licenses under uncertainty," *Journal of Public Economics* 5: 193–208.

Schmalensee, R. 1996. "Greenhouse policy architecture and institutions." Paper prepared for National Bureau of Economic Research conference *Economics and Policy Issues in Global Warming: An Assessment of the Intergovernmental Panel Report*, Snowmass, CO.

Schmalensee, R., Joskow, P. L., Ellerman, A. D., Montero, J. P., and Bailey, E. M. 1998. "An interim evaluation of sulfur dioxide emissions trading," *Journal of Economic Perspectives* 12: 53–68.

Stavins, R. N. 1988 (ed.). *Project 88: Harnessing Market Forces to Protect Our Environment* (sponsored by Senator Timothy E. Wirth, Colorado, and Senator John Heinz, Pennsylvania), Washington, DC.
  1991 (ed.). *Project 88 – Round II Incentives for Action: Designing Market-Based Environmental Strategies* (sponsored by Senator Timothy E. Wirth, Colorado, and Senator John Heinz, Pennsylvania), Washington, DC.
  1995. "Transaction costs and tradable permits," *Journal of Environmental Economics and Management* 29: 133–48.
  1996. "Correlated uncertainty and policy instrument choice," *Journal of Environmental Economics and Management* 30: 218–32.
  1997. "Policy instruments for climate change: how can national governments address a global problem?" *University of Chicago Legal Forum 1997*: 293–329.

1998. "What have we learned from the grand policy experiment: lessons from SO_2 allowance trading," *Journal of Economic Perspectives* 12: 69–88.

2000. "Market-based environmental policies," in P. R. Portney, and R. N. Stavins (eds.). *Public Policies for Environmental Protection.* Washington, DC: Resources for the Future, pp. 31–66.

2002. "Lessons from the American experiment with market-based environmental policies," in J. D. Donahue, and J. S. Nye, Jr. (eds.). *Market-Based Governance: Supply Side, Demand Side, Upside, and Downside.* Washington, DC: Brookings Institution Press, pp. 173–200.

2003. "Experience with market-based environmental policy instruments," in K.-G. Mäler, and J. Vincent (eds.). *Handbook of Environmental Economics.* Amsterdam: Elsevier Science, pp. 355–435.

Stavins, R. N., and Whitehead, B. W. 1992. "Pollution charges for environmental protection: a policy link between energy and environment," *Annual Review of Energy and the Environment* 17: 187–210.

Tietenberg, T. 1985. *Emissions Trading: An Exercise in Reforming Pollution Policy.* Washington, DC: Resources for the Future.

1995. "Tradeable permits for pollution control when emission location matters: what have we learned?" *Environmental and Resource Economics* 5: 95–113.

US Environmental Protection Agency, 1991. "Economic incentives: options for environmental protection." Document P-2001, Washington, DC.

1992. "The United States experience with economic incentives to control environmental pollution." EPA-230-R-92-001, Washington, DC.

2001. "The United States experience with economic incentives for protecting the environment." EPA-240-R-01-001, Washington, DC.

Weitzman, M. 1974. "Prices vs. quantities," *Review of Economic Studies* 41: 477–91.

6   US experience with emissions trading: lessons for CO_2 emissions trading

A. Denny Ellerman

The experience with emissions trading in the United States over the past twenty-five years[1] provides the material for drawing five lessons in this chapter for the use of this market-based instrument in controlling greenhouse gas (GHG) emissions. The first two lessons concern how well emissions trading has worked as a regulatory instrument and what makes it work. The other three lessons concern features that are important for GHG emissions trading, namely, temporal flexibility, voluntary participation, and the allocation of allowances.

Lesson 1: Emissions trading works

The main lesson from the US experience with emissions trading is that it works. This conclusion stands in clear contrast to the interim verdict drawn from the research associated with Robert Hahn in the mid and late 1980s (Hahn, 1989, Hahn and Hester, 1989a, 1989b) that emissions trading, although theoretically attractive, didn't seem to work in practice.

Hahn coined a wonderful metaphor to explain the disparity between theory and practice as observed in the early attempts by the EPA to introduce flexibility into the implementation of the Clean Air Act: the patient wasn't following the doctor's prescription. This assessment was not only blunt, but also hopeful in predicting improvement if the patient

The organizers of the 2002 Egon Sohmen conference on Climate Protection and Emissions Trading are not alone in seeking lessons from the US experience with emissions trading. The Pew Center on Global Climate Change concurrently commissioned Paul Joskow, David Harrison, and the author to write a report on this same subject (Ellerman *et al.*, 2003). Since the Pew Center report constitutes the basis for much of what is presented here, Paul Joskow and David Harrison are virtual co-authors of this chapter and my debt to them is great. At the same time, the Pew Center report also provides a point of departure for further extensions and for a more personal interpretation than would have been appropriate in that report or than what would necessarily be agreed to by my co-authors. They are certainly not implicated in any of these new interpretations, nor for any errors in fact, emphasis, and reasoning, which remain uniquely my own. I am also indebted to Gert T. Svendsen for helpful suggestions.

would only take the medicine (Hahn, 1989). The prediction would be substantiated in the decade of the 1990s and in particular by the "grand policy experiment" (Stavins, 1998) with SO_2 emissions trading in the Acid Rain Program.

Emissions trading can be said to work if it reduces cost without detracting from the environmental goal. These two dimensions – the economic and the environmental – are the principal lines of debate about emissions trading, with advocates citing the cost savings while critics focus on potential environmental damage. The US experience provides lessons with respect to both.

Cost savings are important but not colossal

Cost savings have been predicted for every emissions trading program proposed, but the predicted cost savings when compared to observed command-and-control regulation have ranged from slight (5–10 percent) to colossal (95 percent) (Tietenberg, 2000). Two careful, *ex post* evaluations of the SO_2 allowance trading program indicate that the cost savings fall between these extremes (Carlson *et al.*, 2000, Ellerman *et al.*, 2000).

Both of these studies are based on observed abatement and costs in the early years of the program and both extrapolate the results into the later more stringent Phase II.[2] They differ in methodology and in some interpretations, but they largely agree on the magnitude of the costs incurred in Phase I and on the existence of cost savings. When calculated from a reasonable command-and-control alternative, the cost savings in this program are on the order of 50 percent, and not the 90 percent that had been claimed and that would seem to make the cost of reaching environmental goals almost costless when trading is employed.[3]

Neither of these studies attempts to determine whether emissions trading has changed the technical choices facing firms. Costs are clearly lower than expected, but the causes are mostly attributable to coincidental changes outside of the Acid Rain Program (Ellerman and Montero, 1998). One insightful observer has pointed out, however, that the flexibility associated with emissions trading can lead to cost savings that, paradoxically, do not require any trading (Burtraw, 1996). The ability to choose among alternative means of abatement, and the threat of not abating at all by buying allowances, creates a competition among suppliers of abatement that seems to lower costs relative to those obtained with command-and-control regulation.

The other emissions trading programs in the United States have not been studied in the same detail as the Acid Rain Program, but cost savings are indicated by the trading activity observed in all of them.

The savings from emissions trading may not be as large as theoretically possible, but there seems little doubt that the cost savings are real and sufficient to justify continued interest in emissions trading.

Environmental performance is improved

The other dimension of emissions trading is the surprising one: emissions trading can enhance achievement of the environmental goal. This feature is illustrated in figure 6.1 for the Acid Rain Program.

The three lines in this figure represent actual emissions (the line beginning in 1985 and extending through 2001), the cap (the line from 1995 through 2010), and an estimate of what emissions would have been without the requirements of the Acid Rain Program. Emissions were reduced by about 4 million tons or 45 percent in the first year of the program, even though the cap was then only slightly constraining. This reduction is much greater than anything observed in any preceding year as far back as the early 1970s when comprehensive command-and-control regulation of SO_2 emissions began. The explanation lies both in the two-phase structure of the program, which imposes much higher marginal costs in the post-2000 phase, and in the ability to bank, which provided the incentive to accelerate the timing of the required cumulative emission reduction.

Accelerated emission reductions are also observed in the other two cap-and-trade programs. The first year of the Northeastern NO_X Budget Program experienced a 25 percent reduction in summer NO_X emissions, about 10 percent more than required; and a comparable reduction in NO_X emissions has occurred in the Los Angeles Air Basin since the RECLAIM program began in 1994, despite an initially non-binding cap.

A major contributing factor to improved environmental performance has been the absence of exceptions to the regulatory requirement. Command-and-control regulations usually apply a uniform standard to all sources equally; however, the standard typically imposes high cost on some sources because of unique conditions at those sources. The result is an appeal for equitable exception that often leads to exemption, deferral, or some other form of relaxation. This inevitably detracts from the achievement of the targeted emission reduction since there is rarely, if ever, a compensating requirement placed on sources for whom the cost of compliance is less onerous. In contrast, cap-and-trade programs provide a readily available, offset mechanism whereby sources facing relatively high costs can purchase reductions from sources facing lower costs.

The inability to know exactly where emissions will be reduced has always raised fears about environmental hot spots in emissions trading programs, but these concerns have proved unfounded (Swift, 2000). A more than proportionate share of the emission reductions in the Acid Rain Program occurred in the up-wind Midwest area, in large part because the lowest costs of abatement correspond to the largest sources of emissions (Ellerman *et al.*, 2000).[4] An early analysis of the North-eastern NO_X Budget Program also notes that "wrong-way trades" were not a problem (Farrell, 2000).

A final point concerning the environmental effect of emissions trading is that its inclusion seems to make agreement on the adoption and implementation of air emission control programs easier. The inclusion of emissions trading in the Acid Rain Program ended a decade-long legislative stalemate in the US Congress on command-and-control pro-posals to accomplish the same emission reduction. The inclusion of emissions trading was an important factor in gaining agreement to phase out the lead content in gasoline and to implement emission reductions in the two RECLAIM programs, the Northeastern NO_X Budget Program, and the mobile source ABT programs. All of these regulatory programs adopted emissions trading to implement emission reductions aimed at attaining national ambient air quality standards for which, in theory, adequate command-and-control authority already existed.

CO_2 implication: emissions trading is especially appropriate

If ever there were an environmental problem designed for emissions trading, global warming is it. The uniform mixing of greenhouse gas emissions in the troposphere and the long lives of greenhouse gases remove the spatial and temporal considerations that often limit the scope of emissions trading in programs aimed at local or regional problems of pollution. As a result, CO_2 trading can be global in scope and there is no reason to limit banking, or perhaps even borrowing. The experience with emissions trading in the US has shown that emissions trading can be effective both in reducing costs and in achieving the environmental goal. There is little reason to think that this lesson would not apply to GHG trading.

Lesson 2: The right to trade must be clearly defined

If emissions trading is to work, the right to trade must be clearly defined and not subject to case-by-case approval. The way the three types of emissions trading treat this right to trade has largely determined the relative success of each.

Three types of emissions trading

A common distinction in emissions trading is that between credit-based and allowance-based systems. In credit-based trading, credits can be created by reducing one source's emissions more than required by some pre-specified standard and transferring the credits to another source, which is thereby allowed to have emissions above the standard. Although sources can propose these trades, the decision to create the credit and make the transfer rests with the regulator. Allowance-based trading operates on an entirely different principle. Tradable rights to emit (allowances) are created initially and distributed in some manner to sources, and there is no presumption that individual sources will limit emissions to the number of allowances each received. They are free to trade allowances and the only requirement is that allowances equal to emissions must be surrendered at the end of every compliance period.

A variant of credit-based trading, called averaging in the United States and a relative target in Europe, has emerged and gained sufficient prominence that it might be considered a third form of emissions trading. In fact, its difference from credit-based trading is revealing of what makes emissions trading work. Like credit-based systems, averaging systems presume a pre-specified standard around which emissions are traded; however, as in allowance-based systems, sources do not need to obtain regulatory approval to trade.

All three forms of emissions trading are found in the United States. Conventional credit-based trading characterizes the early EPA emissions trading programs for netting, offsets, bubbles, and banking; the lead phase-down and mobile source ABT programs are averaging programs; and the Acid Rain, RECLAIM, and Northeastern NO_X Budget programs are allowance-based or cap-and-trade systems. In theory, all three forms introduce cost-saving flexibility and all should work, but in practice, credit-based trading has not worked well, essentially because of the high transaction costs associated with the creation and transfer of credits.

Relatively little trading occurred in the early EPA emission trading programs because the cost involved in getting individual trades approved exceeded the potential cost savings from trading. The problem was the desire both to avoid creating credits for "anyway" tons, emission reductions that would be made without trading, and to ensure that the use of the credits does not lead to violation of air emission standards. The process of regulatory approval, which meant creating a market and negotiating the terms of trade anew for each trade, limited trading. In contrast, averaging and cap-and-trade programs require no review of individual trades and the trading observed in both has been much greater.

The real issue: who makes the abatement decision?

The case-by-case certification characterizing credit-based trading is only the surface manifestation of a deeper difference that has been pointed out in a recent article by Shabman *et al.* (2002). The fundamental difference is in who makes the firm-level decision on abatement. Although the firm in a credit-reduction program may propose a level of abatement that differs from the pre-specified standard, the final decision rests with the regulator. In cap-and-trade and averaging systems, the firm is no longer the executor of the regulator's decision; the abatement decision is transferred to the firm, which must operate within the constraint of the cap or the averaging standard. Letting firms trade abatement responsibilities in this way allows markets to emerge; and it should not be surprising that this decentralization of the abatement decision leads to more efficient results.

The transfer of authority for firm-level abatement in these programs does not imply that the government has no role in them. The non-appropriability of environmental benefits and costs means that the government will have to decide the level of the cap or the averaging standard; however, once this constraint and the associated market rules are decided, the role of government can and should be limited to enforcement. The error of command-and-control regulation lies not in defining the environmental goal, but in presuming to know how each firm should contribute to achieving the goal. In all the programs where averaging or allowance-based systems have been employed successfully in the United States, the government has imposed the default standard or the cap and enforced it. The new element has been the government's willingness to step aside and let firms decide how, where, and when to abate.

The government's withdrawal from micro-managing abatement has also contributed to better environmental performance. For firms facing relatively high abatement costs, a functioning market significantly reduces the cost of finding trading partners, while in a credit-based system the costs of gaining regulatory approval and of finding the partner are little different from the costs of negotiating a relaxation in the standard. Applicants can credibly claim not to know of other sources willing to create credits for trading and the regulator is unlikely to know of or to be willing arbitrarily to impose an offsetting, more demanding requirement on sources facing less hardship. By letting a market emerge, the regulator makes special pleading uneconomic, to the benefit of the environment.

CO_2 implication: "download" CO_2 rights

The Kyoto Protocol has certainly recognized the value of emissions trading for the control of GHGs, but whether that recognition includes understanding what makes emissions trading work is not so certain. In Kyoto jargon, national quotas should be "downloaded" to emitting entities. The European Union Directive on emissions trading seems to conform to this lesson, but it is too early to say whether it will be broadly applied.

Lesson 3: Banking improves performance

All of the US emissions trading programs, except the RECLAIM programs, have included banking and they have shown both that banking can lead to significant "early action" when coupled with phased-in emission reduction requirements and that banking can dampen the volatility of allowance prices.

Banking as an accelerator of emission reductions

Figure 6.1 illustrates the extent to which banking has accelerated the timing of the required cumulative emission reduction in the Acid Rain Program. Of the allowances distributed for use during Phase I, 31 percent were not used then but banked for later use in Phase II. In all, 11.65 million tons were banked, which means that 11.65 million tons of SO_2 emissions were reduced ahead of schedule, on average by about six years. Since banking is a response to the cost savings possible by trading across years, cost savings are implied. The recent finding by Ellerman and Montero (2002) that the pattern of accumulation and draw-down through 2001 has been surprisingly optimal suggests that these cost savings are being realized.

Similar patterns of accelerated emission reduction can be observed in other programs with banking. Banking was an important feature in accomplishing the tenfold reduction of lead content in gasoline in the mid-1980s and it has been a heavily used feature of the mobile source ABT programs. The Northeastern NO_x Budget Program is distinct in placing restrictions, known as Progressive Flow Control, that require that banked allowances be surrendered at a ratio of 2:1 when used beyond a certain amount. Nevertheless, the proportions of allowances banked in the first three years of the program were 20%, 11%, and 12%. Moreover, banked allowances are not being held exclusively for use when the cap is lower. About 40% of the bank accumulated in 1999 and 2000 was used in 2001, two years before the more stringent Phase III cap applied; and 40% of these allowances were surrendered at the 2:1 ratio.

Banking (or borrowing) to dampen price fluctuations

The current use of banked allowances in the Northeastern NO_X Budget Program suggests that banking provides a form of inventory to be used in meeting unexpectedly high demand in the next year, thereby dampening allowance price fluctuations. In fact, a correspondence can be observed in the three principal cap-and-trade programs between the volatility of allowance prices and the spatial and temporal dimensions of the allowance market. The program with the greatest flexibility, the Acid Rain Program, which allows nationwide spatial trading and unlimited banking, has experienced price fluctuations of no more than 3:1 when measured as the ratio of the highest observed price to the lowest. The Northeastern NO_X Budget Program, which is more restricted both in spatial scope and in the use of banked allowances, has experienced a ratio of 15:1, with the high price occurring only in the first year when there was no accumulated inventory. The RECLAIM NO_X program has experienced the most extreme price fluctuation – 60:1 – and it is by far the most restricted program in the scope of spatial trading and it allows virtually no temporal trading.[5] The experience with these programs suggests that price volatility reflects the scope of potential trading, both spatial and temporal, and that banking is especially important when spatial trading is limited, as it will be for many environmental problems.

The need for temporal flexibility in spatially limited programs was vividly illustrated by the experience with the RECLAIM NO_X market in 2000–01. The conditions precipitating the California electricity market crisis in late 2000 and early 2001 caused the prices of RECLAIM Trading Credits (RTCs) for NO_X to rise to extremely high levels ($40,000/ton on average in the fourth quarter of 2000), the temporary removal of electric utility generating units from the cap, and the institution of a mitigation fee of $15,000 per ton for uncovered emissions. The immediate cause of the problem was the extraordinary demand placed on old electric utility generating units in the Los Angeles Basin that were not equipped with NO_X emission reduction equipment and that had previously been used for relatively few hours of the year (Joskow and Kahn, 2002). When it became clear that these units could not obtain sufficient RTCs in the limited spatial market and that they could

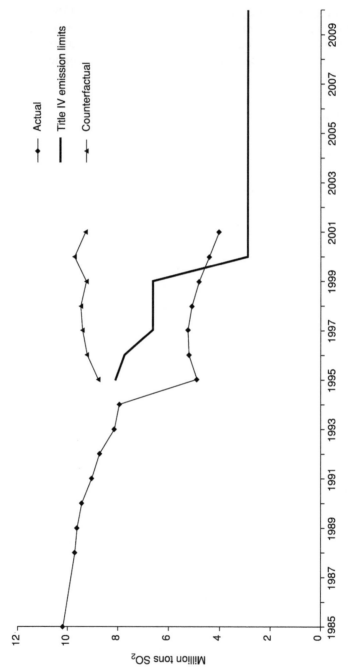

Figure 6.1. The Acid Rain Program in historical perspective: Phase I units.

not be shut down, *de facto* borrowing was adopted by collecting the mitigation fee on uncovered emissions and using the proceeds to acquire future offsets from sources outside the program. Although the fundamental cause of the high prices in the RECLAIM NO_x market was the flaws in the restructured electricity market in California (Joskow, 2001), the effects on RECLAIM NO_x prices would have been much less had banking or borrowing been allowed.

CO$_2$ implication: banking should be included

Just as the uniform mixing of GHG emissions in the atmosphere provides no basis for limiting the spatial scope of trading, so the long lives of GHG emissions offer no basis for restricting banking. Moreover, if GHG emission caps decline over time, as will likely be required, banking will play a large role and deliver a greater near-term reduction. The role of banking in dampening price volatility would not seem to be as important since the spatial dimension of GHG markets can be broadly defined; however, concerns about price volatility continue as evidenced by the arguments in support of a safety valve.[6] Allowing carry-over of allowances from one period to another provides an alternative means of dampening price volatility.

Lesson 4: Voluntary features present a difficult trade-off

The Acid Rain Program included provisions that allowed sources outside the cap with relatively low abatement cost to opt into the program and thereby to reduce the overall cost. The lesson emerging from this experience is highly relevant for GHG trading, but also capable of significant misunderstanding.

Transaction costs matter

The two categories of voluntary participants could opt into the Acid Rain Program: electric utility sources that were not subject to the program until Phase II and industrial sources that were not subject to the Acid Rain Program in either Phase I or Phase II. The response of the two groups was strikingly different and revealing of the trade-off presented by opt-in provisions. Over 200 voluntary electric utility units participated in one or more years of Phase I, and 110 of them participated in all five years. In contrast, only a few sources participated in the industrial opt-in program.

The transaction costs associated with participation explain the difference (Atkeson, 1997). The cost of monitoring was the largest obstacle cited by industrial sources considering participation but deciding not to do so; and the few that did participate already had monitoring equipment in place as a result of other environmental requirements or otherwise did not need to install monitors.[7] In contrast, the transaction costs for electric utility units considering voluntary participation in Phase I were low because continuous emissions monitors had been required on all units from 1995, even for those not subject to the cap until 2000. In addition, the costs of establishing a baseline for units opting in did not have to be incurred because a set of easily applied mathematical formulae determined the number of allowances each would receive if it chose to receive the allowances and be subject to the program's requirements. Finally, the utilities owning the units eligible for voluntary participation in Phase I were already incurring the overhead costs of managing emissions and accounting for allowances.

Adverse selection

While the voluntary participation in the Acid Rain Program was heartening, an analysis of the units that opted in and those that did not reveals a strong element of adverse selection (Montero, 1999). Units for which emissions were expected to be lower than the predetermined baseline tended to opt in, and units with emissions expected to be higher did not. Other features of the voluntary program, such as allowing the owners of these units to take eligible units in and out of the program from year to year and to wait until nearly the end of the compliance year to decide whether to opt in, also encouraged opportunistic behavior.

The source of the adverse selection was the impossibility of specifying a true contemporaneous baseline. The pre-specified baseline, which had the benefit of reducing transaction costs, relied mostly on 1989–90 data; however, changes in coal markets and in the utilization of electric generating units in the intervening years caused the true counterfactual emissions for eligible units in 1995–99 to be different. In particular, units that had already switched to lower-sulfur coal for purely economic reasons because of changes in coal markets could receive allowances in excess of their true baselines by opting in. These units were not so much low-cost abaters, as they were units that were abating anyway.

While the evidence of this selection bias is very strong, the environmental effects must be kept in perspective. Since units opting in still had to cover emissions, most of the allowances issued were not excess. The number of allowances that could be considered excess amounted to only

3 percent of the total issued during 1995–99 and the inflation of the cap during Phase II, when these banked allowances will be used, is only about 2 percent. These magnitudes are not great and they cannot be said to have threatened the overall integrity of the SO_2 cap. In addition, many of the units opting in also abated emissions in response to allowance prices and thereby contributed some cost savings to the program.

CO_2 implication: the trade-off must be recognized and managed

The lesson from this experience with voluntary provisions is both encouraging and cautionary. On the one hand, if monitoring and other overhead costs can be kept low enough, significant voluntary participation is possible, especially through the use of pre-specified baselines. On the other hand, the price of reducing these transaction costs is some amount of adverse selection since the true counterfactual will never correspond exactly to any pre-specified baseline.

It would be tempting to avoid voluntary features altogether; however, opting into a GHG emissions trading program has a strategic value that was lacking in the SO_2 program. Initially, GHG trading will almost certainly encompass only some countries, some greenhouse gases, and probably, some sectors; yet, to be successful the cap on GHG emissions must eventually become comprehensive in all aspects. Extending the cap will require the development of new techniques for measuring and monitoring non-CO_2 emissions and CO_2 sinks or for otherwise ensuring reasonable environmental integrity. Opt-in projects provide small experiments for working out these problems and increasing familiarity with emissions trading. The eventual extension of the cap will require motivation additional to the economic incentives underlying voluntary participation, but the opt-in projects prepare the way. Also, as is evident from Harrison *et al.* (2000), much has been learned from the experience with voluntary features in existing programs and rules for voluntary participation can be designed that will keep opportunistic behavior to a minimum while not discouraging participation by those who can offer cheaper abatement. In sum, the lesson for GHG emissions trading is that the problem of adverse selection must be recognized, addressed, and to some extent accepted.

Lesson 5: Allocating allowances is part of the solution

Cap-and-trade programs have the peculiarity of requiring the regulator to allocate allowances. Although rights to emit are implied and traded in all emissions trading programs, the explicit grant of these rights in cap-and-trade programs creates controversy as well as some benefits. Several regularities can be observed in the US cap-and-trade programs and these regularities suggest that allocation is an integral part of adopting emissions reduction programs.

The first regularity is that allowances have been "grandfathered"[8] entirely to incumbent emitters. This phenomenon is surprising in view of the policy implications that are being drawn from the considerable body of research on fiscal and regulatory interactions and on distributional implications that generally favors the auctioning of allowances.[9] Most of this research is recent so that it is possible that these larger welfare effects were simply not recognized when the three US cap-and-trade programs were adopted. However, the same preference is evident in the three CO_2 cap-and-trade programs being set up in Europe after these implications have become recognized.[10]

A second regularity, which may explain the predominance of grandfathering, is the political use of allowances in gaining consensus for adopting or implementing emissions reduction programs. The clearest study of this phenomenon is the analysis of the allocation of allowances in the Acid Rain Program by Joskow and Schmalensee (1998). They conclude that no single interest group theory explains the many deviations from the basic principle for allocating allowances in that program and that the final allocation reflects a "majoritarian equilibrium" that enabled enactment by the US Congress. In the other two programs, the relevant state and local regulatory bodies charged with NAAQS compliance[11] adopted cap-and-trade approaches (with grandfathered allowances) even though they had the authority to reduce emissions through conventional command-and-control measures. In both cases, award of allowances to the incumbents who would have borne the costs of the command-and-control regulations that were not adopted appears to have facilitated previously elusive agreement on implementing the required emission reductions.

A final common feature of the allocation process is that the specific allocation of grandfathered permits does not seem to have influenced program performance. Despite initial fears about market power and hoarding, nothing in the US experience suggests that the allocation of allowances among affected parties has altered the gains from trading or the achievement of the environmental goal.[12] A reasonably good Coasian separation of equity and efficiency seems to obtain. This is more than can be said of command-and-control and tax solutions, where dealing with political concerns nearly always detracts from program performance.

CO_2 implications: allocation cannot be ignored

Although adoption of a cap and allocation of allowances are often viewed as analytically distinct, the two are fused in practice. The political use of allowances is likely to be an integral part of the decision to adopt a GHG emissions constraint. Adoption of an emissions reduction program should be made easier by being able to use allowances to gain consent and this suggests that the instrument would be a cap-and-trade program since it alone creates its own currency to deal with problems of equity and influence without detracting from the program's goal.

At the same time, the ratio of the value of the endowment represented by grandfathering allowances to the cost incurred in a GHG cap-and-trade program dwarfs anything heretofore known and this makes the larger welfare and equity implications far greater than before. Also, since there is no pre-existing regulation concerning GHG emissions, and no viable alternative in the US context to a cap-and-trade system, the calculations and implicit rules that seem to have decided allocation before may not apply.[13] Finally, the earlier circumstances, when no one seems to have questioned whether there was any better way to distribute allowances than by giving them away to incumbents, no longer exist. Allocation promises to be contentious and the question is whether it will be a complicating issue or simply a sign that the debate about the adoption of GHG constraints is serious.

Conclusion

The Canadian economist J. H. Dales made two observations in his 1968 book, *Pollution, Property and Prices*, that presage the later experience with emissions trading.

If it is feasible to establish a market to implement a policy, no policy-maker can afford to do without one. (p. 100)

It is high time that we begin to devise some new forms of property rights, not to air and water, but to the *use* of air and water. (p. 76, emphasis in the original)

The several experiments with emissions trading in the United States have demonstrated the feasibility of establishing environmental markets and they constitute a beginning in the development of property rights to the use of air and in constructing markets to implement environmental policy. That experience affirms the desirability of continuing in this direction, not just because emissions trading programs lower the overall costs of reducing pollution, but because they also provide superior environmental results. As carefully noted by Dales, not all problems can be solved by devising novel new forms of property rights, but the limitation of anthropogenic greenhouse gas emissions is one where doing so seems clearly feasible.

Notes

1 The programs that constitute the main US experience with emissions trading are six in number and they are described more fully in the aforementioned Pew Center report. They are: (1) the early EPA emissions trading programs that introduced netting, offsets, bubbles, and banking to the Clean Air Act; (2) trading lead content in gasoline in the phase-down program of the mid-1980s: (3) SO_2 allowance trading in the Acid Rain Program, created by the 1990 Clean Air Act Amendments, which began in 1995; (4) NO_X and SO_2 trading in the Regional Clean Air Incentives Market (RECLAIM) program for the Los Angeles Air Basin from 1994 on; (5) mobile Source averaging, banking, and trading (ABT) programs that began in the late 1980s but saw the most application in the 1990s; and (6) NO_X trading under the Northeastern Ozone Transport Commission Budget Program, which started in 1999.

2 Phase II, which began in the year 2000, differs from Phase I in both the stringency and the scope of the required emission reductions. In Phase I, units larger than 100 MW capacity and with 1985 emission rates of 2.5 lbs. SO_2 per mmBtu of heat input (#/mmBtu) or higher were required to be subject to the SO_2 cap and to reduce emissions to an average emission rate equal to 2.5 #/mmBtu times average 1985–87 (baseline) heat input. In Phase II, all fossil-fired generating units greater than 25 MW were subject to SO_2 caps, regardless of historical emission rates, and they were issued allowances in an amount that is less than half the Phase I rate: 1.2 #/mmBtu times baseline heat input. Units with a 1985 emission rate less than 1.2 #/mmBtu received allowances equal to baseline heat input times the 1985 emission rate.

3 See Smith *et al.* (1998) for an analysis of the claims that the costs in the SO_2 program were a tenth of what had been expected.

4 Assertions that imply the contrary by anti-trading advocacy groups in the United States are incorrect. About 77 percent of the SO_2 emission reductions attributable to the Acid Rain Program have been accomplished by sources in the eight Mid-Western states that would otherwise have accounted for 59 percent of emissions. An example of the misleading comparisons can be found in "Darkening Skies" (Clear the Air, 2002), a report from an advocacy group that faults the Acid Rain Program for accomplishing little by comparing 1999, before the more stringent Phase II came into effect, with 1995, after the major reduction attributable to the program had taken place.

5 The RECLAIM programs overlapping compliance cycles allow a very limited amount of *de facto* banking and borrowing for six-month periods.

6 These arguments are provided in a series of publications by researchers at Resources for the Future in Washington DC. See Kopp *et al.* (1998, 1999, 2000). Jacoby and Ellerman (2004) provide an interpretation of this debate.

7 For instance, by shutting down the industrial boiler and purchasing power and steam from an electric utility whose emissions are already monitored, as was indeed the case for one industrial opt-in project.

8 The term "grandfathering", which means that allowances are distributed gratis, has become enshrined in trading terminology, but it is not entirely appropriate. In other contexts, such as tax provisions or environmental requirements, it implies an exemption from the relevant provision. Recipients of allowances are not exempt from any aspect of compliance, i.e. surrendering allowances equal to emissions; their only exemption is from having to purchase allowances to cover emissions equal to or less than the allowances allocated to them.

9 An introductory sampling of this literature can be made by consulting Harrison (1996), Goulder et al. (1999), Burtraw et al. (2001), and Dinan and Rogers (2002).

10 Both the Danish electric utility cap and the UK Emissions Trading Scheme grandfather allowances to incumbent emitters. More significantly, the latest iteration of the European Commission's Emissions Trading Directive limits auctioning to no more than 10 percent of allowances.

11 In the RECLAIM programs, the regulatory authority is the South Coast Air Quality Management District, which is responsible for air quality in the Los Angeles Basin. In the Northeastern NO_X Budget program, allowances were allocated by the individual states, which are the entities responsible for regulating emissions within their borders to achieve compliance with national NAAQS for ozone.

12 For example, arguments about whether the gains from trade in the SO_2 allowance trading program have been fully realized concern the influence of public utility regulation, not the allocation of allowances.

13 To judge by current proposals from left and right, a consensus on this issue is being reached in the United States: there will be some grandfathering, but it will be phased out over some period of time. There is, however, no agreement on percentages, the phase-out schedule, or the use of auction revenues.

References

Atkeson, E. 1997. *Joint Implementation: Lessons from Title IV's Voluntary Compliance Programs*. Cambridge, MA: MIT Center for Energy and Environmental Policy Research.

Burtraw, D. 1996. "The SO_2 emissions trading program: cost savings without allowance trades," *Contemporary Economic Policy* 14: 79–94.

Burtraw, D., Palmer, K., Bharvirkar, R., and Paul, A. 2001. *The Effect of Allowance Allocation on the Cost of Carbon Emission Trading*. RFF Discussion Paper 01–30, Washington, DC: Resources for the Future.

Carlson, C. P., Burtraw, D., Cropper, M., and Palmer, K. 2000. "SO_2 control by electric utilities: what are the gains from trade?" *Journal of Political Economy* 108: 1292–326.

Clear the Air: National Campaign Against Dirty Power 2002. "Darkening skies: trends toward increasing power plant emissions." Washington, DC (http://cta.policy.net/fact/darkening_skies/).

Dales, J. H. 1968. *Pollution, Property and Prices: An Essay in Policy-Making and Economics*. Toronto: University of Toronto Press.

Dinan, T., and Rogers, D. L. 2002. "Distributional effects of carbon allowance trading: how government decisions determine winners and losers," *National Tax Journal* 55: 199–221.

Ellerman, A. D., Joskow, P. L., and Harrison, D. Jr. 2003. *Emissions Trading in the US: Experience, Lessons, and Considerations for Greenhouse Gases*. Washington, DC: Pew Center on Global Climate Change.

Ellerman, A. D., Joskow, P. L., Schmalensee, R., Montero, J.-P., and Bailey, E. 2000. *Markets for Clean Air: The US Acid Rain Program*. Cambridge: Cambridge University Press.

Ellerman, A. D., and Montero, J.-P. 1998. "The declining trend in sulfur dioxide emissions: implications for allowance prices," *Journal of Environmental Economics and Management* 36: 26–45.

2002. *The Temporal Efficiency of SO_2 Emissions Trading*. Cambridge, MA: MIT Center for Energy and Environmental Policy Research.

Farrell, A. 2000. "The NO_X budget: a look at the first year," *Electricity Journal* 13: 83–93.

Goulder, L. H., Perry, I. W. H., Williams III, R. C., and Burtraw, D. 1999. "The cost-effectiveness of alternative instruments for environmental protection in a second best setting," *Journal of Public Economics* 72: 329–60.

Hahn, R. W. 1989. "Economic prescriptions for environmental problems: How the patient followed the doctor's orders," *Journal of Economic Perspectives* 3: 95–114.

Hahn, R. W., and Hester, G. L. 1989a. "Where did all the markets go? An analysis of EPA's emissions trading program," *Yale Journal on Regulation* 6: 109–53.

1989b. "Marketable permits: lessons for theory and practice," *Ecology Law Quarterly* 16: 361–406.

Harrison, D. Jr. 1996. *The Distributive Effects of Economic Instruments for Global Warming*. Paris: Organization for Economic Cooperation and Development.

Harrison, D. Jr., Schatzki, S. T., Wilson, T., and Haites, E. 2000. *Critical Issues in International Greenhouse Gas Emissions Trading: Setting Baselines for Credit-Based Trading Programs – Lessons Learned from Relevant Experience*. Palo Alto, CA: Electric Power Research Institute, Inc.

Jacoby, H. D., and Ellerman, A. D. 2004. "The safety valve and climate policy," *Energy Policy* 32: 481–91.

Joskow, P. L. 2001. "California's electricity crisis," *Oxford Review of Economic Policy* 17: 365–88.

Joskow, P. L., and Kahn, E. 2002. "A quantitative analysis of pricing behavior in California's wholesale electricity market during summer 2000," *Energy Journal* 23: 1–35.

Joskow, P. L., and Schmalensee, R. 1998. "The political economy of market-based environmental policy: the U.S. acid rain program," *Journal of Law and Economics* 41: 37–83.

Kopp, R. J., Morgenstern, R. D., and Pizer, W. 2000. "Limiting cost, assuring effort, and encouraging ratification: compliance under the Kyoto Protocol." CIRED/RFF Workshop on Compliance and Supplemental Framework (http://www.weathervane.rff.org/features/parisconf0721/summary.html).

Kopp, R. J., Morgenstern, R. D., Pizer, W., and Toman, M. A. 1999. *A Proposal for Credible Early Action in U.S. Climate Policy*. Washington, DC: Resources for the Future (http://www.weathervane.rff.org/features/feature060.html).

Kopp, R. J., Morgenstern, R. D., and Toman, M. A. 1998. *The Kyoto Protocol: The Realities of Implementation*. Washington, DC: Resources for the Future (http://www.weathervane.rff.org/features/feature027.html).

Montero, J.-P. 1999. "Voluntary compliance with market-based environmental policy: evidence from the U.S. acid rain program," *Journal of Political Economy* 107: 998–1033.

Shabman, L., Stephenson, K., and Shobe, W. 2002. "Trading programs for environmental management: reflections on the air and water experiences," *Environmental Practice* 4: 153–62.

Smith, A. E., Platt, J., and Ellerman, A. D. 1998. *The Costs of Reducing Utility SO2 Emissions: Not as Low as You Might Think*. Cambridge: MIT Center for Energy and Environmental Policy Research.

Stavins, R. N. 1998. "What can we learn from the grand policy experiment? Lessons from SO$_2$ allowance trading," *Journal of Economic Perspectives* 12: 69–88.

Swift, B. 2000. "Allowance trading and SO$_2$ hot spots – good news from the acid rain program," *Bureau of National Affairs Environment Reporter* 31: 954–59.

Tietenberg, T. H. 2000. *Environmental and Natural Resource Economics*. Reading, MA: Addison Wesley Longman Publishing Co.

7 Climate change policy viewed from the USA and the role of intensity targets

Charles D. Kolstad

Introduction

With the very emphatic withdrawal of the Bush Administration from the Kyoto Protocol, it might appear that there is no US policy on climate change. This view is reinforced by the 2002 Valentine's Day announcement from the Bush Administration that the cornerstone of its climate policy was to *set a goal* to reduce the greenhouse gas intensity of the US economy by 18 percent over the coming decade; never mind that this was roughly the rate at which the economy had been "de-carbonizing" over the previous decade.

But politicians come and go. This is particularly true in the case of climate change. It was President Bush's father who participated in the setting up of the treaty underlying the Kyoto Protocol, the Framework Convention on Climate Change, and no doubt climate policy will outlive the current President Bush. Furthermore, there is other positive activity on climate change in the United States, though relatively modest. There are federal government programs, mostly in research and development, as well as activities by state governments, private parties, and non-governmental organizations.

In this chapter we provide a review of the assorted actions that are being taken in the United States to deal with the climate change problem. The review is by no means comprehensive – just indicative of the types of activities that are under way. In addition, we consider some of the remaining problems that are not addressed by Kyoto, problems which must be addressed regardless of whether Kyoto becomes effective.

The work was conducted during 2002–03, while I was 3M Professor of Environmental Economics at MIT. I am grateful for information on federal activities from John List and Billy Pizer; on state activities, from Jill Gravender of the California Climate Action Network and Dale Bryk of the NRDC in New York. Denny Ellerman provided valuable insights on the greenhouse gas intensity dimensions of the Bush proposal. Insightful comments of Gernot Klepper and an anonymous referee are appreciated. Of course, none of them is responsible for my omissions, misinterpretations, or other blunders.

96

We conclude by a re-examination of the much-maligned Bush approach of focusing on declining greenhouse gas intensity in the economy. Although its voluntary nature makes it not much of a policy, the approach has innovative dimensions, addressing at a general level some of the problems associated with the quantity targets approach of Kyoto.

The policy arena

In March 2001, US President George W. Bush announced that the United States would not be a signatory to the Kyoto Protocol. There is no point in providing another review of the context of the President's withdrawal of the USA from the Kyoto Protocol; in any event, it is unclear whether the US Senate would ever have ratified the Protocol.[1] On February 14, 2002, the President announced his "new approach" to climate strategy.[2] This new approach has charitably been called weak. However, an ancillary benefit of the federal government relinquishing its leadership role in addressing the climate change problem in the USA is that a number of non-federal organizations, including state governments, have stepped forward and taken steps toward controlling precursors of climate change.

The Bush "initiative"

On February 14, 2002, the Bush Administration unveiled its new initiative on climate change, a set of unilateral actions to be undertaken by the USA. Although many observers feel the initiative is weak and largely ineffective, it is important to separate the strength of the initiative from the substantive approaches to the climate problem suggested by the initiative. In other words, there are innovative ideas in the proposal; it is in large part because they are applied weakly or voluntarily or both that the net effect is so modest.

The cornerstone of the Bush proposal is a focusing on reducing the greenhouse gas intensity of the US economy,[3] rather than setting a quantitative cap on emissions, as proposed in Kyoto. The four key dimensions of the proposal are, in brief:

- reduce the greenhouse gas intensity of the US economy by 18 percent over 2002–12
- strengthen the Emission Reduction Registry
- fund climate R&D
- introduce tax incentives for renewable energy, cogeneration, fuel cells, and hybrid vehicles.

There are a number of other miscellaneous actions[4] that are either not new, very modest, or of negligible consequence for climate, including:

- increased funding for idling farm acreage (ostensibly for carbon sequestration)
- fund R&D in energy, including automobile fuel efficiency
- fund climate change technology transfer programs with the developing world
- issue "challenges" to the business community to reduce greenhouse gas emissions
- fund debt-for-nature swaps.

The goal of a reduction in greenhouse gas intensity seeks to decouple growth in output and consumption from greenhouse gas emissions reduction. Although decreases in GDP are a way of reducing emissions (witness the case of Russia in the 1990s), it is not a popular strategy, nor likely to be very effective in the long run. A country whose economy is in the doldrums is unlikely to want to invest much in environmental protection. A reduction in the greenhouse gas intensity of production inevitably means a change in the structure of production (moving away from industries which are intensive in the production of greenhouse gases) as well as pursuing proactive measures to control emissions, such as switching from coal to natural gas in electricity production and reducing vehicle miles traveled by auto.

Of the two major flaws in the Bush proposal on greenhouse gas intensity, one is that the reductions are modest. Table 7.1 shows the reduction in greenhouse gas intensity in the USA and selected other countries over the decade of the 1990s. As can be seen, the greenhouse gas intensity of the US economy "naturally" declined by 17 percent over the 1990s, with most of that occurring in the last five years of the decade.[5] It is unlikely that this was due to any action by the US government; rather, it results from structural change in the economy with a gradual movement away from greenhouse gas intensive industry. Consequently, setting a goal of a reduction of 18 percent over the decade ending in 2012 is not very ambitious and should be an easy target to hit.

In terms of improvements in the greenhouse gas intensity of the economy, the record of other Annex I countries during the period is quite similar to that of the USA.[6] Germany and the UK did very well (much better than the USA) in reducing the greenhouse gas intensity of its economy, though the absorption of East Germany made this somewhat easier for Germany and the introduction of North Sea gas (and the phasing out of coal) made this easier for the UK. The EU minus Germany performed almost identically to the USA in terms of reducing

Table 7.1. *Greenhouse gas emissions (excluding LULUCF) and emission intensity, 1990–2000*

Country/region	GHG emissions			GHG change (%)		GHG intensity			Intensity change(%)		
	1990	1995	2000	90–95	95–00	1990	1995	2000	90–95	95–00	90–00
USA	6131	6482	7001	5.7	8.0	0.94	0.88	0.78	−6.0	−11.8	−17.1
EU-15	4216	4088	4068	−3.0	−0.5	0.53	0.47	0.41	−9.8	−12.6	−21.2
EU-14 (EU-15 less Germany)	2993	3017	3077	0.8	2.0	0.52	0.49	0.43	−6.0	−11.8	−17.1
EU-13 (EU-15 less Germany & UK)	2251	2332	2428	3.6	4.1	0.48	0.46	0.42	−3.0	−10.0	−12.8
Japan	1247	1373	1386	10.1	0.9	0.26	0.26	0.24	−0.5	−6.0	−6.4
Australia	424	443	501	4.5	13.1	1.33	1.19	1.11	−10.9	−6.7	−16.9
Germany	1223	1071	991	−12.4	−7.5	0.54	0.44	0.37	−19.1	−15.4	−31.5
Italy	521	527	547	1.2	3.8	0.51	0.48	0.45	−5.0	−5.4	−10.2
UK	742	685	649	−7.7	−5.3	0.71	0.60	0.50	−15.3	−17.7	−30.3

Units for GHG: millions of metric tonnes of CO_2 equivalent.

Units for GDP: 1995 US$, converted at 1995 exchange rates.

GHG intensity: kg of CO_2-equivalent per $GDP.

GHG emissions omit LULUCF (Land use, Land use change, and Forestry).

Source: GDP data from OECD National Accounts (OECD 2004); GHG data from FCCC database.

greenhouse gas intensity (though the overall intensity is considerably lower than that of the USA). The EU minus Germany and the UK did not do as well as the USA in terms of the decline of intensity. On the other hand, all European countries have economies which are much less greenhouse gas intensive than the USA. Focusing on the reduction of greenhouse gas intensity, the USA looks good; focusing on the absolute level of greenhouse gas intensity, it looks much less noble.

The second major flaw in the Bush proposal on reducing greenhouse gas intensity is that there are precious few ways of implementing the goal of reduced intensity. The goal is just that – a goal – and there are no regulations and few other steps proposed to accomplish the goal. That makes it largely meaningless. The Bush proposal does indicate that there will be a reassessment in 2012 and if progress is slow or the "science" is more alarming, further steps will be taken. However, the public record is littered with goals in energy conservation, environmental clean-up, and other arenas, goals which are subsequently not met; generally the only consequences of unmet goals are expressions of regret over the optimism of goals set in an earlier more naive time.[7]

There are a few steps proposed by the Bush Administration to push the United States toward achieving the goal. Most of the proposals are for continuations of activities of the Clinton Administration or of even earlier administrations. Although they are meritorious, it is unlikely they will have much impact.

Strengthening the greenhouse gas registry can have a positive effect on voluntary actions to reduce greenhouse gases. With policy uncertainty, there is a tendency for firms to delay greenhouse gas reductions until the uncertainty is resolved. This is particularly true if any greenhouse gas reduction serves to define a lower baseline from which future reductions must occur. The strengthening of the greenhouse gas registry serves to eliminate or at least greatly reduce the incentive for individual firms to postpone action.

The Bush Administration has indicated it will push tax incentives for investment in renewables and new transportation technology. Tax incentives for solar and renewables were part of the Carter Administrations energy program. Though meritorious, they will probably not have significant impact. In any event, they require Congressional action for passage and it is unclear whether that will happen.

Another major thrust of the Bush proposal is continued high levels of R&D funding in energy, including automobile fuel efficiency. There have been decades of research on fuel efficiency in automobiles and much progress has been made. A cynic would conclude that this has made possible even larger SUVs. Highly fuel-efficient autos have been available for many years. However, without incentives for consumers and automakers, fuel efficiency *of the average vehicle purchased* will not improve. Ultimately, consumers see a menu of vehicles on display at their automobile dealer and make a free choice among alternatives.

The Bush Administration has also indicated it will continue to invest in R&D in the climate arena. Certainly the US government has been a leader in funding research in many dimensions of climate science. This is to be lauded. However, this is not new; nor is it likely to result in significant reductions in US greenhouse gas emissions.

In sum, the Bush Administration proposal is a very modest proposal that is unlikely to do much to US greenhouse gas emissions, over what would occur from the natural evolution of the economy. Leaving aside the modesty of the Bush proposal, there are some dimensions of it which merit closer attention, particularly the shift to greenhouse gas intensity. We return to this issue later.

Missing incentives

Two conspicuously absent dimensions of the Bush initiative are incentives for reduced energy consumption in transportation and incentives for switching away from GHG-intensive coal in electricity generation. These are tremendously important determinants of the greenhouse gas intensity of the economy.

Within the transportation sector, a major source of greenhouse gas emissions is the private automobile. To address emissions from this sector, one must concentrate on two things: the efficiency of the fleet of automobiles and the annual distance each vehicle is driven. A high tax on gasoline provides incentives for both – driving becomes expensive which gives incentives for consumers to seek high-efficiency vehicles and to drive those vehicles less. One of the quirks of American politics is that high gasoline taxes appear to be politically impossible. This is a mystery to some but it certainly seems to be an accepted truth by most politicians. Consequently, one must rely on other mechanisms to achieve the same effect.

To increase the fuel efficiency of vehicles (which would occur automatically with a high gasoline tax), Congress adopted fuel efficiency standards in 1975 – the CAFE (Corporate Average Fuel Economy) standards. These standards required auto companies gradually to increase the average fuel efficiency of the cars they sell (averaged over a company's total sales). This worked fairly well except for an exemption that started small but eventually became big enough to drive a large SUV through: light trucks were subject to much weaker standards. The auto companies responded to CAFE legislation by constructing a whole new set of vehicles which were technically trucks – minivans and sport utility vehicles.

In the early 1990s (during the elder Bush Administration) there was a movement in Congress to strengthen further the CAFE standards and close the light truck loophole (National Academy of Sciences, 1992, 2002). This effort failed, in part because of a lack of a clear and present need for more fuel efficiency. In 2001 the National Academy of Sciences again studied the question and recommended tightening the CAFE standards. The Bush Administration opposed this, ostensibly on the grounds of safety. Safety is influenced both by the size of vehicles and by the size heterogeneity of the mix of vehicles on the roads. An increase in fuel efficiency would reduce the average size of vehicles but also have the effect of bringing more homogeneity to the fleet. The President's climate initiative calls for continuing study of this issue but most view such study as merely a delaying tactic.

Another major source of greenhouse gas emissions is coal combustion, primarily in electricity generation. Coal involves a much higher level of carbon dioxide emission per unit heat content than either natural gas or petroleum. Coal is used for electricity generation because it is cheap. Without incentives to switch to less carbon-intensive fuels, electricity generators will continue to use the least cost source of energy. The President's initiative is totally silent on this issue, except to encourage the use of renewables for electricity production.

Non-federal initiatives

One of the positive ancillary benefits of inaction at the federal level in the United States is that other actors have stepped in to fill the void. As political theory would suggest, the abrogation of responsibility by one branch of government results in the (partial) filling of that void by other branches of government.

In much the same way that action by member states of the EU can substitute for action by the EU, over a dozen states are considering or have instituted programs that might be found in a more proactive federal program.[8] To gain a true picture of what the United States is or is not doing on the climate front, it is important to look at individual states as well as the federal government. Table 7.2 lists a selection of state activities in the area of greenhouse gas management.

Energy conservation programs have been a mainstay of state energy and environmental policy from the 1970s, and remain so today. This is true in part because of the historic role of the states in regulating public utilities. A number of states have aggressive building and appliance

Table 7.2. *Selected US state actions in climate change*

State	Nature of actions
California	Voluntary greenhouse gas registry
	AB 1493 (2002): Mandated greenhouse gas emission reductions from autos for 2009 model year
Oregon	HB 3283 (1997): New energy facilities required to reduce or offset greenhouse gas emissions
New Hampshire	HB 284 (2002): CO_2 emissions to be reduced to 1990 levels by 2010
	Voluntary greenhouse gas registry
Wisconsin	Voluntary greenhouse gas registry
New Jersey	Voluntary greenhouse gas registry
	Committed to reducing GHG emissions to 3.5 percent below 1990 levels by 2010
Massachusetts	CO_2 emissions from six largest power plants capped and to be reduced

Note: Most states have energy conservation and renewables programs; these have not been detailed here.
Source: Rabe, 2002; personal communication, Jill Gravender, California Climate Action Registry; NESCAUM: Jones *et al.*, 2002.

efficiency standards as well as conservation programs, often implemented through the regulated energy utilities. Furthermore, there are a number of state programs aimed at encouraging the use of renewable sources of energy. Some of these also date from the 1970s.[9] These include renewable portfolio standards, requiring a minimum level of use of renewable energy sources. In many areas where the electricity system has been deregulated ("restructured"), consumers are given the choice of purchasing "green power," electricity produced from renewable sources. Energy conservation and renewable energy programs obviously play a major role in reducing greenhouse gas emissions. Such programs are so varied and common that they will not be reviewed here.

Four states (California, New Hampshire, Wisconsin, and New Jersey) have implemented greenhouse gas registry programs, all voluntary. Other states are considering such action. It is not clear to what extent these overlap, duplicate, or augment the voluntary federal registry program. Several bills have been introduced into Congress to institute mandatory greenhouse gas registries.

At a more proactive level, California recently passed a law which can be interpreted as a state fuel-efficiency standard for new cars. The law (which is being challenged in court) calls upon the California Air Resources Board (CARB) to set emission standards for carbon dioxide emissions from new cars. CARB has been setting standards for automobile emissions of other pollutants since the 1960s. In many cases, California standards have led the country. With respect to greenhouse gas emissions, these standards are effectively fuel-efficiency standards, since, unlike other automobile pollutants, there are no ways to make engines cleaner burning without simply using less fuel. These fuel-efficiency standards are to take into account technology and cost, and are to be applied to the 2009 automobile model year (new cars only). As Californians like to point out, the state's economy is exceeded in size only by the economies of Germany, France, Japan, the UK, and the USA.

Oregon has one of the first state laws requiring emission reductions from major energy sources in the state. House Bill 3283, passed in 1997, requires new fossil-fuelled power plants either to meet strict emission standards for carbon dioxide or to acquire offsets of their emissions in excess of these strict standards.

In May 2002, New Hampshire passed House Bill 284, which sets aggregate greenhouse gas emission limits on power plants in the state, to be achieved by 2010. The bill also includes provisions to further tighten the cap for the post-2010 period. Massachusetts has a similar cap on state emissions from power plants.

There is a variety of private initiatives to reduce greenhouse gas emissions. Two interesting market approaches are the Chicago Climate Exchange,[10] created to trade greenhouse gas emission among sources in several Mid-Western US states. The Exchange is not yet operating and without legal mandates for greenhouse gas reductions, it is unclear exactly what will be traded. Another interesting enterprise is the market in offsets for carbon dioxide generated from international air travel.[11] This allows traveler on international flights (a loophole in the Kyoto Protocol) to offset the emission from their seat on a particular flight.

The issues: quantities versus intensity rates

One of the major components of the Bush climate plan is the concept of moving away from committing to a national emissions cap by a specified date (such as is embodied in Kyoto) to a targeted *rate of decline* in the emissions intensity of the economy. Leaving aside the issue of the strength of the Bush proposal, it is worth examining the relative merits of a cap on overall emissions versus an agreement on a rate of reduction in emissions intensity.

It is appropriate to emphasize that a targeted rate of decline in the emissions intensity is not the same as a growth-indexed cap.[12] A targeted rate of decline (say 3 percent per year) applies indefinitely and specifies a continuing rate of decline in intensity. A cap applies to a particular point in time and is not a continuing target. Thus there is no real symmetry here.

There are two fundamental dimensions of climate policy upon which we will focus this comparison: dynamics and uncertainty.

Dynamic issues

It is important to realize that the Kyoto Protocol has been a long time in the making. The protocol was negotiated (at least in its initial form) in 1997 and keyed off of emissions some years earlier, in 1990. The protocol calls for each developed (Annex I) country to reduce annual emissions in the period 2008–2012 to about 5 percent below what they had been twenty years earlier (1990). As this is written, it is 2005, eight years after Kyoto, and we are still debating the ratification of the protocol. These are very long time-frames. Furthermore, no sooner will we have settled on Kyoto targets and the signatories than it will be time to embark on another round of negotiations, for the so-called second commitment period, possibly with associated additional emission reductions.

This is a key issue. The use of national caps on emissions implicitly involves repeated negotiations. The same parties must come together every decade or two to renegotiate new emission targets. This leads to dynamic incentive problems, first identified in the context of central planning in the Soviet Union. The incentive problem has been termed the *ratchet effect*. If an agent knows that his performance in the current time-period will influence his negotiating position in the next period, there is an incentive to bias current performance in order to enhance the negotiating position.

There are many environmental examples of the ratchet effect. Consider the problem of setting automobile emission standards. In the USA in the 1970s, the government promulgated challenging automobile emission standards. The auto companies were faced with a conundrum. If they tried hard and met the tough standards, they knew their reward would be to be subject to even tighter standards in the next negotiating period – their good performance would be rewarded by a ratcheting up of expectations in subsequent regulatory interactions.

In the context of the Kyoto Protocol, a country that does well in meeting its commitments will be rewarded by further required reductions in the subsequent commitment period. Germany is, of course, a good example of this. Not only is this not fair but it creates incentives for poor performance.

This problem can be solved by precommitting to a path of emissions, eliminating the need for repeated renegotiation. Of course, there are many ways of defining a path of emissions, though there is some appeal to simplicity and a formulaic path. The idea of committing to a rate of reduction in the greenhouse gas intensity of the economy (x percent per year) has the advantage of simplicity while at the same time providing a continually changing target for emission reductions, with the changes predetermined. Of course, if the agreed rates of reduction are subsequently viewed as inadequate, then renegotiation will be necessary.

Uncertainty

One of the major concerns with the Kyoto Protocol for many countries has been the cost of meeting the targets. Will it be easy (cheap) or tough (expensive)? Information on control costs is sketchy since the world has had very little experience with reducing emissions of greenhouse gases; in any event, the reductions will not be at their strictest until 2012 or so – far into the future. The fear has been that a country would commit to a cap on emissions and then find that the cost of abatement is exceptionally high. For instance, if a marketable permit system were implemented for a country's cap, the fear was that the price of a permit might be very high. The fear was not helped by the great deal of variation in the estimates of the marginal cost of emission control associated with Kyoto limits.

Several proposals for dealing with this uncertainty involve putting a cap on the marginal cost of emission reductions. These proposals have taken many forms (Kopp *et al.*, 1997, McKibbon and Wilcoxen, 1997) but one of the most popular is associated with domestic trading schemes for carbon. The assumption is that the Kyoto targets would be implemented with some sort of cap-and-trade system for greenhouse gases: a country would issue permits for its allowed emissions and trading in those permits would proceed. The "safety valve" idea is that the government would sell additional permits at a predetermined price – for example, $25 per ton of carbon. This is a variant on the permit system proposed by Marc Roberts and Michael Spence some years ago (Roberts and Spence, 1976).

On the one hand, the safety valve approach assures that the marginal cost of carbon control would never exceed the price of extra permits. On the other hand, should extra permits be issued, then the quantitative limits of the protocol would be abrogated. This has made many, particularly environmentalists, wary of allowing a safety valve of this sort.

For an individual country, uncertainty over the cost of meeting the Kyoto targets comes from two primary sources. One is that there is uncertainty about the overall level of economic activity in the country, come 2012. High levels of growth over the 1990–2012 period would mean that the target would be much harder to "hit." Low or negative levels of growth (e.g. Russia) make for easy targets. The second source of uncertainty concerns the cost associated with reducing greenhouse gases, holding the level of economic activity constant.

The simple analytics of quantities versus intensity changes

In the previous section we reviewed some of the broad issues related to an emissions cap – the approach taken in the Kyoto Protocol – and a target rate of reduction in greenhouse gas intensity – the approach proposed by the current US administration. We first take a look at the dynamics of stabilizing greenhouse gas concentrations, the goal of the Framework Convention on Climate Change (FCCC), to which the United States and many other countries are signatories. We then look at the question of uncertainty and the nature of a safety valve under either an emissions cap or a targeted rate of reduction in emissions intensity.

Decomposing intensity

The stabilization of greenhouse gas concentrations is the stated goal of the FCCC. Fundamentally, this translates into eventually achieving zero growth in net emissions; presumably that will ultimately be reflected in Kyoto, son-of-Kyoto, or subsequent protocols to implement the FCCC. Let $G(t)$ be the global emissions of greenhouse gases in year t and $Y(t)$ the net economic output in year t. Define the greenhouse gas intensity, $g(t)$, as

$$g(t) = G(t)/Y(t) \tag{1}$$

Solving equation (1) for G, differentiating with respect to t, and manipulating yields:

$$\frac{\dot{G}}{G} = \frac{\dot{Y}}{Y} + \frac{\dot{g}}{g} \tag{2}$$

The interpretation of equation (2) is that the growth rate for greenhouse gas emissions is the sum of the growth rate for economic output and the growth rate for intensity. Since the growth rate for intensity is typically negative (see Table 7.1), the growth rate in output exceeds the growth rate in greenhouse gas emissions. In order to stabilize concentrations, it is necessary to ultimately achieve zero net growth in emissions, which means that the growth rate in output must eventually equal the rate of decline of greenhouse gas intensity.[13]

Clearly, zero net growth in emissions can be attained either by ratcheting up the rate of decline in greenhouse gas intensity or by reducing the rate of economic growth. Most countries, however, would probably prefer to focus efforts on reducing the intensity without retarding growth. In fact, this has been a big issue for developing countries, which have strongly argued that their economic development should not be slowed by greenhouse policies.

We can decompose the greenhouse gas intensity into two parts, an autonomous technological part, dependent only on the passage of time, t, and an abatement effort part, E. The former part has to do with the overall level of technology in the economy as well as the structure and composition of the economy; it is largely outside the control of national governments. The abatement effort part, E, involves costly resources being invested to reduce the intensity of production:

$$G(t) = F(t, E(t), Y(t)) \tag{3}$$

The function F in equation (3) should be homogeneous of degree 1 in E and Y: a doubling of the size of the economy and the amount of effort should lead to a doubling of the greenhouse gas emissions.[14] We can divide equation (3), and F, through by $Y(t)$, letting effort normalized by the overall level of output be denoted by $e(t) \equiv E(t)/Y(t)$:

$$g(t) = F(t, e(t), 1) \equiv f(t, e(t)) \tag{4}$$

Differentiating equation (4) and rearranging yields:

$$\frac{\dot{g}}{g} = \frac{f_t}{f} + \frac{f_e \dot{e}}{f}$$

or

$$\frac{\dot{g}}{g} = \frac{f_t}{f} + \frac{\dot{e}}{e} \div \sigma_e(t) \equiv r_A + r_E \tag{5}$$

where

$$\sigma_e(t) = \frac{f}{ef_e} = \frac{G}{EF_E} \approx \frac{\frac{\Delta E}{E}}{\frac{\Delta G}{G}}$$

and r_A and r_E are, respectively, the rates of growth in autonomous greenhouse gas intensity and endogenous greenhouse gas intensity. Equation (5) can be interpreted as saying that the rate of decline in greenhouse gas intensity is composed of an autonomous part, related to the passage of time, and a part that requires effort on the part of a country.

What is the interpretation of $\sigma_e(t)$? As the rightmost expression suggests, it is roughly the percentage change in effort associated with a percentage change in emissions. If effort is denominated in dollars, than this is closely related to the marginal cost of emission control, expressed as an elasticity. In fact, it is the change of expenditure on control effort necessary to achieve a unit change in aggregate emissions, expressed as a percentage change rather than an absolute change – it is the elasticity of control costs with respect to emissions. The elasticity is a function of time because we would expect it to decrease over time, as the marginal cost of emission control drops.

Rewriting equation (2), using equation (5), we obtain:

$$r_G = r_Y + r_A + r_E \qquad (6)$$

which states that the rate of growth in emissions of greenhouse gas is the sum of the rate of growth of output (GDP) plus the autonomous rate of growth of greenhouse gas intensity (generally negative) plus the rate of growth of intensity due to proactive efforts (hopefully also negative). The autonomous rate of change in intensity is difficult to estimate, although from Table 7.1 we see that during the 1990s a rate slightly less than 2 percent per year was common.[15]

In other words, r_E is the term that balances various growth rates to manage growth in greenhouse gas emissions. The net difference between the growth rate in output and the autonomous rate of decline of intensity must be made up by conscious abatement efforts, r_E.

The bottom line here is that committing to ultimately reducing intensity at the same rate that GDP is rising is a simple and robust way to commit to a dynamic greenhouse abatement path. It is a more natural target than a quantity target that must subsequently be revised. Of course, agreeing on a rate of reduction and adjusting it as additional information becomes available is not easy.

Uncertainty

One of the concerns that many have had regarding the Kyoto Protocol is the cost of meeting the agreed targets. Ironically, for some countries, the cost is zero (or even a net gain); for other countries, the cost is substantial. The playing field appears somewhat level in that most Annex I countries need to reduce emissions by about 5 percent from the baseline year. But the targets are in terms of greenhouse gas emissions some twenty years after the baseline of 1990. Much can happen in those intervening years resulting in a great deal of uncertainty in costs.

Several things can influence the uncertainty over a country's cost for meeting a target. One is the size of the required reduction relative to "business-as-usual." A 20 percent reduction in emissions is obviously more difficult to accomplish than a 2 percent reduction. The second source of uncertainty in cost is simply how much it costs to reduce emissions, holding constant the required emission reduction. Although there are estimates of how much it might cost to achieve a 10 percent reduction in emissions in a country such as the United States, there is considerable uncertainty over that figure.

These uncertainties can be decomposed into uncertainty regarding the overall level of economic activity and uncertainty regarding the cost of emission control at the margin, given the level of economic activity. Let ε be a random variable reflecting the uncertainty regarding GDP in the commitment period. Certainly with a lead of ten to fifteen years between negotiating something like Kyoto and the commitment period, ε will have a great deal of variability. The fact that US GDP grew so much in the 1990s resulted in much higher levels of economic output than had been expected. Recall that the United States has for sometime had lackluster GDP growth.

The other source of uncertainty regards the "ease" with which the economy can achieve the target greenhouse gas intensity during the commitment period. How that intensity declines over time is not well understood nor easily predicted. Let η be a random variable that reflects the uncertainty in the marginal cost of greenhouse gas control conditional on the level of economic output; thus we can define marginal cost as $c(\eta, Y)$. We make the assumption that η and ε are independent, though that may be somewhat of a stretch.

It is clear that under a quantity target for emissions, the cost is more uncertain: $c(\eta, Y(\varepsilon))$, depending on two random variables. On the other hand, with a commitment to a reduction in emissions intensity, the uncertainty is less, since the costs are conditional on the level of output, Y, and hence the realization of the random variable, ε. What is the significance of this? Simply that safety valves or other mechanisms to ameliorate the risk of cost uncertainty will result in far less variability in greenhouse gas emissions and, in fact, are less likely to be exercised when operating under a target for the rate of reduction in intensity.

Conclusion

We have taken a close look at what appears to be a non-proposal: President Bush's climate initiative, unveiled on February 14, 2002. The proposal is conspicuous for the absence of any strong measures to address greenhouse

gas emissions in the United States. However, there are ideas in the proposal, ideas that have some merit when combined with a higher level of
stringency. In particular, the idea of focusing on the rate of reduction of the
greenhouse gas intensity of an economy (greenhouse gas emissions per
unit of real economic output) would seem to have real merit.

One advantage is that such a focus addresses the problem with the
emissions cap approach of Kyoto that requires continual renegotiation of
the caps as we proceed through time. Focusing instead on achieving a
rate of reduction in emissions intensity that equals the long-run rate of
growth of GDP effectively stops the growth of global greenhouse gases.
(Of course, that may not be enough – it may be important to stabilize at
an even lower level.)

Another advantage of the intensity measure is that it does not penalize
countries for economic growth. This has been a major problem with
the developing world, who view Kyoto-like caps as hindering growth.
Decoupling growth from intensity largely neutralizes this criticism.

Another advantage of the intensity measure has to do with reducing
the uncertainty over emission control costs. A major impediment to
ratification of the Kyoto Protocol by some countries has been the
wide-ranging potential costs associated with the protocol. The cost
uncertainty arises from a combination of uncertainty over how much
an economy may grow by the time the commitment period arrives (2012
is fifteen years after Kyoto). Cost uncertainty also arises from simple
uncertainty over how difficult it is to control emissions, given a particular
level of economic activity. The rate of reduction in intensity target has
the advantage of resolving the uncertainty over economic growth –
emissions are conditional on the level of economic activity. Thus overall
uncertainty is reduced.

In sum, there would appear to be more advantages to targets for the
rate of reduction of emissions intensity than might at first appear. They
may be worth examining more carefully in the context of the second
commitment period.

Notes

1 It is far from clear how damaging Bush's decision was to global climate
  policy. It could be argued that dragging out the Kyoto process only to have
  it rejected by the US Senate some time in the future would be worse. Refer to
  David Victor (2001a) in the *New York Times*. See also Victor (2001b).
2 For   details: http://www.whitehouse.gov/news/releases/2002/02/climate-
  change.html.
3 Although the focus on reducing intensity has achieved new prominence
  through the emphasis it has received in the Bush proposal, it is not a new

concept. In fact, German industry has couched its voluntary agreement on reducing greenhouse gases as a commitment to reduce the intensity of greenhouse gas emissions in individual German industries.

4 The plan includes dozens of actions which are very modest or a repackaging of existing programs: for instance, plans for a meeting with the Japanese to discuss opportunities for joint climate change research.

5 Table 7.1 excludes land use, land use change, and forestry (so-called LU-LUCF) from net greenhouse gas emissions. Had those been included, the figures would be somewhat different, though the general picture would remain the same.

6 An examination of other Annex I countries for the 1990–99 period indicates a similar pattern. The FCCC and the OECD report data on eighteen Annex I countries for 1990 and 1999. The median decline in greenhouse gas intensity (excluding LULUCF) is 14.1%; the US decline is 16.1%; Germany and the UK have the greatest decline, of approximately 29%; intensity in Ireland, Switzerland, and Italy, on the other hand, goes up by 10–15%.

7 One classic unmet goal is the goal of attaining air and water ambient quality standards, a goal set out in the Clean Air and Clean Water Acts of the early 1970s. After thirty years, the best measure of the extent to which the goal has been met is the number of days a year the standards are violated – for air pollution, down to less than one hundred in some of the most polluted cities, such as Houston and Los Angeles.

8 The organization NESCAUM (Northeast States for Coordinated Air Use Management) maintains a comprehensive set of data on non-federal actions to control greenhouse gas emissions (www.nescaum.org/Greenhouse/). See also Jones *et al.* (2002).

9 For example, New Mexico was one of the first states to implement sizeable tax credits for the installation of solar energy facilities – a quarter-century ago.

10 Refer to http://www.climateexchange.com/.

11 See http://travel.500ppm.com/. In the context of the conference on emissions trading for climate policy in Dresden, on which this book is based, I purchased an offset for my flight from Boston to Dresden and back through this service. My share of Lufthansa's CO_2 emissions was estimated to be 1.53 tons, for which I bought an offset at a cost of £13.34. The offset involved a share of an afforestation project in the Brazilian Amazon region.

12 See Denny Ellerman, "Growth indexed caps: a better idea?", presented at the Global Trading Workshop, Kiel Institute for World Economics, Kiel, Germany (September 30–October 1, 2002).

13 The US economy grew by 38% in the 1990s yet the intensity declined by only 17% (Table 7.1), leaving a substantial gap. The economy of the EU minus Germany grew by 24% while its intensity declined by 17%, leaving a more modest gap.

14 Homogeneity is easy to see through a thought experiment. Take a country like the US or the UK and divide it in half. Each half has half the GDP, half the effort to reduce emissions, and half the emissions.

15 An examination of eighteen Annex I countries for the period 1990–1999 indicates a median reduction in greenhouse gas intensity of 14.1% per decade, which translates into slightly less than 1.4% per year. There is, however, considerable variation around this figure, as was mentioned in an earlier footnote.

References

Framework Convention on Climate Change "Online searchable database of greenhouse gas inventory data" (http://ghg.unfccc.int/).

Jones, B., Monash, N., Bubenick, D., and Vaurio, K. 2002. *Survey and Evaluation of State-Level Activities and Programs Related to Climate Change.* Prepared for Natural Resources Defense Council. Boston: M. J. Bradley & Associates.

Kopp, R. J., Morgenstern, R. D., and Pizer, W. 1997. *Something for Everyone: A Climate Policy that Both Environmentalists and Industry Can Live With.* Washington, DC: Resources for the Future.

McKibbon, W. J., and Wilcoxen, P. J. 1997. *A Better Way to Slow Global Climate Change.* Brookings Institution Policy Brief 17, Washington, DC: Brookings Institution.

National Academy of Sciences 1992. *Automobile Fuel Economy: How Far Can We Go?* Washington, DC: National Research Council.

  2002. *Effectiveness and Impact of Corporate Average Fuel Economy (CAFE) Standards.* Washington, DC: National Research Council.

NESCAUM (Northeast States for Coordinated Air Use Management) (http://www.nescaum.org/).

OECD (Organization for Economic Cooperation and Development) 2004. National Accounts of OECD Countries, Main Aggregates, vol. I, 1991–2002. Paris (http://www.oecd.org/document/28//document/39/0,2340,en_2649_34245_1914151_1_1_1_1,00.html).

Rabe, B. G. 2002. *Greenhouse & Statehouse: The Evolving State Government Role in Climate Change.* Washington, DC: Pew Center on Global Climate Change.

Roberts, M. J., and Spence, M. 1976. "Effluent charges and licenses under uncertainty," *Journal of Public Economics* 5: 193–208.

Victor, D. G. 2001a. "Piety at Kyoto didn't cool the planet," *New York Times* (March 23).

  2001b. *Collapse of the Kyoto Protocol and the Struggle to Control Global Warming.* Princeton, NJ: Princeton University Press.

8   Design issues of a domestic carbon emissions trading system in the USA

Richard D. Morgenstern

Introduction

As every student of diplomacy knows, broad international agreements are far easier to craft than specific ones, especially when compliance involves potentially costly domestic actions. While committing the United States and more than 150 other nations to the goal of stabilizing atmospheric greenhouse gas (GHG) concentrations at a level that would "prevent dangerous anthropogenic interference with the climate system," the UN Framework Convention on Climate Change (FCCC) was mostly silent on implementation. The Kyoto Protocol is an attempt to move beyond the convention's general obligations and establish specific reduction targets for industrial nations for an initial accounting period, 2008–12.

Scholars will no doubt continue to debate whether an alternative protocol design, perhaps one starting with more modest emission reductions among a broader group of nations, might ultimately have yielded stronger results. However, neither the limitations of the protocol's architecture, nor even the gaping hole in coverage among industrial nations caused by the withdrawal of the United States from the agreement alters the fact that, once ratified, the Kyoto Protocol is likely to endure for many years as the only functioning international mechanism for achieving near-term emissions reductions.

A glance into the crystal ball suggests we are entering a period of relative quiescence in the international climate policy process. During this period, the focus of attention will likely shift to the domestic actions undertaken in industrial nations. Yet, by withdrawing from the protocol, the United States has not only eliminated any obligations to reduce its own GHG emissions but has effectively lowered the bar for everyone else. Thus, in all likelihood, the next few years will serve as a period of modest experimentation. Industrial nations – acting under the aegis of the protocol or outside it – will undertake a limited series of domestic steps to reduce their GHG emissions, probably combined with some mitigation-oriented investments in developing countries. At some point in the future, perhaps in a time-frame suitable for establishing second budget-period commitments under the Kyoto Protocol, either the full group of FCCC signatories or a pragmatic subgroup of nations will likely come together to try to fashion a new or revised international strategy for mitigating GHG emissions.

Recognizing that actions taken now to mitigate domestic emissions could serve as potentially powerful models for future international negotiations, the present chapter focuses on what domestic policies the United States might pursue over the next few years outside the framework of the Kyoto Protocol. Notwithstanding President Bush's Valentine's Day 2002 announcement of a new program to expand existing voluntary efforts by offering transferable credits against future obligations for verifiable GHG emissions reductions undertaken now, the option of stronger, mandatory economic signals to encourage emissions reductions is clearly relevant to ongoing domestic policy discussions. There is already considerable support for some form of mandatory approach in Congress, the NGO community, and the general public.

The benefits of an emissions trading system – efficiency, transparency, flexibility, and political acceptability – have already been demonstrated to a broad swath of US businesses, NGOs, and academics, as well as to the authors of several bills recently introduced in Congress. While a competing approach may yet emerge, the principal option for a mandatory policy to reduce US carbon emissions is an emissions trading system.[1] This chapter addresses the key design issues of such a system. While suitable credits for carbon sequestration as well as for reductions of other GHGs would inevitably be included in an emissions trading system, the focus herein is on the *per se* control of the largest single component of US carbon emissions, namely those from the energy sector.

The experience with the acid rain provisions of the Clean Air Act has demonstrated that a well-designed emissions trading system represents both an environmentally effective and a highly efficient means of reducing emissions of a widely disbursed pollutant like SO_2, where major sources face highly varied control costs. The fact that CO_2 emissions are even more widely disbursed than those of SO_2, and the variability of mitigation costs among sources is probably greater, suggests that emissions trading is a particularly attractive policy option for controlling carbon emissions.

Arguably, however, a great policy triumph like the Clean Air Act can be dangerous if it establishes policies and perspectives that get uncritically applied to other situations. While the success of the SO_2 program is important as a model for future policies, it is also clear that the control of

CO_2 poses significantly different challenges. In contrast to the case of acid rain precursors, carbon emissions do not emanate principally from a small number of large, highly regulated sources in a single industry. And, unlike the situation prevailing before the SO_2 control program was adopted, there is not a broad consensus that relatively low-cost technical solutions are readily at hand. Thus, it is not surprising that the preferred design for a carbon emissions trading system would differ from that adopted for the SO_2 program.

Although the acid rain system principally involved the electric utility sector, included a *gratis* allocation of permits, and did not have an explicit mechanism to protect against price spikes (i.e. no safety valve), other options are clearly possible, and likely preferred in the case of carbon controls. Recognizing that the degree of stringency of a carbon reduction program should reflect a broad range of considerations – including the level of effort undertaken by other large carbon-emitting nations – the focus at this stage in the policy process is on the basic architecture of the system. Over the long term the stringency level can be adapted to evolving economic, scientific, political, and legal situations. The following sections consider the coverage of the program, the initial allocation of the permits, and the use of fixed or flexible targets (prices vs. quantities). An additional section reviews the results of a comparative analysis of different approaches prepared by the US Congressional Budget Office. A final section offers concluding observations.

Coverage of the system

While a host of non-economic factors are clearly relevant to the ultimate decision, efficiency considerations are certainly a critical element in the choice of the point of regulation for a carbon control program. The basic options, as discussed below, are for an upstream, downstream, or some form of hybrid system. For the majority of pollutants, quantitative limits can only be enforced at the point where emissions are released into the ambient environment. This is because the actual level of emissions depends not just on input use (e.g. coal quantities and types) but also on combustion engineering parameters or post-combustion control devices. For example, the same quantity of coal can produce drastically different quantities of sulfur dioxide or nitrogen oxide emissions, depending on the nature of the control equipment used.

The control of carbon emissions involves a quite different calculus. No amount of control equipment can alter the carbon ultimately released from a ton of coal.[2] Carbon emissions depend simply on *fuel use* and not on *how the fuel is used*. Since it is not necessary actually to monitor the emissions from final end-users, there is a real choice about where to place the point of control in a carbon management system.

A downstream system tracks allowances and measures emissions at the point where they are released into the atmosphere, e.g. smokestacks. An upstream or economy-wide system operates by controlling emissions at the point where potentially damaging substances enter the economy – coal-mines and processing plants, oil refineries, processing plants and pipelines associated with the distribution of natural gas. In the United States this amounts to an estimated two thousand entities. To sharpen the focus on potential environmental impacts, and to reduce unwarranted economic impacts, a control system designed to track the releases from these two thousand entities could be augmented by a permit requirement which also covered imported fuels and exempted non-combustion uses and exports.

To date, the US experience with emissions trading has been entirely with downstream systems, e.g. the SO_2 control program. Recent Congressional and NGO proposals similarly focus on downstream systems for carbon controls. For some sectors, direct measurement of carbon emissions is currently in place or readily feasible. The Clean Air Act already requires that electric power plants measure carbon emissions and report them to the EPA. Other large industrial processes that use significant amounts of fossil fuels, e.g. petroleum refining, metals, and machinery, could measure their emissions through the extension of existing surveys and other relatively simple procedures. Together, the utility and large industrial sources represent slightly less than one-half of total US carbon emissions.

The main problem lies in the residential, commercial, transportation, and smaller industrial sectors. In the case of SO_2, these sectors contribute a negligible portion of total emissions. Thus, excluding them from the control system is not critical. In the case of carbon emissions, however, these sectors contribute slightly more than half of total emissions. Yet, it is obvious that a system requiring tens or hundreds of millions of small and medium-sized entities to measure and report the types and volumes of fuels used would not be workable in the United States. Even if non-covered sectors were covered by other forms of mandatory regulation – for example, energy efficiency standards for vehicles and furnaces – these alternatives would be more costly and less certain tools for carbon reduction than cap-and-trade systems. Such standards typically apply to new products only and do not address the emissions from the existing capital stock. In fact, research has shown that such standards can slow the rate of capital turnover – thus offsetting a significant portion of the gains achieved from the efficiency standards themselves (Gruenspecht, 1982). In general, efficiency standards do not encourage the most cost-effective emission reductions throughout the covered sector(s).

Excluding the residential, commercial, transportation, and smaller industrial sectors from controls would be inefficient and could potentially create some serious inequities across industries, consumers, and other groups. Although at modest levels the per-ton control cost differential between upstream and downstream systems would be small, the possibility of economic distortions under a downstream system would increase with more stringent environmental goals. Depending on the rules adopted for the system, a patchwork set of policies may actually encourage the construction of certain types of high-emitting facilities For example, a downstream system with only partial coverage may cause homeowners or small businesses to choose their heating fuels simply because they are excluded from the carbon control system rather than on an economic basis, even after accounting for the environmental damages associated with the use of different fuels.

One reason sometimes offered in defense of a downstream system is that individuals and institutions may be more responsive to the costs of buying and selling permits than they are to comparable changes in fuel prices. As Keeler (2002) has noted, from an economic perspective, this is highly dubious, since the impacts of a carbon permitting system on the effective prices of fuels will be the same regardless of where in the supply chain permits are held or traded. Another reason offered in support of a downstream system is that even if the financial implications are identical, business managers may be more conscious of energy-saving opportunities if they are directly involved in permit trading than if they are simply paying a higher price for energy. While this is an interesting argument, it is, none the less, conjectural. There is no simple way to confirm or refute it. What is clear, however, is that if the carbon cap for the covered sector is the same under both upstream and downstream systems, total carbon emissions will be identical. The fact that managers may overlook particular reduction opportunities in an upstream system would be reflected in higher permit prices. The higher prices, in turn, would provide greater incentives to search for energy-saving opportunities. Thus, it is likely that any initial inefficiencies in an upstream system would tend to be self-correcting as managers become more aware of emission reduction opportunities.

A more interesting issue is whether it is feasible to start with a downstream system – presumably in the electric utility sector – and then make the transition to an upstream system once the program is successfully demonstrated. From an administrative perspective the transition would simply involve a change in the point of compliance from the downstream to the upstream entities. For example, even if the emission allowances were initially given to the electric utilities, the utilities would no longer be required to match their emissions with allowances. Rather, the burden of holding the allowances would shift to the producers of carbon-based fuels. The fuel producers, in turn, would purchase allowances from whoever owned them – in this case the electric utilities. At the same time, the fuel producers would seek to pass along the costs of the allowances to their customers, including to their utility customers.[3] While shifting from a downstream to an upstream system in this manner may lead to conflicts between electric utilities and fuel producers, the administrative aspects of the shift are quite manageable.

The principal challenge in starting with a downstream system and then trying to move the compliance point upstream is that strong economic incentives may work against the transition. For example, if the electric utilities were allowed to purchase offsets outside their own sector, then those firms selling the offsets, e.g. the auto companies, would have an incentive to resist inclusion in the upstream system, as such a shift would effectively change their "business-as-usual" baseline to a considerably less favorable one. Alternatively, if at the outset electric utilities were barred from purchasing offsets outside their own sector – thereby eliminating this particular problem – then the overall compliance costs for achieving any given carbon reduction would be higher.

However unlikely it may be, one can imagine a relatively smooth transition to an economy-wide system. For example, it is conceivable that despite their initial resistance to any mandatory carbon control measures, once (or if) it became clear that there was sufficient political will to support a downstream, electric-utility-based emissions control regime, the utilities might quickly shift tactics and try to expand the system coverage, thereby spreading compliance costs across a broader base.

Overall, two points are clear. First, the strong efficiency advantages of an upstream system suggest that if the United States is to achieve major reductions in carbon emissions it will ultimately need to rely on such a system. The second point concerns the transition strategy. Ideally, one would start with a viable long-term policy architecture – one that was both effective and efficient – and then be in a position to adjust the stringency level to changing scientific, economic, and political circumstances. However, if that is not politically possible, a more viable course may involve starting with a downstream system on one or more sectors and subsequently enlarging it to other sectors before attempting to establish a fully upstream system. At a minimum, more work needs to be done to think through the feasibility and practicality of such an approach.

Allocation of permits

Who will pay for new policies to reduce carbon dioxide and other greenhouse gas (GHG) emissions in the United States? Not surprisingly, disagreements on the magnitude of the costs imposed on different household or industry groups can stymie efforts to reach consensus on the basic GHG mitigation strategy to be undertaken. Disagreements on the distribution of the burden can also impede the development of compensatory policies designed to offset the economic damages imposed on particular groups or industries. As Mancur Olson (1965) argued almost four decades ago, the more narrowly focused the adverse impacts of a given policy, the more politically difficult it is to sustain that policy. For example, claims of high and unfair burdens imposed on selected industries or households are widely seen as having doomed the BTU tax advanced by the Clinton Administration in 1993.

Emissions allowances or permits are potentially quite valuable assets. Any individual entity in a cap-and-trade system will be better off if they are allocated permits gratis instead of having to buy them. Beyond that basic point, however, two key issues are particularly relevant to the decision on the initial permit allocation. The first concerns the technical limitations, if any, that might inform the choice of an upstream vs. a downstream system. The second concerns the basic fairness of providing permits gratis to producers, consumers, or other groups.

The answer to the first question is relatively straightforward. There are no major technical limitations regarding initial permit allocation that would influence the decision to adopt an upstream as opposed to a downstream control system. In either case, permits could be allocated to any group deemed to be worthy. While permits were allocated gratis to electric utilities in the SO_2 trading program, there is no technical or administrative reason why that same decision needs to be made for either an upstream or a downstream program established to control carbon emissions. Congress could choose to allocate carbon permits directly to consumers, workers, basic energy producers, particular geographic locales, or to any other group it chooses. Alternatively, Congress could decide to incorporate the carbon control system into the federal budget process. In that case the government could auction some or all of the permits and count the proceeds as revenues. The revenues from such an on-budget system, in turn, could be used to reduce individual tax burdens (or otherwise compensate taxpayers and/or those individuals below tax thresholds), to fund investments in energy research or designated technologies, to compensate particular industries, or to others deemed worthy. From a technical perspective, Congress has complete discretion on who receives the potentially valuable assets known as emissions allowances, and whether the transactions are treated on or off the federal budget. While some of the options might involve higher transaction costs than others, the differences are probably modest, certainly when compared to the overall cost of controlling carbon emissions in the first instance.

The second question, concerning the "fairness" of a particular allocation system, is more complex. Here the issue is not about administrative/ technical concerns. Instead, it focuses on the distributional implications of alternative schemes to allocate permits (or permit revenues). Using a numerically solved general equilibrium model to examine the economy-wide costs of mitigating adverse distributional impacts of carbon policies on important fossil fuel industries, Goulder (2002) finds that the costs of offsetting, via a rebate mechanism, the losses in profit to fossil fuel industries associated with a carbon tax are relatively modest. Underlying this finding is the recognition that cap-and-trade systems tend to restrict the output of carbon-intensive industries. Such output-restricting policies cause carbon-supplying industries to behave like a cartel, potentially leading to higher revenues or "rents." If the tradable permits are auctioned, then these potential rents are collected as government revenue. If the permits are allocated gratis, the potential rents are retained by firms, and yield increases in profit. To create a level playing-field, the government needs to freely allocate only a fraction of the permits. Based on his model simulations, Goulder finds that the gratis allocation of about 13 percent of the permits could offset losses of profit to the major affected industries.

A paper by Burtraw et al. (2001) focuses exclusively on the impacts on the electricity sector associated with electricity-only carbon policies. Burtraw et al. consider the cost-effectiveness and distributional impacts of three alternative approaches for distributing carbon emission allowances within the electricity sector: 100 percent auctioning, 100 percent gratis allocation (grandfathering), and a so-called generation performance standard (GPS). Burtraw et al.'s main finding is that the auction is significantly more cost-effective than the other approaches – approximately one-half the societal cost of either grandfathering or the GPS. These differences, they argue, arise from the effect of each permit allocation approach on electricity prices. The GPS provides an incentive for generators to increase electricity production in the form of a grant of additional emission allowances. These additional allowances constitute an output subsidy.[4] While the GPS mitigates electricity price increases, it raises economic cost, since it tends to amplify existing economic distortions in electricity markets resulting from economic regulation and other inefficiencies in electricity pricing. In contrast, the auction approach increases electricity prices the most, but the efficiency cost of the price changes is less than under the other approaches.[5]

Table 8.1 displays the Burtraw *et al.* estimates of the changes in economic surplus and cost-effectiveness of the three alternative approaches for distributing carbon emissions allowances.[6] Under the auction approach, consumers face the highest electricity prices but the lowest natural gas prices. The GPS yields the opposite results: the lowest electricity prices and highest natural gas prices. Grandfathering falls midway between the other two approaches with respect to both electricity and natural gas prices.

Consistent with the Goulder results, Burtraw *et al.* find that under a grandfathering allocation system, producer profits and asset values increase substantially compared to the baseline, making producers better off with a carbon policy than without one, but leaving consumers substantially worse off. Even though grandfathering is the intermediate approach with respect to its effect on electricity and natural gas prices, it is the most extreme approach with respect to transfers of wealth. In fact, the compensation implicit in the allowance allocation is substantially greater than the cost of compliance activities for industry – that is, grandfathering actually over-compensates industry for its costs. The auction and GPS approaches have much more moderate distributional effects. According to Burtraw *et al.*, industry could be fully compensated under an auction approach for all of the change in the value of the existing assets with a gratis allocation of less than 10 percent of the total allowances, and the remaining 90 percent could be auctioned.

Table 8.1. *Change in economic surplus, and cost-effectiveness of policies in 2012 ($ billion 1997; 35 million mtC reduction)*

	Auction	Grandfathering	GPS
Consumer surplus	−13.9	−8.0	−1.4
Producer surplus	−1.7	4.9	−1.6
Total surplus	−15.6	−3.1	−3.0
Revenue to Government	14.8	0.0	0.0
Net direct surplus	−0.9	−3.1	−3.0
Cost-effectiveness ($/ton of carbon)	26.5	88.7	87.2

Source: Burtraw *et al.*, 2001.

The Burtraw *et al.* analysis raises an interesting paradox: producers do better paying for emission allowances (through the auction) than receiving them for free (under the GPS). The reason for this, according to Burtraw *et al.*, is that the GPS yields the lowest electricity price, which erodes the value of existing assets. The auction yields the highest electricity price, which preserves or enhances the value of many assets.[7]

The auction approach also has institutional features that make it more readily expandable to an upstream scheme for regulating carbon emissions. Even apart from its lower societal cost, it provides policy-makers with flexibility through the collection of revenues that can be used to meet distributional or other needs. Further, because it is more cost-effective, it will have less effect on economic growth than the alternative approaches when used to achieve the same environmental goals. This, in itself, is an important distributional benefit.

Analyses by Smith (2002) and Ross (2002) critique the Burtraw *et al.* approach as understating the true economic costs of controlling carbon emissions in the utility sector, largely because of Burtraw *et al.*'s reliance on a partial equilibrium model. The key analytic issue hinges on the size of the revenue loss to the US Treasury resulting from decreased economic activity under a carbon mitigation policy. The decreased activity would lead to less revenue from corporate and personal (labor) income taxes. A large revenue loss – as shown by Smith and Ross in their general equilibrium model – would likely require the imposition of new (distorting) taxes which, in turn, would increase the overall cost of the carbon policy. Alternatively, the government could withhold a larger share of the revenues from the auction of carbon emission permits in order to make up for lost revenue elsewhere. This would leave less revenue available to reduce other taxes, or to compensate firms in the utility sector for the cost of the carbon policy. However, using a general equilibrium model similar in many respects to the one adopted by Smith and Ross – albeit with different economic assumptions including the responsiveness of labor supply to changes in the real wage – Goulder (2002) estimates a much smaller revenue loss. While more research is clearly needed on this issue, at this stage of the analytic debate it is fair to say that the revenue loss issue highlighted by Smith and Ross is potentially important to understanding the true economic costs of any new carbon policy. At the same time, the Goulder analysis indicates that the size of this effect may not be as large as suggested by Smith and Ross.

Overall, there are few technical/administrative restrictions on how permits could be allocated in either an upstream or downstream system. The system can be readily designed so that virtually any combination of producers, consumers, regions, or other groups could directly receive the permits or, in the case of an on-budget system, the revenues associated with those permits. The question of "fairness" is more complex. Recent research suggests that grandfathering all the permits to a single industry – as was the case with the SO_2 permits – is not the most equitable solution for carbon. Given the widespread nature of the expected impacts of a carbon policy, some broader allocation would clearly be appropriate to share the burdens associated with either a sector-specific (downstream) or an economy-wide (upstream) policy.

Prices vs. quantities

The fact that SO_2 allowance markets have been remarkably stable and prices well below forecast levels has enhanced the reputation of emissions trading as a desirable mechanism for controlling widely disbursed pollutants like CO_2. Unfortunately, not all emissions trading programs have worked out so well. As Jacoby and Ellerman (2004) note, the Regional Clean Air Incentives Market (RECLAIM) is a case in point:

In 1994 the South Coast Air Quality Management District of California implemented a cap-and-trade program for NO_X emissions in the Los Angeles Basin [including in natural-gas-fired units] that worked well until the California electricity problems appeared in 2000 . . . When these . . . little-used [natural gas] units were called upon to run full-time in 2000, the price of NO_X allowances, which had previously been relatively stable in a range between $1,000 and $3,000 per ton, went as high as $80,000 per ton before the system broke down.

The solution adopted in California to this marked increase in permit prices was to introduce a "mitigation fee" of $15,000 per ton that could be paid in lieu of a permit. This mitigation fee limited the cost to the utilities and maintained relative calm in the market for NO_X permits.

At least two key differences between the SO_2 and the RECLAIM models are relevant to the design of a carbon-based cap-and-trade system. First, the SO_2 program allows for both borrowing and banking; RECLAIM allows for neither. Second, unusual meteorological conditions in California occurred at the same time that electricity demand was soaring – thereby driving up prices of NO_X permits by two orders of magnitude. So far, at least, the SO_2 market has not experienced similar jolts.

The RECLAIM situation is, perhaps, the most dramatic example of the age-old conflict between binding targets (quantity instruments) and emissions taxes (price instruments). A key question in designing any mandatory regulatory structure is whether quantity and price instruments yield the same environmental results and, if so, whether there is any reason to prefer one over the other? Most of the current discussion concerning the choice of policy instruments for carbon controls has focused on political, legal, and revenue concerns. In the United States, environmentalists' desire for fixed emissions targets have combined with a broad political aversion to energy taxes to give the rhetorical edge to pure quantity-based instruments as the leading method for implementing climate policies.

In a tradable permit system where each permit gives the holder the right to emit a specified amount of GHGs into the atmosphere it is possible, in principle, to control CO_2 emissions precisely. However, unexpected economic growth, a sharp increase in electricity demand, or other factors can drive up allowance prices considerably above projected levels. Thus, the costs of control, in terms of higher prices for fuel and reduced productivity, are uncertain under such a system. While the recent experience with SO_2 trading suggests that the costs are lower than expected, the RECLAIM experience demonstrates that the opposite case is also possible. Certainly, the *fear* that carbon mitigation policies will be costly has become a deterrent to action on carbon.

Apart from the uncertainties about the level of future GDP growth and baseline emissions, there are also uncertainties about the cost of reducing carbon emissions below baseline, and about the overall efficiency of the emissions trading system. For example, simulations developed by the Stanford Energy Modeling Forum suggest that, depending on the particular models used, the costs of the Kyoto Protocol may vary by roughly an order of magnitude (Weyant and Hill, 1999).

In general, if the cost of limiting emissions is known with certainty and the benefits of reduced emissions are similarly known, the price and quantity approaches are perfect policy substitutes. However, as Weitzman (1974) demonstrated a quarter-century ago, when abatement costs and/or benefits are uncertain the situation can be quite different. On the one hand, quantity restrictions are preferred when incremental damages increase rapidly with the level of emissions or when marginal costs are relatively flat and predictable. In that case, quantity restrictions prevent emissions from rising above a "safe" level and do not risk cost surprises. On the other hand, when health or environmental damages are not very sensitive to short-term emission levels or when concerns exist about potentially high costs, the undesirable side effects of quantity restrictions may dominate. In that case, price-based instruments are preferred.

Which of these situations applies to greenhouse gases? The first observation is that GHGs represent a canonical example of what are known in the literature as "stock pollutants," ones in which the damages are a function of total accumulation in the environment and annual emission flows are a relatively small part of the total stock. Thus, there is little basis to believe that *short-term* increases in emissions cause large environmental damages. Following from Weitzman's intuition that relatively flat marginal benefits/damages favors taxes, Pizer (1997) finds that an optimal tax designed to control GHGs yields significantly higher gains than the optimal permit policy.

What about the longer-term damages as concentrations rise over time? A great deal of attention has been given to the possibility of some "extreme event", e.g. a shift in the Gulf Stream that destabilizes global temperature and weather. Recent research by Schneider and Thompson (2000) highlights the potential importance of such extreme events. Notwithstanding the importance of this issue, most scientists believe that climate change will occur gradually in response to growing atmospheric concentrations of GHGs. Accordingly, most evaluations of potential consequences of climate change are based upon this assumption. However, the potential clearly exists – with unknown probability – for disproportionately large responses to even small disturbances in the climate system.

It is, of course, possible to combine price and quantity policies by establishing binding emissions targets as long as costs remain reasonable, and allowing the target to rise somewhat if costs are unexpectedly high. One way to achieve this goal is to establish a predetermined penalty per unit of emissions in excess of the quantity restriction. Such a policy (1) fixes emissions targets that are binding as long as costs remain reasonable and (2) allows the target to rise somewhat if costs are unexpectedly high. In practical terms this hybrid or "safety valve" approach would involve an initial allocation of permits followed by the subsequent sale of additional permits to be made available at a fixed trigger price.

The safety valve guarantees that emissions will not exceed the target as long as the price of the tradable permits (i.e. the marginal cost of GHG control) does not rise above the trigger price. For environmental advocates who believe that the cost of reducing GHG emissions is low, the permit price is not likely to reach the trigger level. In that case, of course, emissions would remain capped. If the permit price did reach the safety valve level, extra permits would be offered for sale and emissions allowed to rise to contain compliance costs.

In effect, the $15,000 per ton mitigation fee established under RE-CLAIM served as a safety valve to prevent NO_x permit prices from rising excessively. A key question is whether a comparable safety valve is also appropriate for a carbon trading system? In principle, some of the benefits of a safety valve could be achieved by establishing an allowance banking system of the type set up in the SO_2 program. For a number of reasons, including the fact that implementation of that program spanned a period of almost twenty years, a considerable cushion of SO_2 allowances has accumulated. This cushion has served to protect the system from major shocks. It is conceivable that had a comparable banking system been in place in the RECLAIM program it might not have been necessary to implement the mitigation fee. However, that cannot be known with any confidence.

In the case of a carbon control system, there are many factors that could lead to an unanticipated increase in allowance prices. In contrast to both the SO_2 and the NO_X programs, there is less *ex ante* consensus among experts about future allowance prices. Certainly, one can imagine scenarios involving large – potentially very large – fluctuations in allowance prices over both the short and long terms. Arguably, and depending on how the rules of the program are written, the issuance of carbon allowances pursuant to President Bush's Valentine's Day proposal could lead to the build-up of a large cushion of allowances. These allowances, in turn, could serve the same function as the SO_2 allowances have served in the acid rain program. Whether that would be sufficient – or whether they would be perceived to be sufficient – to protect against major price shocks is unknown. However, since the safety valve would not come into effect unless prices actually rose to unacceptable levels, it can be seen as a form of free or very low cost insurance. Thus, on balance it might well be prudent to include it in the design of a carbon cap-and-trade system.

The CBO analysis

A recent report by the US Congressional Budget Office (2001) examined four different proposals for domestic action which vary in terms of their coverage, allocation, and the use of fixed or flexible targets. CBO analyzed these four options according to a number of specific evaluation criteria:

- *Ease of implementation.* Would the policy be easy to carry out and enforce?
- *Carbon-target certainty.* Would the policy achieve the target level of carbon emissions?
- *Incremental cost certainty.* Would the policy place an upper limit on the cost the US economy might bear?
- *Cost-effectiveness.* Would the policy reduce carbon emissions at the lowest possible cost to society?
- *Distributional effects.* How would the costs and financial benefits of the policy be distributed among US households of different incomes and among US producers?

Table 8.2. *How various cap-and-trade options measure up against CBO's evaluation criteria*

	Upstream trading		Downstream trading	
Criterion	Option I[a]	Option II[b]	Option I[c]	Option II[d]
Is relatively easy to implement	Yes	Yes	No	Yes
Provides certainty about meeting carbon target	No	Yes	Yes for large emitters; no for the economy	Yes for the electricity sector;[e] no for the economy
Places upper limit on incremental cost	Yes	No	No	No
Cost-effectiveness				
• Creates incentives for least-cost emission reductions	Yes	Yes	Yes for capped sources; no for other sources	No
• Uses revenue to offset tax-interaction effect	No	Yes	No	No
Distributional effects				
• Creates regressive price increases	Yes	Yes	Yes	Yes
• Creates windfall gains for selected industries	No	No	Yes	Yes
• Overall effect on households	Progressive	Regressive	Regressive	Regressive

Notes: [a] Similar to the "Sky Trust" proposal by Resources for the Future and Americans for Equitable Climate Solutions. Suppliers of fossil fuels would be required to hold emission allowances, which the government would sell by auction with the price per allowance capped. Auction revenue would be distributed evenly to all US residents and to some companies hurt by the policy.
[b] Similar to the previous option except that allowance prices would not be capped and auction revenue would be used to cut corporate income taxes.
[c] Similar to a proposal by the Progressive Policy Institute. Large sources of carbon emissions would receive allowances free of charge on the basis of their current emissions. Their allocations would shrink by 1 percent per year.
[d] Similar to three bills introduced in the 106th Congress (H. R. 2569, H. R. 2980, and S. 1369). Only carbon emissions from electricity generators would be capped. Generators would receive free allowances on the basis of their annual production multiplied by a generation performance standard.
[e] Assuming that the government could adjust the generation performance standard each year to maintain the target level of emissions.
Source: US Congressional Budget Office, 2001.

The results of the analysis are shown in Table 8.2. While no one proposal stands out in terms of all the criteria, CBO's Option I – which resembles the "Sky Trust" proposal developed by several experts at Resources for the Future and advanced by the Climate Policy Center (formerly known as Americans for Equitable Climate Solutions) – received the most favorable rankings of any of the options. Like several of the other options, this proposal is both cost-effective and relatively easy to implement. Unlike the others, it is the only one that places an upper limit on incremental cost and the only one that yields an overall progressive effect on households. Not surprisingly, the major criterion on which the proposal falters is its failure to provide certainty about meeting a carbon target. As CBO notes, however, neither of the downstream options provide such certainty either, once one looks beyond the covered sector(s).

Because of the absence of certainty about meeting the target, a number of influential environmental organizations have expressed strong reservations about the RFF/Sky Trust approach. Yet, given the obvious concerns about the potentially high costs of action, it seems unlikely that a proposal without some limit on costs, such as a safety valve, is achievable in the near term.

Concluding observations

Over the coming decade national policies to reduce GHGs will be developed and implemented along two distinct tracks. The first of these involves those nations operating under the terms of the Kyoto Protocol, which is expected to enter into force – *sans* US participation – over the next few years. Most of the announced signatories are already starting to implement policies, acting either singly or in combination with others, to meet the emission targets established under the protocol. The evolving experiences of these nations will provide valuable information on the effectiveness, as well as on the cost-effectiveness, of the various measures employed. The second track involves the United States and any other nations which decide to reduce their GHG emissions outside the aegis of the Kyoto Protocol. Like the Kyoto signatories, the so-called Track Two group will gain experience with their own policies, including information on the effectiveness and cost-effectiveness of the chosen options.

At some point over the next decade, the cumulative results of the policies adopted around the world will become known. In all likelihood, the results will indicate fairly modest changes in the emission paths of the industrial nations. None the less, the results should provide at least some information about the relative performance of the alternative approaches.

In addition to being useful in its own right, information on the performance of the policies adopted in different nations is likely to help shape the expectations of negotiators in future efforts to create a new or revised international strategy for GHG reductions.

The path the United States will pursue over the coming decade is still very much an open issue. President Bush has proposed a very limited expansion of the voluntary programs adopted during the 1990s. In light of the considerable experience with the existing programs, however, it seems unlikely that this initiative will lead to any significant change in the status quo. The failure to stipulate at least a conditional set of mandatory policies that might be adopted in the event even the modest goals established for the program are not met, as well as the failure to set a date prior to 2012 at which an interim policy evaluation would take place, are further indications that progress in reducing US emissions below baseline levels over the coming decade is likely to be limited.

In some respects the outlines of an effective and efficient long-term policy are quite evident. If the overall goal is to control aggregate US emissions of GHGs, then a cap-and-trade system with broad-scale, economy-wide coverage is clearly preferred to a single-sector policy which, by its very nature, cannot assure emission reductions across the entire economy. If a further goal is to avoid placing a disproportionate cost burden on a particular sector, then the preferred policy must distribute the permits – or at least the revenues associated with the permits – to those groups most disadvantaged by the new policy. And, if a further goal is to avoid unexpectedly high or uncertain fuel prices, as occurred in California's RECLAIM program, then some form of safety valve may be appropriate. While inclusion of a banking provision in the cap-and-trade system – of the type used in the SO_2 program – might be able to cushion the economy against some unanticipated shocks, it may not provide adequate protection. Accordingly, at least in the early phases of the program, it may be appropriate to include a safety valve in the overall architecture.

The real challenge for policy-makers – especially those in Congress who are pushing for a near-term, mandatory program – is how best to design a GHG control program to achieve near-term results without, at the same time, creating obstacles to longer-term and broader-scale policy solutions. Issues of system coverage (i.e. upstream or downstream) and permit allocation (i.e. the extent of gratis allocation to producers) are of the greatest concern. At a minimum, it is clear that near-term policies must be explicit about the need for a transition to a long-term policy architecture. For example, even if near-term policies include a generous allocation of permits to producers, a phase-down over time in the gratis allocation would send a signal about the required longer-term transition.

Similarly, to avoid establishing expectations about a generous baseline for sectors not initially included in the system, it might be appropriate to limit the use of project credits from uncovered domestic sectors that could be used to offset the obligations of the covered sector(s). In these ways a near-term mandatory program can begin to make environmental progress without poisoning the prospects for more comprehensive policies that might be adopted at a later date. Whatever the outcome of the US policy process in the next few years, the results are certain to weigh heavily in future international negotiations. The more credibly the United States can point to its own successful policies, the more likely it is to persuade other nations to follow a parallel course.

Notes

1 Emissions trading works by issuing a fixed number of total allowances. All firms in the system that emit carbon dioxide must hold an allowance for each unit of emissions. In general, total emissions cannot exceed the capped amount, but allowances may be bought and sold as individual parties pursue their own emissions reduction strategies.
2 Of course, biological or mechanical sequestration could alter the amount of carbon that ever reaches the atmosphere. As noted earlier, however, credits for effective sequestration, as well as for other GHGs, would be an essential component of any emissions trading system.
3 It is possible that some kind of bundled transactions could evolve in this situation.
4 Simulations by Burtraw *et al.* indicate that in the absence of an efficient system for crediting energy conservation actions, much of this subsidy persists even when utilities are able to receive credit for such programs.
5 Under the auction policy examined by Burtraw *et al.* the revenues from the auction are returned to households as lump-sum transfers. The authors point out that alternative "revenue-recycling" methods – for example returning revenues via cuts in marginal income tax rates (as in some of the experiments performed by Goulder) could further reduce the costs of the auction policy.
6 Price changes are virtually proportional to changes in economic surplus.
7 Although consumer expenditures increase under the auction approach, substantial revenues are also raised and they can be used to compensate consumers. A portion of the revenues could also be used to compensate producers, or they could be directed to support energy conservation or other benefit programs.

References

Burtraw, D., Palmer, K., Bharvikar, R., and Paul, A. 2001. *The Effect of Allowance Allocation on the Cost of Carbon Emission Trading*. RFF Discussion Paper 01–30, Washington, DC: Resources for the Future.

Goulder, L. 2002. *Mitigating the Adverse Impacts of CO_2 Abatement Policies on Energy Intensive Industries*. RFF Discussion Paper 02–22, Washington, DC: Resources for the Future.

Gruenspecht, H. K. 1982. "Differentiated regulation: the case of auto emission standards," *American Economic Review* 72: 328–31.

Jacoby, H. D., and Ellerman, A. D. 2004. "The safety valve and climate policy," *Energy Policy* 32: 481–91.

Keeler, A. 2002. "Designing a carbon dioxide trading system: the advantages of upstream regulation." Mimeo, Americans for Equitable Climate Solutions, July.

Olson, M. 1965. *The Logic of Collective Action*. Cambridge, MA: Harvard University Press.

Pizer, W. A. 1997. *Optimal Choice of Policy Instrument and Stringency Under Uncertainty: The Case of Climate Change.*" RFF Discussion Paper 97–17, Washington, DC: Resources for the Future.

Ross, M. T. 2002. "Analyses of GHG permit allocation and compensation issues." Presentation before OECD Expert Meeting on the Allocation of GHG Objectives, Paris. Charles River Associates.

Schneider, S. H., and Thompson, S. L. 2000. "A simple climate model used in economic studies of global change," in S. J. Decanio *et al.* (eds.), *New Directions in the Economics and Integrated Assessment of Global Climate Change.* Washington, DC: Pew Center on Global Climate Change, pp. 59–80.

Smith, A. E. 2002. "Analyses of GHG Permit Allocation and Compensation Issues." Presentation to the Electric Power Research Institute's 7th Annual Global Climate Change Research Seminar, Washington DC (June 4–5). Charles River Associates.

US Congressional Budget Office (CBO) 2001. "An evaluation of cap-and-trade programs for reducing US carbon emissions." Washington, DC.

Weitzman, M. L. 1974. "Prices vs. quantities," *Review of Economic Studies* 41: 477–91.

Weyant, J. P., and Hill, J. N. 1999. "Introduction and overview," *Energy Journal*, Special Issue: costs of the Kyoto Protocol, pp. vii–xiv.

Part 3

European policies to control
greenhouse gases: the EU directive
on emissions trading

9 Regulation or coordination: European climate policy between Scylla and Charybdis

Mikael Skou Andersen

Introduction

One might have expected deliberations toward a European climate policy to have passed the stage of infancy long ago. It was in 1986 that the European Parliament passed its first resolution calling for measures to counteract the rising concentrations of carbon dioxide in the atmosphere (European Parliament, 1986). With the recent signing of the Kyoto Protocol, European climate policy deliberations have become encapsulated in a global framework, but despite widely celebrated European leadership in this process, "internal" EU climate policy has scarcely matured to the level one would expect from an eighteen-year-long policy process. The stabilization target agreed in 1990 for CO_2 emissions has been exchanged for a more complex and demanding 8 percent reduction target for six greenhouse gases, but the policies and measures required to accomplish the desired reductions remain fragmented and incoherent. That the European Union succeeded in achieving a stabilization of greenhouse gas emissions from 1990 to 2000 was largely due to the combination of industrial restructuring in the former GDR and a phase-out of coal in the UK. Both the European Environment Agency and the International Energy Agency now warn that the temporary relief provided by these gratis effects is likely to be swallowed by substantial emission increases in most member states in the coming decade. The foreseen increases seem to reflect a lack of ability on the part of the European Union to develop a viable and effective climate policy on an internal basis.

This chapter addresses "domestic" European climate policy. It would perhaps be more appropriate to refer to the subject of this chapter in the plural, as there is barely yet a uniform European climate policy. Each of the fifteen (since 2004: twenty-five) member states is required to develop a domestic climate policy to accomplish its own share of the EU target. A number of pioneering member states have done so already, while others lag behind and scarcely seem to have taken notice of their violation of allowable emission levels. At the same time, the European Union itself has endeavored to develop a framework climate policy based on common approaches toward, for instance, mineral oil taxation, emissions trading, and energy efficiency standards.

Policy-making in the European Union is a complex affair, no matter what the issue in question. It is a multi-level governance system, with no clear locus of decision-making. On one hand, the various member states evidently have different and, on occasion, conflicting interests. On the other hand, the Union institutions (the Commission, Council, Parliament, and Court being the four major ones) also have their own agendas and interests. The ongoing integration process implies that the system of policy-making is far from stable, being very dynamic and somewhat unpredictable. One political science scholar has described policy-making in Brussels as a giant "roundabout," where new actors are continually arriving and where alliances are formed on an *ad hoc* basis, with only scant attention to previous coalitions at member-state level (Richardson, 1995). The literature offers several interesting accounts of the European policy-making process, with different theoretical perspectives (Leveque, 1996, Andersen, 1998, Barnes and Barnes, 1999, Weale *et al.*, 2000). More recent contributions emphasize that despite the somewhat chaotic character of policy-making, institutionalized patterns of policy-making have formed and are much stronger than the roundabout reference would lead us to suspect.

European political science scholars have, following on from the above, identified an *institutionalized reciprocity* of European policy-making (Heritier, 1992, Heritier *et al.*, 1994, Andersen and Liefferink, 1997). This concept refers to the dynamic reciprocity between, on the one hand, domestic policy-making processes at member-state level, and on the other, policy-making at Union level in Brussels. We have previously identified the specific European characteristics of this type of two-level game as related to its (1) reiterative and (2) legally binding character, evolving from (3) the specific triangular relationship among community institutions, one that frequently is (4) asynchronous, involving significant time-lags (Liefferink and Andersen, 1997, pp. 10–12). The "roundabout" perception of European policy-making was perhaps true in the early years of the integration process, but as European institutions have matured, the policy-making process has become more familiar to everyone, a learning process having taken place. Despite the ongoing Treaty revisions changing the rules of the game, there are, in fact, institutionalized features of the European policy process, guarded by the Treaty and the careful legal distinctions enshrined in it. However, when it comes to implementation, the animal rarely moves in unison; a great deal of divergence is apparent between the actions of the individual member states and between the various parts of the institutions in Brussels.

The purpose of this chapter is to contribute toward disentangling the dynamics of European climate policy. Particularly relevant to the climate policy case is the possible phenomenon of "reverberation" identified in the institutional reciprocity approach. Reverberation refers to the effect of EU-level policy-making processes on domestic politics in as far as the "tailwind" of EU decisions can be said to alter the powers, preferences, and coalitions of interests at the member-state level. This perspective poses the question of whether agreement on a common approach to climate policy provides feedback, impacting the way interested parties at member-state level define their preferences. Moreover, the question is raised of whether this, in turn, leads to an acceptance of coordinated approaches – e.g. emissions trading – being more likely than would be the case in the absence of the integration process.

The chapter is structured so as to focus on the ideas, interests, and institutions involved in European climate policy. With respect to ideas, the eco-modernist philosophy behind European climate policies is contrasted with "conventional wisdom" regarding relations between environmental and economic policies. With respect to interests, the Triptique policy-making approach to the conciliation of member-state interests, involved in the design of the EU greenhouse gas bubble, is explained. With respect to institutions, the implementation of a European approach through adequate policies and measures is analyzed, the perspective of institutional reciprocity being applied.

The eco-modernist philosophy

European environmental policy builds on a perception of the fundamental relationship of environmental policy to economic viability, this differing in many ways from the perception that tends to dominate among decision-makers in the United States. Although concerns about the implications for economic development and growth should not be neglected, especially among the cohesion countries (those EU member states which receive financial support from the EU cohesion funds), the requirements and directions of community environmental policies are – at least in the medium term – believed to be reasonably congruent with some basic European objectives.

According to a statement from one key Commission official, in line with the official rhetoric on the relationship between environmental protection and economic issues, the European Union "is focused on the integration of environmental considerations into economic and sectoral policies, and on the broadening of the range of environmental instruments, in order to improve both the effectiveness and efficiency of environmental management." Especially emphasized is "the need simultaneously to protect Europe's environment and to maximize the competitiveness of European industry" (Sors, 1996, p. xi).

Some scholars refer to the philosophy on economy–environment relations prevailing in European institutions and policies as one of "ecological modernization" (Jänicke, 1988, Mol, 1995, Andersen and Massa, 2000). Instead of regarding economy-environment interactions as a zero-sum game, environmental protection measures are viewed rather as a component of economic efficiency. One of its early pronouncements was the 1993 Delors White Paper on "Growth, employment and competitiveness", chapter 10 of which established the argument concerning the "double dividend" of environmental and employment benefits from innovative environmental regulations.

A long controversy among various scholars has been apparent in the aftermath of the Delors White Paper. However, if one considers a specific tax shift where environmental taxes replace existing distortionary taxes, the evidence of several European modeling experiences points toward the existence of a moderate employment dividend. With significance for climate policy, the comprehensive European research projects which have taken place on this issue since the early 1990s have established a modeling capacity that is now able to deal with the challenge of the Kyoto Protocol and which represents detailed relations reflecting the economic dynamics of energy taxation and energy efficiency issues.

The first European Commission-funded study aimed at modeling the costs of attaining the 8 percent reduction by the EU as demanded by the Kyoto Protocol (i.e. for all greenhouse gases, not just CO_2) was published in 2001 (see CEC 2001). The study is based on the models PRIMES and GENESIS, of which PRIMES is a traditional general-equilibrium model that has been developed for DG-Energy. The costs of the Kyoto Protocol are estimated to be €3.7 billion per year, or about 0.06 percent of GDP in 2010, provided sufficient flexibility exists between sectors and countries to allow advantage to be taken of least-cost opportunities. The cost increases would be limited for most sectors; average electricity costs increasing by about 10 percent, and costs for all household energy services and related equipment increasing by about €56 per household per year. The results have received only limited attention across Europe, although they compare favorably with results of the Intergovernmental Panel on Climate Change, whose socio-economic group expects costs in the range of 1–2 percent of GDP for Annex I countries.[1]

The Commission's proposal for a European carbon tax (now transformed into a proposed revision of the Mineral Oil Directive) was feasible because it mirrored a long-standing concern and preoccupation in Community institutions with the security of energy supply. The tax was not only a potential instrument to reduce greenhouse gases, but also one for cashing in on the profits of oil-producing countries, while at the same time reducing European dependence on foreign energy supplies.

The Triptique approach

At first glance, the various reduction targets that have been fixed for individual EU member states under the EU Kyoto bubble look as if they are primarily the result of "domestic politics," rather than one of common EU deliberations. A number of member states have pledged to reduce emissions, some even considerably, such as Germany and Denmark with 21 percent. On the other hand, the four cohesion countries (Spain, Portugal, Ireland, and Greece) plus Sweden have been allowed to increase emissions (Table 9.1 below). Finland and France have agreed to a stabilization. The apparent diversity of the various emissions targets would make it difficult for the lay observer to grasp the specific logic behind the national commitments.

The member-state reduction targets agreed under the EU bubble reflect the outcome of a negotiation process in which the so-called "Triptique" approach was used to allocate targets among member states according to criteria of fairness and equity (Ringius 1999). The approach reflects a combination of different concerns, and was developed prior to the Kyoto meeting in order to allocate reductions within the original 15 percent CO_2 reduction target, this constituting the original EU proposal for Kyoto. The Triptique approach, developed by European energy specialists at Utrecht University in the Netherlands for the then Dutch presidency of the European Council, combined available data on energy supply systems and industrial energy efficiency to allocate fair shares of CO_2 emissions. Basically, it separated energy demand into three different subsystems: (1) the light domestic sector (including households), (2) energy-intensive and export-oriented industries, and (3) the electricity generation sector.

CO_2 emissions per capita from the domestic sector did not appear to vary significantly across member states, but the cohesion countries generally exhibited lower emissions in this category. A per capita approach was used to calculate comparable emission allowances, account being taken of climatic differences and expected population changes.

Table 9.1. *Burden-sharing in the EU: from the Triptique approach via the Council compromise to the Kyoto agreement*

Member state	Triptique approach: altern. I	Council compromise (1997)	Final emission reduction targets (1998)
Austria	−1	−25	−13
Belgium	−12	−10	−7.5
Denmark	−12	−25	−21
Finland	−4	0	0
France	−4	0	0
Germany	−17	−30	−21
Greece	+2	+30	+25
Ireland	−2	+15	+13
Italy	−5	−7	−6.5
Luxembourg	−17	−30	−28
Netherlands	−6	−10	−6
Portugal	+21	+25	+27
Spain	+11	+17	+15
Sweden	+26	+5	+4
United Kingdom	−17	−10	−12.5
EU-15	−9	−10	−8

In the case of heavy industry and the power generation sector, however, considerable divergence was apparent throughout the Union. For energy-intensive industries across member states, the Triptique approach sought to minimize adverse effects on competitiveness by setting identical targets. The approach assumed that similar rates of economic growth should be available to these sectors in all member states, and that similar rates with regard to energy efficiency improvements were achievable.

The electricity sector exhibited a large degree of disparity, and for this reason a more tailored approach was employed for calculating emission allowances. The cohesion countries were allowed a 1.9 percent increase in electricity consumption, whereas other member states were allowed only a 1 percent increase. The tailor-made approach took account of national preferences for nuclear power, but otherwise allocated similar rates of change in the use of renewable and fossil fuels.

Application of the Triptique approach would produce a 9% reduction of CO_2 emissions. Since this was short of the desired EU reduction of 15%, it was not until the final stages that domestic climate policy targets could be established. The national targets involved a 30% reduction for Germany and 25% reductions for both Austria and Denmark, while a 5% increase was set for Sweden. Adding together the impact of national climate targets led to the EU as a whole being able to present an overall 14% reduction in CO_2 emissions.

The Triptique approach was developed in typical EU manner by independent experts and was refined during informal workshops involving diplomats and civil servants from member-state administrations. It formed a prepared basis for the final decisions on burden-sharing in the EC Council of Ministers. The then Dutch presidency proposed national emissions reduction targets on the basis of the Triptique approach, but adjusted the targets to accommodate concerns from cohesion countries. In addition to strengthening the domestic targets of Germany, Denmark, and Austria, the Dutch presidency proposed more stringent targets for Finland, Sweden, Italy, and the Netherlands. Spain's allowable increase in emissions, on the other hand, was adjusted from 11% to 15%, and Portugal's from 21% to 25%.

A further moderation of the national emissions targets took place subsequent to the Kyoto agreement which required a smaller emissions reduction than foreseen by the EU.

Table 9.1 compares the emissions targets agreed under the final EU bubble in 1998 with those proposed according to the Triptique approach (9% emissions reduction) and the preliminary compromise struck among member states in 1997 (10%). Despite discrepancies between the figures the logic which led to the final burden-sharing agreement, which was composed of two steps – first the technical Triptique approach and then the political-diplomatic inclusion of unilateral commitments plus some bargaining – is demonstrated.

The EU proclaimed its leadership in climate policy both prior to the Kyoto meeting and following the Bush Administration's denouncement of the Protocol. This leadership does not relate, however, to the actual greenhouse gas emissions reduction targets, where the EU target of 8 percent is only marginally more stringent than the US target of 7 percent. In fact, it can be argued that a lot more hot air is involved in the EU target than in that of the USA. Of the EU reductions, 80 percent will have to be achieved by only two countries, Germany and the UK (Grubb et al., 1999). In the case of both countries there are, moreover, structural gratis effects easing attainment of the target. If there can be said to be an EU leadership, it would seem to relate rather to the relatively sophisticated approach to mitigation of the many and diverse interests involved in "domestic" greenhouse gas policy of the Union, than to the EU target itself.

Policies and measures: a troubled path toward a coherent European climate policy

Emission Trends

Following the analysis above of the process which led to the reduction targets for individual member states, and as an introduction to the current section which analyses the introduction of policies and measures, the trend in greenhouse gas emissions in the period 1990–2000 may be considered briefly. Figure 9.1 provides an overview of the greenhouse gas emissions trends in the member states and in the EU as a whole, and contrasts them with the burden-sharing targets for 2008–12 (emissions targets are to be attained as an average for this five-year period).

From 1990 to 2000, the greenhouse gas emissions of the EU declined by 3.5 percent. This decline is the outcome of a very uneven pattern among different member states. On one hand, the two most substantial contributors to the EU reduction target, Germany and the UK, are already currently close to meeting their commitments. On the other hand, it appears that in the cohesion countries, especially Spain and Ireland, the increase in greenhouse gas emissions is out of control. Furthermore, some smaller member states, otherwise known for a high environmental profile, such as Austria, Denmark, Belgium, and the Netherlands, are not performing as well as might be expected in terms of the trend in greenhouse gas emissions relative to the declared targets.

Figure 9.1 suggests that the general trend in greenhouse gas emissions is less a matter of greenhouse gas *policy*, and more one of the structural effects arising from "business as usual." (This observation should not be carried too far, though, as previous research has disentangled and sub-stantiated the effects of domestic CO_2 emissions control policies in specific sectors, particularly industry [see Enevoldsen and Brendstrup, 1998].) The report from the European Environment Agency (2002a) reveals, however, that emissions increases in other sectors, such as transport, tend to outweigh the decreases achieved in the more traditional sectors.

Policies and measures

The first specific climate initiative of the European Union was the Commission's 1990 proposal for a European carbon-energy tax. This initiative suffered an early strategic reverse at the European Summit in Essen in 1994 (for a detailed analysis of the proposal's fate, see Andersen 1996). The Commission's revised approach to taxation took the form of a proposal to amend the Mineral Oil Directive. Negotiations on this Directive went on from the mid-1990s, and thanks to a compromise at the Barcelona Summit in 2002, where Spain's acceptance in principle was secured, a final agreement was reached. The attention drawn to the battle on energy taxation has in many ways overshadowed other attempts to develop a common European climate policy.

More recently, and following the Gothenburg Summit in 2001, the Commission has launched a European Climate Change Program (ECCP), which lists policies and measures within ten different areas. This program puts emphasis on emissions trading as a cross-cutting approach to climate policy, but also lists initiatives regarding, for instance:

- effective implementation of the IPPC directive
- linking of Joint Implementation (JI) and Clean Development Mechanisms (CDM) to the Emissions Trading Directive
- energy-efficient public procurement
- promotion of combined heat and power production
- public awareness
- promotion of biofuels for transport
- regulation of fluorinated gases.

When presenting the European Climate Change Program at the conference of the World Business Council for Sustainable Development in October 2001, the Environment Commissioner, Margot Wallström, stressed that, for the EU, emissions trading is a "cornerstone in a low-cost strategy for reducing greenhouse gas emissions." (Wallström, 2001) However, the Emissions Trading Directive will cover 12,000 large installations and deal initially only with CO_2 emissions, i.e. about 45 percent of CO_2 emissions or 35 percent of total EU greenhouse gas emissions. As to the timetable for the introduction of this potentially important instrument, the ECCP freely admits that the "objective is to start a learning by doing phase by 2005 in order to have useful experience at EU level by 2008, i.e. the start of the 1st Kyoto Protocol Commitment Period" (when establishment of an international trading scheme is foreseen). This ambition may prove too modest for those member states which are hard pressed to meet their present commitments in a cost-effective way. Governments in the Netherlands, Denmark, and Italy have already announced that their present reduction targets can only be attained by extensive use of flexible mechanisms, in particular emissions trading.

The absence of desired trends with regard to emissions targets in several member states provides a strong impetus to develop more active

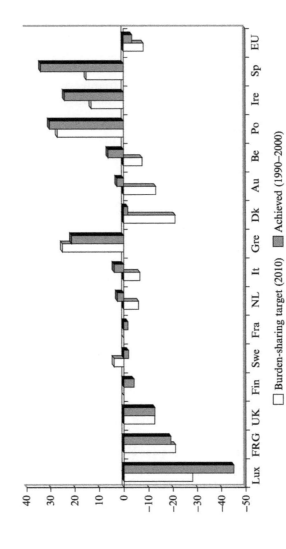

Figure 9.1. Status year 2000: distance to greenhouse gas emission target for 2008–12 of EU and member states. (*Source*: European Environment Agency, 2002b).

climate policies at the domestic member-state level. Whether some member states may opt for a certain amount of free-riding on reductions attained in other member states is not clear. Emission increases in Spain are particularly worrying, Spain being one of the larger member states, with the potential to affect EU emissions targets as a whole. Emissions trading might be a way to smooth out reduction progress among member states. However, since the transport sector is one of the key drivers behind emissions increases, emissions trading among large installations may not prove sufficient.

Emissions trading

The adoption of emissions trading in the EU has been favored by one institutional aspect; unlike the energy tax proposal, unanimity in the Council has not been required. An emissions trading scheme could be agreed with qualified majority voting, although the consent of both the Council of Ministers and the European Parliament was still required in accordance with normal procedures for decision-making in the European Union. In June 2003 the EU finally succeeded in reaching a compromise between the Council and the Parliament, allowing the system to begin operating from 2005. The protracted stalemate between the two institutions threatened to block the agreement, but ultimately the Parliament gave way. Further disagreement could have postponed implementation to beyond 2006 and endangered activities in the initial trial period (2005–08), delaying effective action until after 2008.

Although emissions trading is more attractive to certain industries than energy taxation, it has been vehemently opposed in some quarters for a number of years. One particularly influential opponent of emissions trading was the German association of industry, the BDI, which favored voluntary agreements and domestic approaches. In 1995 the association committed its members to a 25 percent voluntary reduction of CO_2 emissions (baseline year 1990), a reduction of about 15 percent (relative to production output) having already been achieved. Until the 2002 elections in Germany, the German government, in fact, opposed the Emissions Trading Directive. A revised position allowed for support to the scheme, but drastic changes to the directive were required, with the result that the directive abandoned strict individual assignment of allowances by allowing for trading pools and other exemptions favoring German industry. The UK also voiced skepticism on the approach proposed by the European Commission to emissions trading as it was not seen as compatible with the voluntary approach applied in the emissions trading scheme which had been introduced in the UK. It is not surprising that opposition came from Germany, which at that time already was close to fulfilling its domestic climate target and whose industry regarded emissions trading as an unnecessary burden. That Germany finally accepted a compromise on the directive can be seen as a typical tailwind effect of European policies. However, if these two high-emission countries allow opt-outs for major sources, the exemption clauses now inserted into the directive may place emissions trading in a more peripheral position than originally foreseen.

Whether emissions trading will be able to deliver on the expectations for it deserves attention. With the number of potential buyers on the market the key question seems to be: who will be the sellers? Many look to the new member states in Eastern Europe, which acceded to the EU in May 2004, as the potential sellers of emissions credits. However, because these member states have agreed to the environmental *acquis*, they will, according to the IPPC Directive, only be allowed to trade such emissions allowances as are beyond a baseline compliance with the *acquis*. Detailed analysis reveals, for instance, that for the Czech Republic allowable trading would amount to only a few percent of current emissions (see Jepma, 2002). Poland is the largest new member state and appears to possess the largest potential for emissions trading; yet its government has taken a rather negative stance on emissions trading.

Between Scylla and Charybdis: regulation or coordination?

In ancient Greek mythology, Odysseus had to navigate between the dangers of Scylla and Charybdis. He managed to find a middle way and to survive. Does the choice between regulation and coordination in EU climate policy represent, in a similar way, two extremes, neither of which is desirable? On one hand, simple coordination of member-state climate policies is favored by strong domestic interests fearing the costs of common EU regulation, and pointing to soft consensual mechanisms for achieving national targets. On the other hand, the European Commission and other European actors view member-state commitment to the burden-sharing agreement as a significant step in the European integration process, and fear retreat and lack of allegiance on the part of member-state authorities, pressed by domestic special interests. Scylla, in this case, can be said to represent climate policy's falling prey to nationalistic go-it-alone, and Charybdis to represent being smashed on the rocks of excessive regulatory costs at Union level.

The EU still needs to find a route between Scylla and Charybdis. How it is possible to combine trustworthy domestic and pioneering climate policies with Union-level regulation in a reliable and cost-effective way remains to be seen. As shown above, the fact that the EU is apparently well on the track to its Kyoto target has more to do with the prior availability of "hot air" in Germany and the UK than with effective policy implementation.

One may well argue that the reciprocity of European policy-making constitutes an institutional logic which will help find a navigable path toward the target. The reiterative character of policy-making ensures that member states will be confronted with their commitments as part of the ongoing policy-making process, and that failure to live up to these commitments can be sanctioned in future policy-making deals, possibly on completely different issues. If Spain continues to ignore its climate target, hence threatening the possibility of the Union achieving its Kyoto target, how will it then affect Spain's credibility in other European issues? Spain may soon find that it needs to implement at least symbolic measures to demonstrate "good will." The fact that European policies are legally binding will gradually strengthen the effects of common measures, e.g. on energy-efficiency standards, in all member states, and help secure a bottom line.

The complex relationship between member states and community institutions explains the frequent periods of standstill, but once decisions have been made, they produce tailwinds which may alter the preferences and perceptions of domestic interest groups. The recent German concession on emissions trading seems to be an example of this process. The tailwind from commitments in international fora, e.g. the Johannesburg Summit, has underlined the commitment of the EU to its burden-sharing agreement and the Kyoto agreement, and has altered the preferences, and perhaps even powers, of domestic constituencies. That Kyoto is important and matters was underlined in the 2002 German elections, where it served to strengthen the Green lobby vis-à-vis conventional competitiveness viewpoints in the Social Democratic Party and German industry. It is evident that the flooding in eastern Germany just before the German elections also played a role in this process, but, without the Kyoto agreement and the burden-sharing agreement, credible mechanisms for climate change policies would not have existed, and the political difference would have been much more blurred.

The main problem with the institutional reciprocity in relation to climate change is the time-lags involved. Decision-making is a drawn-out process, and the differences in tempo are felt at member-state level.

The Emissions Trading Directive is a good example of this. On one hand, some member states, such as the Netherlands and Denmark, whose policy-making systems are flexible and innovative, are eager to see emissions trading introduced. On the other hand, decision-making and implementation at EU level awaits consideration by and consent from the whole convoy of member states. The interpretation of the reciprocity of the European Union policy-making process, presented above, indicates a possible institutional trajectory that might be leading toward more mature and credible climate policies within the coming five to eight years. The "if" is very much related to possible stalemates and time-lags, and the inherent implementation problem.

Note

1 According to the ENDS News Service (September 13, 2002) the European results have been attacked by an American think-tank, the American Council for Capital Formation, which claims that the EU's GDP will decline by 5 percent at the end of the first commitment period, a figure almost 100 times higher. In the other direction, the European Commission believes the American results are flawed. The technical aspects of the debate are, however, beyond the scope of the present chapter.

References

Andersen, M. S. 1996. "The domestic politics of carbon-energy taxation," in M. S. Andersen and D. Liefferink, *The New Member States and the Impact on Environmental Policy*. Final report to the Commission (DG-XII), part I. Aarhus: Dept. of Political Science, Aarhus University (http://www.statsbiblioteket.dk/).
  1998. "Environmental Policies in Europe," in *The European Yearbook of Comparative Government and Public Administration*. Baden-Baden: Nomos Verlag, vol. III, pp. 205–26.
Andersen, M. S., and Liefferink, D. 1997 (eds.). *European Environmental Policy: The Pioneers*. Manchester: Manchester University Press.
Andersen, M. S., and Massa, I. 2000. "Ecological modernization: origins, dilemmas and future directions," *Journal of Environmental Policy and Planning* 2: 337–45.
Barnes, P., and Barnes, I. 1999. *Environmental Policy in the European Union*. Cheltenham: Edward Elgar.
CEC 2001. "Economic evaluation of sectoral emission reduction objectives for climate change." Brussels (http://europa.eu.int/comm/environment/enveco/climate_change/sectoral_objectives.htm).
Enevoldsen, M., and Brendstrup, S. 1998. "Considering feasibility and efficiency: the Danish mix of CO_2 taxes and agreements," in M. S.Andersen and R.-U. Sprenger (eds.). *Market-Based Instruments for Environmental Management*. Cheltenham: Edward Elgar, pp. 148–75.

European Environment Agency 2002a. "Energy and environment in the European Union." Environmental Issue Report no. 31, Copenhagen.

2002b. "EU makes insufficient progress in reducing its environmental impact," press release, Copenhagen (May 30).

European Parliament 1986. "Resolution on measures to counteract the rising concentration of carbon dioxide in the atmosphere (the 'greenhouse' effect)." *Official Journal* C 255 (October 13), p. 0272.

Grubb, M., Vrolijk, C. and Brack, D. 1999. *The Kyoto Protocol: A Guide and Assessment*. London: Earthscan.

Heritier, A. 1992. "Policy Netzwerkanalyse als Untersuchungsinstrument im europäischen Kontext," *Politische Vierteljahresschrift Sonderheft* 24: 432–47.

Heritier, A., Mingers, S., Knill, C., and Becka, M. 1994. *Die Veränderung von Staatlichkeit in Europa*. Opladen: Leske und Budrich.

Jänicke, M. 1988. "Ökologische Modernisierung. Optionen und Restriktionen präventiver Umweltpolitik," in U. E. Simonis (ed.). *Präventive Umweltpolitik*. Frankfurt: Campus, pp. 13–26.

Jepma, C. 2002. "Editor's note," *Magazine on the Kyoto Mechanisms* 8: 2.

Leveque, F. 1996 (ed.). *Environmental Policy in Europe: Industry, Competition and the Policy Process*. Cheltenham: Edward Elgar.

Liefferink, D., and Andersen, M. S. 1997 (eds.). *The Innovation of EU Environmental Policy*. Copenhagen and Oslo: Scandinavian University Press.

Mol, A. 1995. *The Refinement of Production*. Utrecht: Van Arkel.

Richardson, J. 1995 (ed.). *European Union: Power and Policy-Making*. London: Routledge.

Ringius, L. 1999. "Differentiation, leaders and fairness: negotiating climate commitments in the European Community," *International Negotiation* 4: 133–66.

Sors, A. 1996. "Foreword," in Leveque (ed.), pp. xi–xii.

Weale, A., Pridham, G., Cini, M., Konstadakopulos, D., Porto, M., and Flinn, B. 2000. *Environmental Governance in Europe*. New York: Oxford University Press.

Wallström, M. 2001. "Combating climate change: the EU strategy." World Business Council for Sustainable Development, Speech 01/496 (October 26) (http://europa.eu.int/rapid/start/cgi/guesten.ksh?p_action.gettxt=gt&doc =SPEECH/01/496 | 0 | RAPID&lg=EN).

10 Lobbying and CO_2 trade in the EU

Gert Tinggaard Svendsen

Introduction

The world's first framework for international greenhouse gas emissions trading was proposed by the European Commission in its new and remarkable Directive Proposal of October 2001. This Directive Proposal was the outcome of a policy process started by the Commission in March 2000 when launching the Green Paper. It started, in the words of the Commission, "a debate across Europe on the suitability and possible functioning of emissions trading." This is so because "Emissions trading is, firstly, an instrument for environmental protection, and, secondly, one of the policy instruments that will least impair competitiveness." (CEU, 2001a) Thus, the idea is that emissions trading could ensure that the stated target levels are achieved without invalidating the stated EU strategic goal of becoming the world's leading economy within a decade (from the Lisbon Summit of 2000; see Svendsen, 2003).

We focus on two main differences between the Green Paper and the Directive Proposal, namely the choice of allocation rule and enforcement. By doing this it is possible to measure the effect of lobbying as the difference in proposed design between the Green Paper (before lobbying) and the final Directive Proposal (after lobbying). Lobbying may lead to an irrational policy outcome for all market participants because the proposed market system is most likely to break down as a result of market distortions. A market breakdown means less economic growth in the EU because the gains from free trade of greenhouse gas permits among firms in member states disappear so that emissions reduction efforts can no longer be carried out in the cheapest places.

Tietenberg (2004) reviews the literature on emissions trading and it is evident that the greenhouse gas market in the EU needs far more academic attention. Svendsen (1998) suggested a market scheme for

This chapter draws, in part, on earlier published work (Svendsen, 1998, 2003). The author is responsible for any errors.

150

greenhouse gas trading in the EU but this idea needs more elaboration concerning the preferences of the main interest groups and the establishment of a politically feasible and workable design. Thus, the research question of whether the EU Directive Proposal on CO_2 trade was influenced by lobbying and whether it can be improved is stimulated by the existing gap in the literature.

Identifying the effect of lobbying and how to improve the design of a forthcoming CO_2 market is important because the EU has committed itself to meet an 8 percent greenhouse gas reduction target level (following the Kyoto agreement). The greenhouse gas emissions trading scheme has been in operation since January 1, 2005 and the idea is to reduce the emission quotas in circulation by the year 2012 at the latest, when the EU must meet its Kyoto target level. Political agreement on the distribution of reduction target levels among the EU member states was reached in June 1998, and is referred to as the "burden-sharing agreement" (Boom and Svendsen, 2000, CEU, 2001b, Grubb and Yamin, 2001).

In the remainder of this chapter, the following section deals with political economy theory and develops two hypotheses. First, it suggests that an institutional structure with power centralization is vulnerable to lobbying. Second, it suggests that industrial groupings will lobby and dominate political decision-making owing to their group size. The next section turns to the empirical evidence in the EU concerning these two hypotheses, and ends with policy recommendations on how to improve the current Directive design proposal based on the US experience. A concluding section summarizes the results.

Lobbying

Power centralization

As argued by Paldam and Svendsen (2000, 2002, 2005), New Institutional Economics can be applied to the issue of the level of decentralization and lobbying. Douglass C. North is an especially prominent representative of modern institutional economics, with its focus on transaction costs in a world with incomplete information. Thus, agents need to construct "rules of the game," i.e. institutions (North, 1990).

New Institutional Economics tends to focus on the institutional circumstances that facilitate successful lobbying and the achievement of "rent" among organized interest groups. Here, Schjødt and Svendsen (2002) emphasize, following North and Weingast (1989), that the rise of England can be attributed mainly to the constitutional change following the Glorious Revolution in 1688–89 and the way political power was divided. The revolutionary settlement stated that Parliament would gain the upper hand in financial matters and the outcome was a complex institutional arrangement of checks and balances in which Parliament became the new focus of power. Because of this spreading of power in Parliament, rent-seeking activities became more difficult, as interest groups had to pay a higher price for favorable regulation than they previously paid under the centralized political system of the Stuarts.

How does this transaction cost perspective relate to the EU and its environmental policy? Here, we simply hypothesize that the more centralized power is in the EU, the easier it is for lobbying groups to achieve favors, for example within environmental regulation. If one institution essentially holds all the power in the EU, an EU pressure group has to lobby in only one place; this compares to the situation where power is spread over many EU institutions, such as the Parliament and the Council, thus forcing interest groups to lobby in many places.

Hypothesis 1: Power centralization in the EU lowers lobbying costs.

Who will lobby?

Mancur Olson introduced the importance of group size when explaining lobbying and the potential redistribution of national income to specific group members. This idea is the starting point for his three most famous books, namely *The Logic of Collective Action* (1965), *The Rise and Decline of Nations* (1982), and *Power and Prosperity* (2000). As argued by Olson, more and more interest groups will form over time, each struggling to maximize its slice of the national income pie rather than contributing to economic growth.

Owing to this logic of collective action, rational EU interest groups will try to redistribute as much money as possible from the EU taxpayers to themselves. Such redistribution, and an irrational economic outcome for the EU as a whole, can be illustrated with the use of theory. Let us, in the context of permit trade, consider the potential "winners" and "losers" when choosing between grandfathering and auctioning permits in the EU. We assume that the "collective good" of auctioning off permits without refund, or of grandfathering, is provided by lobbying. The results from this analysis lead to a hypothesis on rational interest-group behavior in the EU and an asymmetrical political pressure in favor of grandfathering. Let us illustrate this logic by a hypothetical example in which we compare the lobbying capability of 200 million EU taxpayers with that of five 5 industrial groups. Note, that none of the groups is organized beforehand.

The hypothetical EU group of non-organized taxpayers is assumed to consist of 200 million identical agents. Furthermore, each taxpayer will earn €10 per year if the auction is chosen because the revenue from this mechanism will be redistributed to all EU taxpayers as a slightly lower income tax. Thus, the total gain for all EU taxpayers amounts to €2 billion. If the total cost for a single taxpayer to stay fully informed about EU policies and successfully lobby EU bureaucrats and politicians amounts to €1 million, then each individual taxpayer will not act because the individual net gain from doing so is clearly negative. Thus, even though the EU taxpayer group as a whole would obtain a total gain from getting the auction worth €2 billion (2000 times higher than the total cost of €1 million), no single EU taxpayer will take the initiative to provide this collective good in the absence of organization. Thus, in this "large" group, the collective good of choosing the auction mechanism will not be provided; see Table 10.1.

Consider now the small group of five industrial pressure groups. Again, let their total gain from achieving grandfathering rather than auction without refund equals the €2 billion that the taxpayers would have gained in the latter case. The five identical industrial groupings would then gain €400 million each. Assume also that the lobbying costs correspond to the previous figure, namely €1 million. Now, it pays each industrialist to act on his or her own even in the absence of organization, with an individual net gain amounting to €399 million (the individual gain of €400 million minus the lobbying cost of €1 million). Therefore, the collective good of achieving the grandfathered allocation rule for this small group of five industrialists will be provided. Furthermore, there will be a strong incentive to meet and share the costs of lobbying thus realizing even greater individual net gains. In this way, the logic of group size demonstrates why, for example, there is an overwhelming political pressure in favor of grandfathering rather than the auction mechanism without refund.

Table 10.1. *Taxpayers, industrialists, and the choice between auction and grandfathering*

	Taxpayers (if auction)	Industrialists (if grandfathering)
Number	200 million	5
Individual gain	€10	€400 million
Total gain	€2 billion	€2 billion
Total cost	€1 million	€1 million
Individual net gain	€10 – €1 million	€400 million – €1 million

Hypothesis 2: Small-sized industrial groups will dominate EU lobbyism and ask for favorable environmental policies.

CO_2 trade in the EU

After hypothesizing how the EU may be vulnerable to lobbying and why some groups may have a strong incentive to lobby, we now turn to the empirical evidence. Initially, we focus on Hypothesis 1 concerning the institutional structure of the EU. Then, we turn to Hypothesis 2 concerning dominant interest groups and try to measure and evaluate their lobbying effect on the EU CO_2 trade system policy.

The Commission and lobbying

Three main points suggest that the Commission holds the reins of power in the EU. First, the Commission has the exclusive right to initiate all legislation by submitting proposals to the Council of Ministers. Second, the Commission promotes the inclusion of affected interest groups in the process of policy formulation in order to draw upon the expert knowledge of external actors. Third, the Commission acts as the enforcement agent of EU law-making, and is by far the most influential institution in the EU. In contrast, the main role of the EU Parliament, with its 626 democratically elected members, is to approve the annual EU Commission budget and fulfill an advisory role; however, it cannot initiate legislation (Svendsen, 2003).

Interest groups facing the Commission and its bureaucratic leadership in the EU may provide new information when lobbying. However, they may also try to affect regulation in their own private interest, which is possible in the present pluralist system with competitive lobbying. As argued by Schmidt (1999), pluralism in the EU is probably even less "pluralistic" than that in the United States because the EU Commission, as the agenda-setter, has more control over the entire process of interest representation.

The number of interest groups in Brussels has grown steadily from 59 in 1954 to 3000 in 1992, i.e. the number has increased more than fifty times since 1954. Also, it has been estimated by the Commission that 10,000 professional lobbyists were active in Brussels back in 1992 as well. Finally, most EU pressure groups (83 percent) are involved in promoting business interests while only very few represent the large groups of consumers and taxpayers (CEU, 1992, Svendsen, 2003).

The findings by Daugbjerg and Svendsen (2001) confirm that consumers do not have much influence compared to business groups, i.e.

business groups are the winners when competing against consumer groups. This claim is documented, for example, by a detailed analysis of the actual design of CO_2 taxation in the five countries which, to date, have introduced it, namely, Denmark, Norway, Sweden, Finland and the Netherlands. Here, a large difference exists between the CO_2 tax rate applicable to the large group of consumers and the one applicable to the small group of producers. In general, CO_2 taxes are non-uniform and consumers would, on average, pay a tax rate which is six times higher than that paid by the producers. Furthermore, producers are subsidized by favorable refund systems. Likewise, the optimal solution of auctioning off permits without refund may not be politically feasible because business interests would oppose it just as they have opposed the CO_2 taxation.

Measuring lobbying

Main interest groups Six main industrial groupings are dealt with in the Green Paper, namely, electricity producers, iron and steel, oil and gas (refining), building materials, chemicals, paper and pulp. In the final Directive Proposal, the chemical sector was left out of the target group because its direct emissions of carbon dioxide are relatively low and because the number of chemical installations – emitting all six greenhouse gases in complicated processes – is high. The risk of substantially increasing the administrative complexity of the whole emissions trading scheme led to the final exclusion of the chemical sector (CEU, 2001a, Svendsen, 2003).

The five sectors included in the final Directive Proposal account for 43 percent of total EU CO_2 emissions.

As seen in Table 10.2 the main emitters of CO_2 are the EU electricity producers with almost a third of total emissions in the EU (30%). The interest of these large electricity producers is mainly represented by Eurelectric at the EU level. The second sector, iron and steel producers, emits 5% and is represented by the European Confederation of Iron and Steel Industries (Eurofer). Oil and gas industry is third, emitting 4%. It is represented by the International Association of Gas and Oil Producers and its daughter organization, Europia. Building materials are fourth, being responsible for 3%. This sector is represented by two main industrial groups, namely the cement industry (Cembureau) and the ceramic industry (Ceramie-Unie). Finally, the paper and pulp sector is fifth, emitting 1% only. The Confederation of European Paper Industries (CEPI) represents the paper and pulp industry in Europe. The position of CEPI is also supported by the Confederation of European Forest Owners (CEPF); see Svendsen (2003) for more details.

Table 10.2. *CO₂ emissions from five industrial sectors in the EU, 1997*

Sector	% of total CO_2 emissions
1. Electricity (and heat) producers	30
2. Iron and steel	5
3. Oil and gas	4
4. Building materials	3
5. Paper and pulp	1
Total	43

Source: CEU, 2001b.

Allocation rule   The Green Paper lists a number of possibilities for the initial allocation rule. The EU Commission itself points to the auction solution because it would clearly eliminate rent-seeking, as existing firms would have to pay for all the permits they need just as new firms would. Such periodic auctioning gives an equal and fair chance to all companies to get access to the desired permits and respects the "polluter pays" principle at the same time (CEU, 2001b). Furthermore, auctioning simplifies the emissions trading system. No politically controversial decisions about how much to give each company covered by the trading scheme would be necessary. Also other politically sensitive issues, such as state aid, for example, would be eliminated. Most prominently, new entrants would have a periodic opportunity to buy the permits that they need in the event that existing sources refused to sell them any (ibid.).

Still, the final Directive Proposal suggests a grandfathered allocation based on historical emissions at the 1990 level, which is clearly the solution that benefits rent-seeking industry the most in theory (as argued above). Grandfathering favors industry in general as it minimizes private emissions reduction costs, and creates a rent for existing firms. Thus, this feature of the design in the Directive proposal points in particular to the presence of powerful national industrial rent-seeking and potential achievement of significant rent in terms of a beneficial allocation rule. Therefore, the choice of allocation rule in the United States' tradable permit systems has been grandfathering too (Tietenberg, 1985, 2000, Hansjürgens, 1998, Svendsen, 1998, Dijkstra, 1999, Ellerman *et al.*, 2000).

In the United States, the well-functioning control system is enforced by a single and neutral authority (the Environmental Protection Agency in Washington DC), so that local authorities do not have full responsibility and as such are not tempted to protect their own firms. The establishment of a common supra-national EU institution independent of local member-state interests is a good idea in view of the US experience. EU member states have strong free-rider incentives to protect their "own" firms against strict control, so some kind of central control is needed. Otherwise, local firms may be given substantial room for cheating because national authorities may accept violations in the interest of attracting industry and a larger tax base (Baumol and Oates, 1988, Oates and Schwab, 1988).

However, not only did industrial groups achieve grandfathering in the EU Directive Proposal, they also achieved implementation and settlement of permit allocation among sectors at the member-state level. The specific allocation of permits is to be decided at the national level, taking the burden-sharing agreement, i.e. the different target levels for different member states, into account. Most troublesome in the political sense is that industry, beside its small-group advantages when mobilizing lobbying efforts, holds an even stronger position at the national level than at the international level. This is arguably so because industry traditionally has influenced governments and built up strong networks for achieving favorable regulation and for fighting the labor unions. In fact, it is clearly in the interest of industrial organizations to lobby in favor of emissions trading to be implemented at the national level, as such a move will increase the likelihood of higher rents when grandfathering and enforcing CO_2 trade in the EU (Daugbjerg and Svendsen, 2001).

A simple way to minimize the risk of member states favoring their own firms when allocating permits, would be to define allocations to industry according to the nominal Kyoto emissions target levels starting in 1990. Denmark, for example, must reduce greenhouse gases by 21 percent according to the Kyoto Protocol. This would simply mean that its participating industrial sectors would have to take on the same 21 percent reduction obligation. Even though competition may be distorted because of differing total reduction costs for Danish and Greek firms, for example (Greece is allowed to *increase* its greenhouse gas emissions by 25 percent), member countries have agreed politically on the burden-sharing agreement. Therefore, this politically feasible starting point is worth considering.

Enforcement   In the Green Paper, it is unclear how the market is to be enforced. However, in both the Green Paper and the Directive Proposal, the Commission states that the control system is intended to make the whole trading scheme credible by assuring that there is a one-to-one correspondence between a permit to emit one tonne of CO_2 and the actual emission of one tonne of CO_2. If the system is to work, avoidance of cheating is crucial.

The problem is that cheating is most likely to take place in member states. For example, a Sicilian firm may sell fictive permits to a Swedish firm without reducing the corresponding amount of emissions. In fact, the northern part of the EU is generally less corrupt and better at implementing EU legislation than the southern part; see Svendsen (2003). If money is generally redistributed from firms in less-corrupt countries to firms in more corrupt countries in this way, total emissions will increase and the value of permits will no longer be credible. Even if sanctions are formally in place, they will not be imposed in corrupt countries. Basically, the risk of cheating puts a ticking bomb under the whole EU CO_2 trading system.

This risk is further increased by the fact that the Directive Proposal relies on self-reporting of emissions data by firms. National authorities are then supposed to compare the two numbers from buyers and sellers of permits on the basis of calculations of emissions from the fuel input. In addition to the risk that corrupt authorities will not do a proper job, this indirect measurement of CO_2 emissions is an uncertain and complicated procedure, especially for the big coal-fired plants; see Varming *et al.* (2000). In contrast, direct measurement, such as the method used when measuring SO_2 emissions in the US Acid Rain Program, has been proved to work. Here, measurement devices placed in all plant chimneys directly report to the computers of the US Environmental Protection Agency in Washington, DC. It is probably not possible to cheat in the US system, for example, by selling permits and earning money without making the corresponding reductions (Stavins, 1998, Svendsen, 1998, Ellerman *et al.*, 2000). Thus, we simply suggest that direct emissions monitoring, such as the equipment employed in the US Acid Rain Program, should be used for measuring CO_2 emissions in the EU permit market system because of the risk of cheating and the uncertainty of calculation.

Conclusion

We answered the research question of whether the EU Directive Proposal on CO_2 trade had been influenced by lobbying, and whether it could be improved, in the following way.

First, we argued theoretically that the degree of power centralization is crucial. In the extreme case where one institution holds all power, a pressure group only has to lobby in one place. In contrast, where power is decentralized, for example when it is spread over the many members in a parliament, interest groups are forced to lobby in many different places, which increases lobbying costs. Second, we argued that lobbying will take place among well-organized and small-sized "Euro groups." The logic of group size gave industrial groupings small-group advantages when attempting to affect policy outcomes and to provide the collective good of favoring, and redistributing resources to, their members.

It was observed that the EU Commission (the EU bureaucracy) holds centralized power because it has the exclusive right to initiate all legislation by submitting proposals to the Council of Ministers. Also, we identified a large increase over time in the number of Brussels-based industrial pressure groups. Therefore, the EU becomes especially vulnerable to lobbying and harmful redistribution, as known in England before the Glorious Revolution. Furthermore we identified the five main industrial groupings targeted in the Directive Proposal and the two main shifts in design issues from the Green Paper to the Directive Proposal. First, the Green Paper pointed to the use of auctions run by member states as the preferable allocation rule for economic reasons. However, in the Directive Proposal, the suggestion was for a grandfathered permit allocation rule like the one found in the US tradable permit systems, and for member states to decide the final allocation of permits among their own sectors. Therefore, to avoid discretionary allocation decisions by national governments, which could be heavily influenced by lobbying and corruption, we recommended that the national industrial sectors should "take over" the national target level following the burden-sharing agreement, as a compromise between economic optimality and political feasibility. Second, concerning enforcement, emissions monitoring

Table 10.3. *Lobbying and CO$_2$ trade in the EU*

Green paper	Directive proposal	Policy recommendation
1. Allocation rule		
Should preferably be an auction run by member states.	Grandfathering based on the right of member states to allocate among sectors.	Grandfathering based on the "burden-sharing agreement" so that sectors "take over" national obligations.
2. Enforcement		
Unclear.	Indirect emission monitoring based on self-reporting.	Direct emission monitoring.
	Member states as authorities.	Independent supranational authority.

should be direct to avoid cheating, and an independent supranational authority to run the whole program should be established; see Table 10.3.

These modifications in design are important to avoid national firms being favored on account of their traditional domestic lobbying strength. As it stands, the current Directive is likely to result in a market break-down, implying lower economic growth in the future if more expensive solutions for reaching the Kyoto target levels have to be applied in the EU member states. Overall, these results are arguably consistent with our Hypotheses 1 and 2 concerning power centralization and industrial pressure groups. Thus, we suggest that lobbying affected the design of the EU CO_2 market in favor of small-sized and well-organized industrial interest groups and at the expense of EU taxpayers.

References

Baumol, W. J., and Oates, W. E. 1988. *The Theory of Environmental Policy*. New York: Cambridge University Press.

Boom, J., and Svendsen, G. T. 2000. "International emission trading systems: trade level and political acceptability," *Journal of Institutional and Theoretical Economics* 4: 548–66.

CEU 1992. *An Open and Structured Dialogue Between the Commission and Special Interest Groups*. Brussels: Secretariat of the European Commission.

  2001a. "Proposal for a Directive of the European Parliament and of the Council establishing a scheme for greenhouse gas emission allowance trading within the Community and amending Council Directive 96/61/EC." (presented by the Commission) Brussels, October 23, 2001, COM (2001) 581 final, 2001/0245 (COD) (http://europa.eu.int/eur-lex/en/com/pdf/2001/en_501PC0581.pdf [accessed at December 12, 2001]).

  2001b. *Green Paper on Greenhouse Gas Emissions Trading Within the European Union*. Brussels: Commission of the European Communities, March 8, 2000, COM (2000) 87 (http://europa.eu.int/comm/environment/docum/0087_en.htm [accessed at June 12, 2001]).

Daugbjerg, C., and Svendsen, G. T. 2001. *Green Taxation in Question: Politics and Economic Efficiency in Environmental Regulation*. New York: Palgrave.

Dijkstra, B. R. 1999. *The Political Economy of Environmental Policy*. Cheltenham: Edward Elgar.

Ellerman, A. D., Joskow, P. L., Schmalensee, R., Montero, J. P., and Bailey, E. M. 2000. *Markets for Clean Air: The US Acid Rain Program*. Cambridge: Cambridge University Press.

Grubb, M., and Yamin, F. 2001. "Climatic collapse at The Hague: what happened, why, and where do we go from here?" *International Affairs* 77: 261–76.

Hansjürgens, B. 1998. "The sulfur dioxide (SO_2) allowance trading program: recent developments and lessons to be learned," *Environment and Planning C: Government and Policy* 16: 341–61.

North, D. C. 1990. *Institutions, Institutional Change and Economic Performance.* Cambridge: Cambridge University Press.

North, D. C., and Weingast, B. R. 1989. "Constitutions and commitment: the evolution of institutions governing public choice in seventeenth century England," *Journal of Economic History* 49: 803–32.

Oates, W. E., and Schwab, R. M. 1988. "Economic competition among jurisdictions: efficiency enhancing or distortion inducing?" *Journal of Public Economics* 35: 333–54.

Olson, M. 1965. *The Logic of Collective Action.* Cambridge: Cambridge University Press.

1982. *The Rise and Decline of Nations.* New Haven: Yale University Press.

2000. *Power and Prosperity: Outgrowing Communist and Capitalist Dictatorships.* New York: Basic Books.

Paldam, M., and Svendsen, G. T. 2000. "An essay on social capital: looking for the fire behind the smoke," *European Journal of Political Economy* 16: 339–66.

2002. "Missing social capital and the transition in Eastern Europe," *Journal of Institutional Innovation, Development and Transition* 5: 21–34.

2005 (eds.). *Trust, Social Capital and Economic Growth: An International Comparison.* Cheltenham: Edward Elgar.

Schjødt, E. B., and Svendsen, G. T. 2002. "Transition to a market economy in Eastern Europe: interest groups and political institutions in Russia," *Nordic Journal of Political Economy* 28: 181–94.

Schmidt, V. A. 1999. *The EU and its Member States: Institutional Contrasts and Their Consequences.* Working Paper 99/7, Cologne: Max Planck Institute for the Study of Societies (MPIfG).

Stavins, R. N. 1998. "What can we learn from the grand policy experiment? Positive and normative lessons from SO_2 allowance trading," *Journal of Economic Perspectives* 12: 69–88.

Svendsen, G. T. 1998. *Public Choice and Environmental Regulation: Tradable Permit Systems in the United States and CO_2 Taxation in Europe.* Cheltenham: Edward Elgar.

2003. *Political Economy of the European Union: Institutions, Policy and Economic Growth.* Cheltenham: Edward Elgar.

Tietenberg, T. H. 1985. *Emissions Trading: An Exercise in Reforming Pollution Policy.* Washington, DC: Resources for the Future.

2000. *Environmental and Natural Resource Economics.* Reading, MA: Addison-Wesley-Longman Higher Education.

2004. "Tradable permits bibliography" (http://www.colby.edu/personal/thtieten [accessed at April 6, 2004]).

Varming, S., Eriksen, P. B., Grohnheit, P. E., Nielsen, L., Svendsen, G. T., and Vesterdal, M. 2000. *CO_2 permits in Danish and European energy policy.* Risø, R-1184(EN), Roskilde, Denmark: Risø National Laboratory.

11 Greenhouse gas emissions trading in the EU: building the world's largest cap-and-trade scheme

Peter Zapfel

Introduction

Economists regard control of greenhouse gas emissions as a natural application for tradable allowances. While the most important existing cap-and-trade scheme – the Sulfur Allowance Scheme in the United States – is largely based on the notion that location does matter, greenhouse gases are uniformly mixed pollutants at the global scale, i.e. the time and place of the emissions does not matter from an environmental point of view. At the same time it is relatively uncontroversial, although subject to some scientific uncertainty, to fix conversion rates between the different greenhouse gases,[1] thereby enabling the establishment of an emissions trading scheme for all greenhouse gases.

However, the framing of international climate change policy – most importantly in setting targets – is a crucial precondition for the implementation of cap-and-trade allowance schemes. This process has turned out to be very cumbersome so far and has rendered a global company-based greenhouse gas emissions trading scheme a distant objective. While climate change was put on the radar screen as a major environmental problem some two decades ago, the incomplete international institutional governance structure has so far allowed only limited progress. The UN Framework Convention on Climate Change, agreed in 1992, contains only non-binding commitments for the industrialized world. The Kyoto Protocol, agreed in 1997, contains legally binding targets for the same set of countries plus the transition economies in Central and Eastern Europe and some successor countries of the former

The author would like to thank participants in the 10th Symposium of the Egon Sohmen Foundation, and in particular Richard Morgenstern, for comments and discussion on a presentation that served as the background for this chapter. The views expressed in this chapter are those of the author and do not necessarily coincide with those of the European Commission.

Soviet Union. Only eight years after its adoption, has the Kyoto Protocol been ratified by a sufficient number of countries for it to come into force, while the withdrawal of the United States in early 2001 constituted a major setback for international climate diplomacy.

The fact that combating climate change has the character of a global public good has proven a difficult hurdle in the climate policy process. Even ambitious countries and regions have been held back by concerned domestic lobbies fearing negative economic effects of an early-mover attitude of their government and the free-riding of other countries. The debate over whether it is in the interest of a country or individual sector to be an early mover in greenhouse gas emissions control is multi-dimensional and continuing.

As a consequence of this intricate situation, policy-making to date has been largely driven by a preference for two types of measures: soft policy instruments, and measures implemented also or primarily for other reasons. In the first category are, for example, research and development policies and information campaigns. In the latter category a number of measures taken for energy or environmental policy reasons have in some cases resulted in quite substantial reductions of greenhouse gas emissions. Energy efficiency programs and the promotion of renewable energy sources, which gained wide popularity and acceptance in the aftermath of the oil crises of the seventies and eighties, are sound climate policies. In environmental policy the objective to cut sulfur dioxide emissions by switching away from coal to other fuels is an example of policies that make sense from the climate angle.

The critical test from an economic point of view is, however, whether these admittedly sound climate policies would have won the public debate and been undertaken solely for climate policy reasons. A key economic criterion for judging the quality of a policy is the implicit or explicit carbon value. It is evident that the carbon value attributed by society to those policies undertaken also for other reasons is lowered by the societal benefits in terms of other policy objectives.

The establishment of a European greenhouse emissions trading scheme (EU ETS) fills a void as the first almost continent-wide attempt to move beyond purely national policies, which suffer from the overarching global public good and free-rider concerns. As such a scheme will not be introduced into a perfect world, however, it is important not to measure it against the theoretical ideal and the economic textbook template. It rather needs to be seen and judged against the motivation to set the ground and make a first step to a global greenhouse gas emissions trading scheme. Climate change cannot be averted effectively by the action of a single country, or even a continent. The success of the nascent EU ETS will depend, among other factors, on whether it will serve as a catalyst that speeds up the shaping of a widely shared policy.

In this chapter we begin by presenting the underlying rationale and proposed design (of October 2001) of the European Commission for an EU ETS. The debate up to early 2004 in the institutions (the Council of Environment Ministers and the European Parliament), as well as among stakeholders, on adoption and implementation is reviewed in the following section. This is followed by our conclusions.

Rationale and design of the proposed EU ETS

The debate about greenhouse gas emissions trading in the European Union commenced in early 1998, immediately after the Kyoto conference. While tradable allowances as a policy instrument were not well known and understood in Europe at this stage, the Kyoto Protocol put them on the European climate agenda.[2]

In the debate it quickly became clear that international emissions trading is most valuable if conceived for the private sector in the form of a cap-and-trade scheme rather than being restricted to countries, as originally envisaged by some in Article 17 of the Kyoto Protocol. Triggered by the proposed design from the European Commission in October 2001 (European Commission, 2001a), the European Union has taken up the challenge to put an EU-wide company-level cap-and-trade scheme into place. This has implied a deviation from the hesitant line followed by the European Union in the Kyoto conference. One of the main driving forces for this development is the desire to provide European business with a tool for low-cost compliance with the Kyoto commitment, even more so in the wake of the US withdrawal from its Kyoto commitment in March 2001.[3] With this step the European Union has also taken on a trailblazing role in the establishment of an architecture and framework for facilitating the development of the largest cap-and-trade scheme in the world. A functioning scheme will serve as a blueprint for company-based international emissions trading beyond the European continent and as a yardstick for other domestic greenhouse gas emissions trading schemes.

Before turning to the individual elements of the design of the EU ETS it is useful to review the underlying rationale. After the long-standing recommendation by economists for such a scheme, the move from theory to practice entails the need to prove the feasibility of the concept "on the ground." The key rationale of the EU ETS is the recognition that the economic textbook scheme cannot be achieved in one step but serves rather as a medium-term goal in an evolutionary process. The practical challenge lies in selecting the most promising pathway to putting the EU and the wider world on track to a comprehensive and well-functioning ETS. As neither individual member states nor the European Union possess much experience with tradable allowances in environmental policy to date, attempting to achieve too much in the first step carries the risk of failing from excessive ambition. In the trade-off between size and robustness the proposed design aimed for "critical mass" by starting with a scheme that is sufficiently large to make the effort worthwhile but not so large that the implementation challenge proves insurmountable by design.

Economic theory would argue in favor of a broad scheme covering all sectors and greenhouse gases from the start. In recognition of the administrative challenge (for example, in the monitoring of emissions) of such a broad scheme, experts frequently recommend an upstream scheme. Such a scheme does not apply at the point of emissions (as the downstream EU ETS) but at the point where the fossil fuel enters the economy. While such an upstream scheme is practically possible for energy-related CO_2 emissions, it is not clear how process-related CO_2 emissions and the other five Kyoto gases could be fitted into such a scheme. Furthermore, the Kyoto Protocol follows the territoriality principle concerning emissions accounting, i.e. the emissions are attributed to the national inventory of the country where the fuel is combusted, and therefore is not fully compatible with an upstream scheme.

Design elements of the EU ETS

In the following the design elements of the scheme are elaborated.

Timing While the commitments at the country level in the Kyoto Protocol only become effective in 2008 the EU ETS is starting with a three-year "warm-up" phase from 2005 to 2007. The second phase would overlap with the five-year Kyoto commitment period from 2008 to 2012. The introductory phase was proposed to provide European regulators and companies with an opportunity to obtain early experience, and to allow for a certain trial-and-error in order to have a solid scheme in place by 2008. In recognition of the fact that emissions trading is a new challenge for environmental law and policy practice in the EU the "warm-up" phase may turn out to be quite valuable. The absence of a binding emissions constraint at the member state and EU level will allow for more leeway in the first allocation decisions. As allocations are likely to prove controversial because of their distributional nature and the substantial asset value of the created allowances at stake, and may also be administratively cumbersome, learning-by-doing would seem to be useful. In view of the experimental nature some provisions are proposed to differ between the first and second phase. Most important is the reduced penalty rate for each unit of uncovered emissions of €50 in 2005 –07 which is proposed to be increased to €100 in 2008–12 (see under the heading "Enforcement and compliance" for more details).

Participation and coverage   Participation and coverage is a key choice in a cross-border scheme. As already discussed the EU ETS is crafted as a downstream scheme applying at the point of emissions. It foresees a harmonized and consistent participation and coverage across the internal market of five major downstream sectors with typically large stationary emissions sources:

- power and heat generation
- mineral oil refineries
- iron and steel (incl. coke ovens)
- pulp and paper
- building materials (cement, ceramics, and glass).

Capacity thresholds apply in order to prevent the inclusion of small plants; for example, in the power and heat sector, installations with an installed capacity of less than 20 MW would be excluded.

The major advantage of the harmonized and consistent coverage is the fact that a firm subject to the rules of the scheme can be certain that any competitor in the European Union would be subject to the same set of rules and face the same market price for greenhouse gas allowances. While the scheme was originally conceived for a European Union of fifteen member states, its size automatically increased with the enlargement of the European Union which took effect in May 2004, i.e. prior to the start of the EU ETS.

As regards greenhouse gases the EU ETS will encompass only one of the six Kyoto gases at the outset, namely carbon dioxide. This substance, however, accounts for the majority of EU emissions, with a share of some 80 percent, and is the one that is best measurable with the lowest uncertainty range.

With its defined scope – representing the operationalization of the "critical mass" approach – the EU ETS covers a manageable number of close to 12,000 installations, i.e. one-third of EU greenhouse gases and close to half of CO_2 emissions. In order to pave the way for a gradual extension over time to more sectors and to the other greenhouse gases, review clauses have been included that mandate periodic examination.

Initial allocation of allowances   The most important step and at the same time the decision that is likely to spark most political controversy both in design and implementation is the fixing of the overall cap and the initial allocation of allowances. The two main ways to allocate allowances at the outset are free of charge (also called grandfathering) and allocation against payment (or auctioning). The two approaches can obviously be mixed as well.

The EU ETS differs in the two important elements in the initial allocation – the allocation methodology and the actual quantities. While the Directive is based on full harmonization regarding the methodology, it delegates a lot of decisions regarding fixing the overall cap and determining quantities to the member states. Free of charge is proposed as the only admissible way of allocating allowances in the "warm-up" phase. The methodology for the Kyoto period is proposed to be fixed later in the light of the experience with the first allocation process. Instead of providing for detailed provisions of how many allowances should be allocated to individual sectors and plants or even creating a central allocation authority at the EU level the Directive mandates the establishment of a national allocation plan in every member state prior to the actual issuance of allowances. In drawing up such a plan certain criteria had to be observed. The plan had to be submitted to the European Commission and made available to the general public. The European Commission was given the possibility of rejecting such a plan within a three-month period, should the criteria be found to have been violated. In addition it had to scrutinize these plans in respect of EU state aid rules.[4]

While this approach relies both on the soft concept of transparency and peer pressure and on the hard concept of the European Commission as a referee, a certain room for maneuver is preserved and might prove quite valuable to achieve political acceptability in these inherently distributional processes.

Technical infrastructure   The technical infrastructure needed for operating a cap-and-trade scheme comprises the development and maintenance of two information systems: an emissions accounting system to monitor, report, verify, and record emissions at the individual plant level and a registry to track allowance holdings. The EU ETS does provide for these two information systems and includes principles for monitoring and verification. Detailed provisions are proposed to be developed subsequently to the adoption of the Directive.

Enforcement and compliance   A crucial design element for a successful cap-and-trade scheme is sound enforcement and compliance provisions. At the end of each year a plant operator must surrender allowances to cover actual emissions in the year. In the event a plant operator does not surrender a sufficient number of allowances, a member state must apply a dual enforcement approach. The first measure is levying a financial penalty per non-surrendered allowance (i.e. excess tonne of carbon dioxide emitted) of €50 in the "warm-up" phase and €100 thereafter. In order to account for the uncertainty of future allowance prices, the fixed amount would not apply in the event of the market price being above €25 in the first period and €50 in the second. In such a situation the penalty to be levied for excess emissions would be set at double the market price. The possibility of the penalty should serve as a strong incentive for all participants to surrender enough allowances. However, the environmental disadvantage of excess emissions is not offset by the payment of a penalty. Therefore the non-delivered allowances would have to be subtracted from the allocated budget of the plant in the subsequent year. These stringent provisions are designed to make non-compliance the least attractive option, as a plant operator should in practice always find it cheaper to purchase additional allowances to make up a shortfall or take additional on-site measures to cut emissions.

Market organization   The market organization is left broadly to the private sector. There are no restrictions on who may purchase allowances, thereby allowing non-participants in the scheme – ranging from companies who are preparing to enter a market which is covered by the EU ETS to charities and schoolchildren – to purchase and hold allowances.

There are also no provisions on how and where the exchange of allowances may take place. This implies that any form (bilateral transactions between two participating plants, transactions brokered by third parties, and organized secondary spot, option, or future markets) of market exchange is permissible, as long as other existing financial market regulations are respected.

A final element of the market organization is the issue of allowance banking, i.e. carrying forward unused allowances in time. There are no restrictions on banking within the individual trading periods. There are also good reasons for allowing banking from one period to the next as it encourages early reduction efforts and could improve economic efficiency. It is also permissible in the Kyoto Protocol. However, when it comes to banking from the first period, in which no Kyoto commitments yet exist, to the period overlapping with Kyoto, banking will have an influence on the overall budget of a member state. Banked allowances would imply that companies have preferential and guaranteed claims to a share of the country's Kyoto budget. In recognition of the trade-off between encouraging early reduction efforts and the implications for the Kyoto commitment the EU ETS leaves the decision to allow banking, and to what extent, to each member state in the implementation of the Directive. The potential drawback of this approach is that, in the event that only a few member states allow banking, substantial flows of allowances to participants in these member states may be triggered towards the end of 2007.

Linkage with other schemes and project mechanisms (including domestic projects)   As an expression of the objective to pave the way for a broader and deeper scheme over time the EU ETS contains a provision to allow geographical extension. If other countries outside the European Union have a greenhouse gas emissions trading scheme in place, a bilateral agreement could be concluded to allow for the mutual recognition of allowances. This provision could also be used to link with domestic schemes maintained by members of the European Economic Area[5] (Norway, Iceland, and Liechtenstein) and other countries like Canada, New Zealand, and Japan.

Another item on the agenda of the European Commission was the creation of a link with project credits, in particular those emanating from the Kyoto project mechanisms, Joint Implementation (JI) and the Clean Development Mechanism (CDM). In parallel with the adoption of the proposal for the EU ETS the European Commission also tabled a strategy paper (European Commission, 2001b) in which it made its intention known that a link with the Kyoto project mechanisms should be in place as of the start of the EU ETS in 2005.

In addition to Kyoto project credits, linking to credits generated from domestic projects[6] can be considered. Allowing domestic projects is desirable from an economic point of view. The criterion for achieving a given target at least economic cost is that every emitter in a country abates up to the same level of marginal avoidance costs. The EU-wide flexibility allows for the fulfillment of this criterion for all ETS participants, whatever collective target is determined. It is however possible, and in view of information constraints even likely, that the collective target (expressed in the number of allowances created) for the trading population is chosen at too high or too low a level from a macroeconomic perspective. Choosing too low a level would imply that emitters outside the scheme would have to spend more at the margin per tonne avoided. Choosing too high a level would imply that emitters outside the scheme spend less than the market price for allowances. The latter problem could be mitigated by admitting domestic project credits into the EU ETS. However, this would only be a second-best solution, as credit-based approaches have turned out in practice to suffer from high transaction costs. Therefore, not all gains from trade could be reaped by allowing domestic projects, and the extension of the coverage of the scheme would be preferable. Admitting domestic projects is prone to administrative complexity and may result in the double-counting of emission reductions, in particular if credits are constituted from domestic projects implemented in sectors directly (e.g. generation of power from renewable energy) or indirectly (e.g. construction of a new transmission line to reduce power transfer losses, insulation of buildings heated with power) covered by the EU ETS.

One element of linking that has been excluded in the EU ETS is the possibility of plant operators surrendering Kyoto-assigned amount units purchased from governments of other countries.

The debate in the institutions and beyond

The proposal by the European Commission triggered an intense debate in the institutions charged with deciding upon the adoption (the Environment Council and the European Parliament), the member states and many stakeholders and observers in Europe and beyond. This section reflects the debate in early 2004, after the European Parliament and the Environment Ministers found consensus on the final shape of the Directive in mid-2003 and Directive 2003/87/EC[7] entered into force in October 2003. This section focuses on the four issues that sparked most debate in the legislative process. It does not touch on issues of timing, technical infrastructure, and market organization. In these matters, all stakeholders broadly supported the European Commission proposal.

The issue of *participation and coverage* was a core issue in the debate from the very start. Many voices argued for deviations from the proposed approach of a harmonized and consistent coverage of some major downstream sectors. "Voluntary" participation became the most frequent buzzword in the debate. A catalyst for this debate was the implementation in April 2002 of the UK Emissions Trading Scheme based on voluntary participation (see Essex, 2002). A second driver of crucial importance was the concern of member states that existing climate policy instruments at the national level, covering some or all of the proposed sectors, would need to be adapted or could even be rendered obsolete by the introduction of the EU ETS. The "voluntary" header included a number of different positions. The decision to participate could be left to member states, sectors, companies, or individual plants.

Each of these options raised a set of questions. What they all had in common was the loss of the major advantage of the approach proposed by the European Commission – namely, prevention of the risk of distorting competition, as any of the choices would imply that all the competitors in a sector would no longer necessarily be subject to the same rules. Positions also varied regarding the time-period for which such an element should be introduced – i.e. in the "warm-up" phase only or beyond.

The demand for voluntary participation materialized in both the European Parliament and the Environment Council introducing articles with similar content to provide for temporary exclusion. The commonalities were that the opt-out would be conditional, limited to the "warm-up" phase, and subject to approval by the European Commission upon application by a member state. The conditions for an opt-out would be the application of national policies of the same environmental quality to excluded installations, the compliance with monitoring, reporting, and verification obligations for each plant, and the introduction of equivalent financial penalties in the event the alternative policies were not successful. In the end, Article 27, providing for an installation-specific opt-out, was agreed.

Demands for deviating from the harmonized list of the proposed EU ETS were also made in the direction of allowing for the inclusion of more sectors (harmonized or unilateral) and other greenhouse gases. A non-harmonized extension of the coverage carries the same drawbacks as an opt-out provision regarding distortions of competition. Although this debate was less passionate than the one about opt-outs, both the Environment Council and the European Parliament included an opt-in provision. Beyond this the European Parliament wanted an extension of the harmonized coverage to the chemical and aluminum sectors from the outset. Furthermore, it demanded to provide member states with the possibility of a unilateral extension for individual plants or whole sectors as of 2005. Finally, it asked to include an article determining that other greenhouse gases in the covered sectors should be automatically covered as soon as data quality is satisfactory and monitoring methods are available. The Environment Council, on the other hand, had included in its common position an article for unilateral extension covering both sectors and gases and being available as of 2008. Furthermore, it favored a very limited unilateral extension clause as of 2005 by giving member states the choice to include installations in the harmonized sectors that would be below the capacity thresholds. In the end, Article 24, providing a limited opt-in below capacity thresholds as of 2005 and a much wider opt-in for other sectors and gases as of 2008, was agreed.

The second major bone of contention in the debate turned out to be issues of *initial allocation* of emission allowances. Opinions among stakeholders differed strongly. The only issue that found broad support was the harmonization of the methodology across member states. Businesses and industrial associations were expectedly very much in favor of allocations free of charge and wanted to have this already laid down for the second period, too. Other stakeholders, including environmental organizations and some member states (e.g. those with existing carbon or energy taxes), expressed an interest in, and fielded demands for, at least part-auctioning. Positions diverged also on when the methodology for the second period should be fixed, with some supporting the proposal by the European Commission to capitalize on the experience from the first allocations and decide at a later stage, while others were in favor of fixing the methodology for the second period in the Directive in order to create more certainty for business.

In the end both the Environment Council and the European Parliament agreed to fix the methodology for the second period upfront. The positions on the preferred methodology differed however. The European Parliament supported a hybrid approach in both periods with 85 percent allocated free of charge and 15 percent auctioned. The Environment Council, on the other hand, was in favor of free-of-charge allocation in the first period and at least 90 percent free of charge in the second period. In the end the full harmonization of the methodology was lost. Article 10 foresees a minimum of 95 percent free of charge in the first period and a minimum of 90 percent free of charge in the second period. This may lead to limited differences among member states, depending on their choices.

The wide delegation of decisions concerning quantities allocated to member states also sparked much debate. Several Member States and industry associations did not feel at ease with this solution and asked for more detail in terms of the criteria to be followed in drawing up national allocation plans. Among the items requiring further detail were the treatment of early action, the determination and possible harmonization of the base year/period, the treatment of newcomers and plant closures, the application of sector-specific benchmarks, and increased transparency by listing plants and allocated quantities. Some member states expressed a preference for non-binding guidelines for allocation as a starting point to facilitate work on the national allocation plan. In the end Council and Parliament introduced a number of changes and additions to Annex III and mandated the Commission to produce guidance on the implementation of the eleven common allocation criteria.

The debate about further detail and more harmonization regarding allocated quantities took place against the background of both a constraint and an uncertainty. The constraint on achieving a perfect degree of harmonization of allocated quantities is imposed by the EU burden-sharing agreement foreseeing a differentiation of the Kyoto targets among member states. Harmonization would imply interference in national decisions on how to share out the burden between sectors participating in the EU ETS and those outside.

The uncertainty lies in not knowing how stringent the Commission will be in exercising its competence when it comes to reviewing national allocation plans for their compatibility with state aid policy and compliance with the criteria laid down in the Directive. The European Parliament was very sensitive to this concern and feared a deterioration of environmental quality, in particular in the phase before 2008, when member states would not yet be subject to economy-wide national limits under the Kyoto Protocol. For this reason it had adopted a provision, which did not find acceptance in Council, that would limit the total number of allowances a member state could create and allocate in the "warm-up" phase.

Issues of *enforcement and compliance* are worth mentioning not because of the lively debate on them but rather for its absence. The EU ETS Directive would be the first piece of EU environmental legislation mandating a member state to impose financial sanctions on companies. Remarkably this approach was widely shared and opposing voices were few. Debate centered around the implication of an opt-out provision for the level of sanctions. In view of an expectation of reduced market liquidity and a perceived higher likelihood of allowance supply shortage due to opt-outs, demands were made to lower the level of the sanction or to waive the requirement to make up shortfalls in the subsequent years. The changes introduced were quite limited. The double market price provision concerning the level of the sanctions was deleted and the sanction in the "warm-up" phase was lowered to €40. In addition, a *force majeure* clause – applicable in the "warm-up" period only – was inserted that would allow a member state to create and allocate additional but non-transferable allowances in *force majeure* circumstances. Application of this provision would be subject to European Commission approval.

Linkage issues also caused intense lobbying and lively debate. Most of it was directed to the project mechanisms rather than the provision to link to other domestic trading schemes via a bilateral agreement. Businesses and an increasing number of member states expressed a keen interest in a simple and early link to the Kyoto mechanisms, while environmental organizations generally expressed a hesitant view on this. The adopted Directive referred to linking as desirable and important to achieve the goals of reducing emissions and increasing cost effectiveness.[8] A change related to the linkage with other domestic schemes was introduced so that such a link may only be considered for Annex B countries that have ratified the Kyoto Protocol.

Conclusions

After the speedy decision-making in the institutions the EU ETS has quickly become more visible on the political radar screen and it is now being implemented. This stage of the process offers the opportunity to draw early lessons and look to the challenges ahead.

The early debate in the European Union – in particular, although not exclusively, prior to the initiation of the legislative proposal in October 2001 – was characterized by the necessity to overcome many fallacies but also by speedy learning among stakeholders. As expected, it turned out that the policy debate was prone to special-interest lobbies that perceived themselves as the short-term losers of climate policy. An interesting facet was that several stakeholders opposed the instrument of tradable allowances in a "proxy war" against climate policy and the Kyoto targets. This may be explained by the fact that the broad societal consensus in Europe – as demonstrated by the overwhelming parliamentary majorities in the ratification decisions in early 2002 – explicitly ruled out opposing the Kyoto Protocol itself.

Besides the opposition to the EU ETS on the grounds of general opposition to a climate policy that results in a positive and robust carbon value, a second major point of criticism mounted against the scheme as proposed was its narrow focus, i.e. the coverage of only about a third of total EU greenhouse gas emissions. This criticism stems from the yardstick of the idealized scheme as portrayed in economic textbooks. In practice the proposed size would imply the largest cap-and-trade scheme in the world to date. The implementation challenge of such a continent-wide instrument is substantial. Furthermore, the coverage of one-third may result in an unexpected effect. While there is no *prima facie* guarantee that abatement in the rest of the economy will be anywhere close to the carbon value as revealed in the EU ETS, the transparent and continent-wide price signal in part of the economy may have an important catalytic effect on policies in the non-covered sectors of the economy. It can be expected that both action and inaction in those other sectors will have to be justified in the future, with the market price for EU allowances as a benchmark.

In particular, in sectors where only light measures are intended to be taken and the implicit carbon value is lower than the allowance price, pressure may arise to take cheap measures and sell them for a profit into the allowance market or be rewarded in any other way possible. From this perspective, attaining by means of an ETS a broadly visible price signal for part of the economy may pave a quicker way to the vision of the economist – an economy-wide scheme.

While the decision-making process in the institutions resulted in a certain move away from the proposal by the European Commission on issues of participation and coverage, the main elements for a successful scheme were retained. The legislative process gives reason for optimism that the scheme emerging may eventually fulfill the catalytic role and lead to a deeper and broader scheme over time.

At the time of adoption of the Directive the focus turned to implementation issues. A first task is the development of the infrastructure for emissions monitoring and allowance registries, which is technically cumbersome and laborious but not politically difficult. Another immediate task is the preparation of the national allocation plans in all member states.[9] This task will obviously turn out to be contentious and tedious. The first allocation process may to a certain extent also be a learning process for both governments and businesses. And an impartial referee will judge the quality of the allocation process – the allowance market. The early level of the market price will serve as a judgement of how "good" the allocation decisions have been. Another major task for member states will be to examine the interaction of the EU ETS with existing instruments, and the potential adaptation of those instruments. This is a task that naturally has to be delegated to the member states as most of these measures are ones taken at national rather than EU level so that the adaptation can only take place at national level.

A lot will be learned and possibly some unexpected lessons may emerge as Europe sets out on the road to the largest cap-and-trade scheme in the world.

Notes

1 While carbon dioxide (CO_2) is the major man-made greenhouse gas, the Kyoto Protocol also covers methane (CH_4), nitrous oxide (N_2O), hydrofluorocarbons (HFCs), perfluorocarbons (PFCs) and sulfur hexafluoride (SF_6). The conversion rates are called global warming equivalents and allow one to express the emissions of all other greenhouse gases as units of carbon dioxide equivalent.

2 A recounting of the debate can be found in Zapfel and Vainio (2002).

3 In this context, see also Christiansen and Wettestad (2003).
4 For information about state aid policy, which is based on Articles 87 and 88 of the Treaty, consult http://europa.eu.int/comm/competition/index_en.html and, in particular, http://europa.eu.int/comm/competition/state_aid/others/vademecum/vademecum_en.pdf.
5 Alternatively, EEA members have the option to accept and implement the Directive as adopted by the EU.
6 The Kyoto project mechanisms always involve actors from two different countries.
7 See *Official Journal of the European Union*, L 275 (October 23, 2003):32–46
8 In July 2003 the Commission tabled a proposal to amend Directive 2003/87/EC to allow for linking of JI and CDM credits (European Commission, 2003a). This proposal was adopted with changes in April 2004.
9 See European Commission (2003b) for guidance on the implementation of the eleven common allocation criteria.

References

Christiansen, A. C., and Wettestad, J. 2003. "The EU as a frontrunner on greenhouse gas emissions trading: how did it happen and will the EU succeed?" *Climate Policy* 3: 3–18.
Essex, B. 2002. "Linking the UK and EU emissions trading schemes: an assessment of the problems and solutions." Imperial College of Science, Technology and Medicine, September.
European Commission 2001a. "Proposal for a Directive for greenhouse gas emissions trading within the European Community." COM (2001)581.
  2001b. "Communication on the implementation of the first phase of the European Climate Change Programme." COM (2001)580.
  2003a. "Proposal for a Directive amending the Directive establishing a scheme for greenhouse gas emission allowance trading within the Community, in respect of the Kyoto Protocol's project mechanisms." COM (2003)403.
  2003b. "Guidance to assist member states in the implementation of the criteria listed in Annex III to Directive 2003/87/EC and on the circumstances under which force majeure is demonstrated." COM (2003)830.
Zapfel, P., and Vainio, M. 2002. "Pathways to European greenhouse gas emissions trading: history and misconceptions." Nota di Lavoro 85–2002, FEEM, Venice.

12 Legal aspects of the European Emissions Trading Scheme

Michael Rodi

In October 2003, the Directive "establishing a scheme for greenhouse gas emission allowance trading within the Community" came into force.[1] After long debates, especially among economists,[2] this represents a first step towards the implementation of a new instrument of environmental policy.[3] Following the examples of member states such as Denmark, the Netherlands, and the United Kingdom, which had already introduced domestic trading schemes,[4] emissions trading will form one of the instruments of European climate policy.

The Directive establishes a specific legal framework for emissions trading. This will lead to a fundamental change in perspective in the debate, from the theoretical advantages and disadvantages of this environmental policy instrument toward concrete and practical questions of implementation and application.

This chapter discusses the legal framework set up by European or national law for the Directive and its implementation in the domestic legal systems of the member states. A comprehensive survey of the legal questions is beyond the scope of this chapter. In the interest of brevity, it focuses on four major issues:

- the leeway of European law-making bodies in relation to the national legislator;
- compatibility of the emissions trading system with public international law, especially in the field of trade and climate protection;
- legal limitations and guiding principles affecting the design of the emissions trading system (especially higher-ranking law); and
- compatibility with other environmental policy instruments.

The leeway of the European legislator

The legality of the European emissions trading scheme depends on whether the Directive exceeds the leeway afforded to the European legislator under Community law. This "internal" law has to be distinguished from the external aspect – the European Community's competence to sign international treaties in the field of climate change policies, which will not be analyzed here. (Both the EC and the member states are contracting parties to the Climate Change Convention and the Kyoto Protocol; these types of "mixed treaties" are, as a rule, used in cases of disputed overlapping jurisdictions.)[5]

Community jurisdiction to establish emissions trading

Legal Basis   To pass the Directive, the Community needs an explicit competence under the EC Treaty (Art. 5 I EC).[6] In its introductory preamble, the Directive itself refers to the general authority of the Council in the field of environmental policy (Art. 175 I EC).

Assuming this view is correct, some important implications follow:

- European rules on emissions trading would not require the unanimous approval of the Council. Tax provisions, in contrast, do require unanimity, whether they are for environmental protection (Art. 175 II EC) or for harmonization (Art. 95 II EC). For that reason, ambitious proposals of the Commission for harmonized energy taxation have generally failed during the last decade (see Krämer, 2000, p. 228); recent attempts at minimum harmonization (see Council Directive 2003) are disappointing in the light of climate change policy. This may explain why the Commission focused enthusiastically on emissions trading as a new policy instrument.
- Choosing this legal basis (and not Art. 95 EC) indicates that the emissions trading system is primarily intended to promote environmental protection; providing a functioning internal market and avoiding restraints on competition can be seen as secondary objectives. Moreover, member states are allowed to take additional measures for environmental protection (Art. 176 EC).

This interpretation of the legal basis held by the Commission and the European legislator is correct (and shared by most observers).

- Art. 175 EC, linking legislative competence to the objectives of environmental protection in Art. 174 EC, is applicable. It is the purpose of the Directive to protect the global climate by reducing the emission of greenhouse gases on the basis of the Kyoto process. Given the interdependence of greenhouse gases and climate change (global warming), this measure serves the purpose of "preserving, protecting and improving the quality of the environment" (Art. 174 I EC).[7]

- Choosing Art. 175 EC (and not Art. 95 EC) as a legal basis is in line with the practice confirmed by the judiciary; in plant-related regulations, as a rule, a preponderance of general environmental protection is assumed.[8]
- Some authors refer to Art. 175 II EC and argue that a Directive on greenhouse gas emissions trading requires an unanimous Council decision. According to them, such a system significantly affects the ability of member states to choose energy sources and the general structure of their energy supply (Spieth, 2002, pp. 34 et seq.). This view is not convincing: an emissions trading system for CO_2 might well disadvantage coal as an energy source, but that would also be the case with other environmental protection measures to limit greenhouse gas emissions. Moreover, it is not the primary intention of the Directive to regulate the general structure of the energy supply in member states

Principle of Subsidiarity   According to the principle of subsidiarity (Art. 5 II EC), measures at the level of the member states have priority. A Community Directive may be enacted only if the goals of a greenhouse gas emissions trading system (1) cannot be sufficiently achieved by member states, and (2) because of the scale of effects of the proposed action, can be better achieved by the Community. The European legislator believes that it has met these criteria (see consideration 30 of the Directive; Commission 2001, no. 23 of the Explanatory Memorandum). Effective climate change policy requires supraregional action, and the instrument of emissions trading requires markets big enough to function. Moreover, the Directive gives considerable regulatory leeway to member states, perhaps enough to endanger gains from trading. This would be true for clauses that let member states decide on the allocation of allowances or choose which sectors of industry should participate.

The new Directive: too much or too little?

The final directive was preceded by an intense discussion about how detailed the legal framework for greenhouse gas emissions trading should be (on that issue, see Green Paper 2000, no. 6.2). Considerations of both environmental protection and competitiveness suggest comprehensive and compulsory provisions in the form of an EC regulation (which has direct legal force without national implementation).[9] Some member states (including Denmark, Germany, and the Netherlands) favored independent national measures to meet the climate change objectives. In this controversy, the Commission adopted a middle course and followed the path of a Directive that builds a framework to be completed by the member states. Within the Directive, the level of regulatory specificity varies considerably.

The Directive embodies some fundamental elements that give no leeway to the member states:

- The trading scheme involves an (obligatory) permit for greenhouse gas emissions (Art. 4–8).
- Participating firms belong to certain defined energy-producing or energy-intensive sectors (Art. 4 and Annex I).
- The greenhouse gases whose emissions are capped (Art. 2 I and Annex II) will begin with CO_2.
- The trading system is based on plant permits; it is a cap-and-trade model involving large-scale fixed or immobile sources; but in a departure from the original Commission proposal, member states may now extend the trading system to smaller or other emission sources according to Art. 24.
- Certificates will almost all be distributed free of charge ("grandfathered"); after intense debates in the legislative process, up to 5 percent (in the first trading period from 2005) or 10 percent (in the second trading period from 2008) may be auctioned (Art. 10).
- Allowances shall be freely tradable all over Europe (Art. 12 I).
- Allowances will be valid during the entire trading period of several years (Art. 13 I), but by April 30 of each year, a certain amount of allowances have to be surrendered and subsequently cancelled, corresponding to the amount of greenhouse gases emitted during the preceding year (Art. 12 III).
- The issue, holding, transfer, and cancellation of allowances will be recorded in consolidated national registries (Art. 19 I) on the base of a standardized electronic database to be fixed by an EC regulation (Art. 19 III); automated checks by a central administrator through an independent transactions log are anticipated (Art. 20).
- The types and extent of penalties will be fixed and binding (Art. 16).

The framework merely provides a number of general provisions in several areas which will be of crucial importance for the success of the program. This is especially true for the procedure through which allowances will be allocated and traded. Art. 9 II and Annex III of the Directive provide only that a national allocation plan be developed and submitted to the Commission, which may reject it after consultations with the committee instituted pursuant to Art. 8 of the Council

Decision on a monitoring mechanism for greenhouse gases (Council Decision 1993). The relevant criteria (apart from the state aid provisions) are vague: member states must provide an adequate quantity of allowances (in line with international obligations to reduce greenhouse gases), account for new entrants, and give credit to early action. Further details are left open (e.g. the distribution of allowances among specific sectors of industry), and only the general goal of a non-discriminatory allocation is mentioned.

The Directive is equally vague about the trading system, even though a functioning market is essential to the success of the system. Aside from establishing holding and transfer registries (Art. 19), it provides only that the transfer between entities within the Community be ensured (Art. 12 I). The details of how the market will be organized – public auctions, participation of stock exchanges, brokers – and how certificates can be traded are left unspecified.[10]

Compatibility with public international law

The use of emissions trading schemes for climate protection is also a subject of international discussion. There, at least for the moment, we have only a small number of rules relevant to national or regional emissions trading. Our consideration of possible conflicts between the future EC emissions trading scheme and international law (both trade law and climate change law) can therefore be short.

World trade law (GATT/WTO)

There are only marginal connections between general world trade law and the planned emissions trading scheme, and thus few possible points of conflict.[11] In theory, there might be a possibility of tensions arising with the General Agreement on Tariffs and Trade (GATT) and the General Agreement on Trade in Services (GATS) if EU allowances became a requirement for the importation, sale, or distribution of energy products and services in the European Union.[12] In the view of most experts, however, emissions allowances are neither products nor services in the sense of the World Trade Organization (WTO) Treaty and are therefore not covered by that regime.[13]

Moreover, as a rule, the implementation of an emissions trading system does not imply subsidies or state aid in the sense of the Agreement on Subsidies and Countervailing Measures 1994 (Wolfrum, 2001, pp. 199 et seq.). Even if emissions allowances are distributed freely, they do not confer any specific advantage; the allocation merely reflects what has been previously defined by command-and-control laws. To the extent that standards are exceeded, the resulting advantage is nullified by the obligation to buy allowances.

The Climate Change Convention and the Kyoto Protocol

In Recitals 3 and 4 of its preamble, the Directive explicitly refers to the European Union's obligations to reduce greenhouse gas emissions in accordance with the Climate Change Convention and the Kyoto Protocol. The instrument of emissions trading is a suitable instrument to meet these obligations, and, moreover, it is suggested and more or less required by the international climate change regime (Art. 17 sent. 2 of the Kyoto Protocol, for instance, mentions international emissions trading).

This has changed to a certain extent with the Linking Directive (Council Directive 2004), which lays down requirements and conditions for participation in the project-based mechanisms of the Kyoto Protocol (Joint Implementation and the Clean Development Mechanism).

Burden-sharing agreement

The European Union and its member states will be obliged by the Kyoto Protocol to reduce greenhouse gas emissions by 8 percent compared with their 1990 levels.[14] The contracting parties mentioned in Annex I may meet their obligations in a joint effort, and thus individual states may contribute differentially (Art. 4 I). This is what the European Union has done in its Council decision approving the Kyoto Protocol (Council Decision 2002). On that basis, the obligations of the member states differ, as some of them are even allowed to increase their greenhouse gas emissions.[15]

Legal constraints on the design of emissions trading schemes

In designing an emissions trading scheme, neither the European legislator drafting a Directive nor the national legislator implementing it into the national legal system can operate without constraints. Both must respect the standards of primary European law (i.e. the establishing treaties, including general legal principles such as fundamental rights,[16] as well as, in the future, a possible constitution for Europe).[17] Moreover, the national legislator must respect national constitutional law and secondary European law, which prevails over national law.

Within this legal framework, however, very different designs for an emissions trading system are conceivable. Certain design aspects have special potential for legal conflicts.

Allocation of emissions allowances

The question of how to allocate emissions allowances concerns several legal spheres. Decisions made at this stage will determine the environmental effectiveness of the instrument. The standard has to respect the material requirements which constitutional law and European law impose on environmental law. These decisions are also highly sensitive because they affect fundamental property rights and the ability of new firms to compete. The allocation decision can create problems of equal treatment on several levels – between firms obliged to participate in the scheme and those outside it, between existing plants and new market entrants, and between polluting firms and those that have taken early action in environmental protection. Finally, the allocation of allowances interferes with competition, especially in activities across state borders.

Despite the significance of these problems, the Directive refrains from setting far-reaching harmonized standards. It grandfathers the allocation of free certificates to the extent of at least 95 percent for the period 2005–2007 (and at least 90 percent from 2008 onwards), contains only vague criteria for national allocation plans, and restricts the ability of the Commission to control them. According to the Directive (Art. 9 I 3), the Commission has developed guidance on the implementation of the criteria (Commission, 2004); this combination of abstract criteria and more specific guidelines has been a success story in the field of state-aid control (Rodi, 2000a, pp. 177 et seq.). But it may be doubted whether this will prevent market distortions and avoid infringements of basic rights.

The leeway of the legislator in setting up the allocation plan is probably most effectively limited by the principle of equal treatment: the design must be systematic and fair. Compared with that, other legal limits are of secondary relevance.[18]

Certainly, the freedom of property protects existing plants with regard to the substance of property; but it also protects them with regard to their use according to prior conditions. Nevertheless, the legislator taking environmental protection measures is rather free in determining the content and limits of property positions; in the end, he or she is bound primarily by the principle of proportionality, requiring a test of necessity, appropriateness, and adequacy. Very few observers question the appropriateness of the emissions trading system as such, by rejecting the need for climate protection measures; equally few challenge its necessity, by arguing that voluntary agreements conflict less with individual rights (Rengeling, 2000, p. 1730). Such objections can be dismissed, at least as legal arguments, as an overinterpretation of fundamental rights (Epiney, 2001, pp. 233 et seq.). The property right does not protect a firm against new financial burdens, at least as long as its economic situation is not fundamentally compromised. Taking into account that, as a rule, allowances will be grandfathered, it is not likely that this benchmark will be reached. The property right does not require the credits to be free.

Firms entering the market can claim (equal) freedom of occupation, and their market access must not be blocked. Thus, it would be problematic to direct them to an allowances market for the certificates they need to operate. If a number of certificates are held back each year, however, they can be distributed at reasonable prices (and not necessarily free of cost). Because new entrants are not protected by the property right, their situation is more like that of existing plants that are expanding production. And unlike established firms, they are not endangered by "stranded assets" (investments made obsolete by policy changes) (Commission, 2004, no. 56; Green Paper, 2000, no. 7.3; for an interesting solution in the US Clean Air Act 1990, see Rehbinder, 2001, p. 237).

The Directive requires that national allocation plans not only accommodate new entrants (Annex III, no. 6), but also take into account environmental protection measures already carried out ("early action") (no. 7). To distribute allowances on the basis of historic emissions alone would not differentiate such firms to the extent required by the equal treatment provision. Such problems could be avoided if allocation were related to the emissions standards of the permit or to (input- or output-related) benchmarks.

Determining which sectors must participate in the emissions trading system raises specific problems of equal treatment. Still, the present approach – to restrict participation to fixed industrial sources of emissions (excluding motor vehicles and private households) and to medium and large energy-intensive firms – can be justified (Epiney, 2001, pp. 239 et seq.; Giesberts and Hilf, 2002, pp. 130 et seq.).

The system of allocation affects competition among enterprises. But the freedom of competition for private business is, at least in Germany, not protected by a special fundamental right; its protection derives from a combination of economic freedoms. Special problems related to transnational competition are treated below.

The functioning of the allowance market

Because the implementation of emissions trading interferes, as a rule, with fundamental rights, the system can be justified only with a functioning emissions trading market; this is not only an economic, but also a legal, precondition.

A basic prerequisite of a functioning market is that certificates can be bought and sold in the first place. The national legal systems will have to establish the legal framework for such transactions (e.g. the question of good-faith acquisition).[19]

Furthermore, the market organization has to be regulated. Here, the Directive leaves considerable leeway for innovative solutions, including the participation of private institutions like stock exchanges or brokers (Commission 2001, Explanatory Memorandum no. 21).

Functioning markets require liquidity and transparency. In its comments, the Commission has always paid special attention to questions of transparency (see Commission 2001, Explanatory Memorandum no. 18). Providing market liquidity requires general measures to prevent market participants from abusing market power; in this respect, member states have to check whether general competition law is sufficient or has to be amended in accordance with the special requirements of emissions trading.

Effective monitoring, reporting, and verification

Strict compliance and enforcement provisions and an effective system for compiling data form a second important pillar of effective allowances trading.

The Commission realized this from the beginning (Green Paper, 2000, no. 9.1). Referring to positive experiences in the SO_2 emissions trading system of the United States, the Directive contains strict harmonized provisions, including sanctions such as penalties or publication of the names of firms violating their obligations (Art. 16), the system of registries (Art. 19 et seq.), and the monitoring and reporting of emissions (Art. 14). Moreover, the Commission has adopted guidelines for monitoring and reporting based on the principles of Annex IV (Art. 14 I) (Commission Decision 2004a). Although the effectiveness of the control and sanction system will depend on many factors, the proposed system promises to be sufficiently effective.

Two major legal problems have to be mentioned. The first is the question of whether the Community has jurisdiction to create such far-reaching and detailed regulations. The suggested system of control and sanctions, including the possibility of Community organs adopting detailed guidelines, may be considered necessary and adequate given the importance of this mechanism for achieving the environmental effects of the emissions trading system. That applies to the monitoring procedure as well as the guidelines for monitoring and reporting, and the registration system managed by a central administrator (Art. 20). Administration remains in the hands of member states, however, and beyond these specific measures, the Commission's influence is restricted to the general system of surveillance according to Art. 211, 226 EC, which is rather inflexible and blunt.

The second legal problem is the question of whether the Commission would infringe on the fundamental rights of enterprises, especially in the field of data protection. Even on the basis of the German understanding of fundamental rights, which champions the protection of data and business secrets, the envisioned system of surveillance is basically unproblematic. Firms do not require as much data protection as private individuals (apart from the economically relevant area of business secrets); legally, this derives from the fact that the use of property is bound to general interests of public welfare. Here again, systematic control, including access to data, is necessary to realize the objectives of environmental protection.

Effects on the Common Market

From an economic perspective, it is understood that the design of national emissions trading systems may have severe consequences for international competition and the functioning of the Common Market. The Commission has focused on this problem from the beginning (see Green Paper 2000, no. 2, 5.2. and 9.3.). Specific legal guidelines have to be derived from the general anti-discrimination clause, and specifically from the right of establishment (Art. 43 EC) and the system of state-aid control (Art. 87et sqq. EC).

The right of establishment would be infringed if a business start-up became considerably hampered by the regulations on emissions trading. Whether this is the case depends on the details. In a very general way, the Directive states in Art. 12 I that member states shall ensure that allowances may be freely transferred between persons within the Community. If this is achieved, there is no violation of the freedom of establishment (on this issue, see Commission 2004, no. 52; Peeters, 2003, pp. 86 et seq.).

Beyond that, international competition could be endangered by an identity of interests between member states and "their" enterprises if, for example, allowances were handed out too generously or control activities were lax. Here the Commission is relying on the general toolbox of state-aid control (Art. 87 et sqq. EC), since the described behavior could be considered state aids (on this issue, see Commission 2001, Explanatory Memorandum no. 12 and Art. 11 III). Those rules are unlikely to apply, however, given that the national allocation plans will only contain elements of state aid in the most exceptional of cases. The European Court of Justice recently specified the concept of state aid (ECJ, case 379/98 of March 13, 2001). It referred only to those measures adopted by the state which have negative effects on the state budget. This criterion will be met by national allocation plans only in exceptional circumstances, as grandfathering is the regular allocation method. Thus it will not even be possible to perceive the allocation as a waiver of state income.

Compatibility with environmental policy instruments

A compulsory, Community-wide emissions trading system will not be the member states' first environmental policy measure. This new instrument will join direct or indirect regulations with identical or similar objectives, such as plant-related command-and-control laws, energy taxes, voluntary agreements, mechanisms to promote renewable energy, or even existing emissions trading systems. How this range of instruments can be made mutually consistent can be approached at two levels. This chapter will focus on contradictions with existing law, *de lege lata*, and how these might be reconciled, *de lege ferenda*. The second question, of how a combination of instruments can be designed for optimal effect,[20] is beyond the scope of this chapter.

Relationship to plant-related law

There is considerable potential for conflicts between the adopted emissions trading scheme and plant-related emissions control law (as discussed in Green Paper 2000, no. 8.1). Most observers agree that the climate is protected by the Integrated Pollution Prevention and Control (IPPC) Directive (Council Directive 1996), which in Consideration 8 aims at a comprehensive protection of the entire environment, especially in relation to transboundary air pollution (Art. 9 IV and 17, IPPC Directive) (Peeters, 2003, p. 87). German national law, for instance, is even more specific in this regard, as the "atmosphere" and the "climate" are expressly mentioned as protected goods.

The Commission recognized this problem early on (see, *inter alia*, Commission 2001; Non-Paper 2002). Art. 26 of the Directive therefore provides that a permit issued under the IPPC Directive shall not include an emissions limit value for direct emissions of gases falling within the scope of the emissions trading system, unless it is necessary to ensure that no significant local pollution is caused. Still, the compatibility of the emissions trading Directive and existing emissions control law remains problematic regarding energy efficiency requirements. The initial Directive Proposal of the Commission expressly stated that it would apply without prejudice to any requirements pursuant to the IPPC Directive that relate to energy efficiency. A controversy arose on that issue and some authors argued that, as a consequence, the IPPC Directive needed to be amended, e.g. by differentiating energy efficiency requirements for enterprises participating in emissions trading (Spieth, 2002, pp. 56 et seq.). The Commission argued that the general standard of energy efficiency set up in the IPPC had to be regarded as the minimum requirement for energy and heat consumption: the "baseline" or "bottom line" (see Commission 2001, Explanatory Memorandum no. 10; Non-Paper 2002). Thus it is possible to avoid a conflict between emissions trading and emissions control law by prescribing modified and graduated energy efficiency standards, as is the case, for example, in the United Kingdom (DEFRA, 2001, pp. 38 et seq.). The same is true for France, where the duty to consider energy efficiency is not a strict and binding individual obligation.[21] German emissions control law is more problematic, since it requires plant operators to use energy efficiently and economically (§ 5 I no. 4 BImSchG); this considerably narrows the scope for emissions trading and could endanger the liquidity of the market for emissions allowances. Under the version of the Directive recently adopted, however, Art. 26 leaves it to the member states to choose not to impose requirements relating to energy efficiency in respect of combustion units or other units emitting carbon dioxide on the site. Specific problems are caused by so-called coupled emissions. The activities addressed by the Directive (Annex I) can result in changes to the emissions of other regulated pollutants (SO_2, NO_X, particulates), which are not subject to emissions trading (see Council Directive 1996, Annex III). The IPPC Directive and national emissions control laws remain applicable despite a firm's participation in emissions trading. Thus, limitations on coupled emissions further restrict the flexibility for trading in CO_2 emissions allowances.[22] The combined application of both systems seems necessary even if it creates efficiency problems for emissions trading. Because of provisions in environmental law (as derived from European law and national constitutional law), "hot spots" of dangerous gases have to be avoided. The US experience shows that emissions trading can also work under these circumstances.[23]

Relationship to energy taxes

No less problematic is the relationship between greenhouse gas emissions trading and environmental taxes implemented as part of climate protection programs, such as the UK "climate change levy" (Richardson and Chanwai, 2003, pp. 39 et sqq. Varma, 2003, pp. 51 et sqq.), and the German ecotax reform (electricity tax and mineral oil tax, both with periodic increases) (see Commission 2001, Explanatory Memorandum no. 7).

Basically, the Commission has been right in considering emissions trading and energy taxes as complementary instruments (Green Paper 2000, no. 8.3). Certainly, the application of both instruments may result in an undesired double burden and thus cause market distortions.[24] Some observers therefore argue that firms taking part in emissions trading should be exempted from energy taxes;[25] another possibility could be to apply already existing tax reliefs for (energy-intense or manufacturing) industries to plants taking part in emissions trading. According to the Commission, it would be "appropriate to take into account the level of taxation that pursues the same objectives, without prejudice to the application of Articles 87 and 88 of the Treaty" (Commission 2001, Explanatory Memorandum no. 7). At least, as the Green Paper suggests, energy taxes could target small and mobile emissions sources and emissions from heating for industrial and commercial buildings, because they are not exposed to the same pressures of international competition (Green Paper 2000, no. 8.3).

For several reasons, the effects of a combination of emissions trading and energy taxes are difficult to untangle.

- The effective costs of emissions trading can be calculated only on the basis of a specific design including the national allocation plan; it is possible, at least, that emissions trading may only make existing burdens more flexible (and tradable), without changing them in substance.
- The financial burdens caused by energy taxes are not clear from an economic point of view; indirect taxes by definition are costs that can be shifted to consumers.
- Tax relief for an industry subject to energy taxes may not necessarily constitute illegal state aid; it could be argued that they are necessary measures to guarantee equal competition with states that have not imposed energy taxes.

The rather complicated relationship between emissions trading and energy taxes demonstrates once again what a challenge it is to develop a rational combination of instruments in the field of climate change policy and energy use. Shortcomings in this regard have, as a rule, no legal consequences. Aside from the issue of state aid, there is only the rather abstract and imprecise legal standard of equal treatment according to European and national law.

Relationship to voluntary agreements

The Commission basically favors voluntary agreements as a policy tool, especially in climate protection and energy efficiency (Green paper 2000, no. 8.2; Commission 2000, p. 11). Germany has some experience in using voluntary measures as instruments of environmental policy, such as the agreement of German industry and German government regarding global climate protection (Voluntary Agreement 2000; for commentary, see BMU 2000; Michaelowa, 2003, p. 35), under which all six greenhouse gases of the Kyoto Protocol will be reduced by 35 percent by 2012 compared to their 1990 levels, and by 28 percent by 2005 (Voluntary Agreement 2000, no. I). The German government has agreed not to impose energy audits and further command-and-control-measures as long as these targets are met (Voluntary Agreement, 2000, no. II). Some observers believe the Directive is incompatible with German industry's voluntary agreement (Working Group 2002, pp. 19 et seq.): They argue that the voluntary agreement creates *relative* obligations to reduce emissions, whereas emissions trading is based on *absolute* targets (Rehbinder and Schmalholz, 2002, p. 9). The additional burden caused by emissions trading, they continue, is neither useful nor necessary, and the voluntary agreement infringes less on individual rights; moreover, the EU violates the principle of good faith by first encouraging voluntary agreements (see Commission, 1996) and then implementing emissions trading (Rengeling, 2000, pp. 1729 et seq.). For these reasons, some suggest that participation in emissions trading should be optional for the duration of the voluntary agreements (Rehbinder and Schmalholz, 2002, p. 9). As a compromise, Art. 27 of the Directive provides a temporary exclusion of certain installations until 2007, if certain requirements are met.

According to the Commission, compatibility can be achieved by adapting existing agreements (Commission, 2001, Explanatory Memorandum no. 8). Under German law, even that would not be required, as the voluntary agreement is not truly binding: industry merely declares that it will try to reduce greenhouse gases, thus committing itself only to the effort, and the German government declares only that it will take no initiative regarding new measures, which does not mean that there will be no new regulations at all (Frenz, 2001, pp. 306 et seq.). Section II of the Agreement, moreover, specifies that the pledge not to initiate new legislative measures leaves the implementation of EU law unaffected. Thus the voluntary agreement has no legally binding effects for the legislator and can be replaced or terminated within an emissions trading scheme on the basis of the Directive (Kloepfer, 1998, ch. 5, annot. 218). The credibility of voluntary agreements as an instrument is not in question (see Rehbinder and Schmalholz, 2002, p. 9), since the parties apparently have addressed such developments.

Still, voluntary agreements and other instruments of environmental protection need to be made compatible with emissions trading. More conflicts can be foreseen, such as the problem of monitoring and verification and the relationship between the obligations of individual operators and branch or sector obligations (see Green Paper, 2000, no. 8.2). Following an amendment in the legislative stage, the directive allows for a temporary exclusion of certain installations in the first trading period (Art. 27) and might thereby help accommodate voluntary agreements in the domestic implementation process.

Relationship to instruments to promote renewable energy

Many member states, including Denmark, Germany, the Netherlands, and the United Kingdom have implemented specific legal instruments to promote renewable energy. The systems are very different, however. For example, Germany has obligations to purchase and compensate, the UK has an agency that purchases renewable energy and auctions the Renewable Obligation Certificates required in proportion to energy sales, and Denmark sets quotas for the use of renewable energy.[26] Initially, the European Union favored a quota model with tradable certificates, but in the Directive for renewable energy, which took effect on October 27, 2001 (Council Directive, 2001), no specific instrument is prescribed as obligatory; the choice lies with member states. A harmonized European system is scheduled for 2010, with a current leaning toward the quota model. The Directive already stipulates a certification of origin for electricity from renewable energy sources. Once quotas are set, these certificates could easily become part of a trading market.

The Commission of the European Communities assumes that emissions trading is compatible with a trading system for renewable energy certificates and that the two systems should be kept separate.[27] In isolated cases, undesired financial burdens (or reliefs) might occur. Promoting electricity production from renewable energy by fixing quotas, for example, might disadvantage sellers of emissions allowances, since production of electricity from renewable energy sources would accompany a reduction in CO_2 emissions.[28] The German system of obligations to purchase and compensate would create a double advantage for producers of renewable energy and a double burden for producers of conventional energy; in this case an adjustment of the system will be necessary.

The question of an ideal instrument mix arises again, as the two schemes overlap in the objective to promote renewable energy. One possibility would be a general emissions trading system that ensures complete internalization of external costs. In the meantime, systems to promote renewable energy will remain necessary in order to promote specific technologies. But here, as well, the issue essentially remains a political question, and a lack of harmonization can only be considered unconstitutional in clear cases.[29]

Relationship to existing emissions trading systems

Considerable legal adjustment will be needed wherever member states have already implemented their own emissions trading systems. The UK Emissions Trading Scheme (ETS) presents special obstacles.[30]

Unlike the cap-and-trade scheme of the Directive, the UK system sets relative reduction goals on the basis of Climate Change Levy Agreements (CCLA) that relate energy consumption or emissions to production units. Whereas the Directive will cap the total amount of emissions at the beginning, the environmental effectiveness of the UK system can only be assessed *ex post:* during the auctions of reduction subsidies, firms make offers to reduce CO_2 equivalents on the basis of economic considerations. Whereas the Directive requires participation in the trading system for certain sectors, the ETS provides for voluntary participation within the framework of the "direct route" (in this case, fixing absolute reduction goals), and the scope of possible participants is very broadly defined. Whereas the Directive is based on an upstream model (including, for example, combustion plants), the ETS follows a downstream concept: not the producers of electricity but the consumers are made responsible for the emissions. Whereas the Directive proposes a strict system of sanctions, the UK system does not impose fines on operators who cannot cover their emissions with a sufficient quantity of allowances.

Such differences would make it difficult to reconcile the two systems. In any case, with the UK ETS designed as a voluntary scheme, any operators covered by the Directive are, first and foremost, required to comply with its compulsory provisions. With a recent decision, the Commission agreed to exclude certain installations from the European scheme on condition that these installations will be subject to no less stringent duties and penalties under the national ETS (Commission Decision, 2004b). By comparison, the Danish model of certificates would require considerably less adaptation (on that issue, see Giesberts and Hilf, 2002, pp. 88 et seq.).

Conclusion

The European legislator had to and still has to overcome many hurdles in designing a harmonized emissions trading system. The same is true for the national legislatures implementing and developing the trading scheme. The most effective limits to their freedom of action are set by the obligation to avoid an unsystematic design that interferes with competition and violates the equal treatment provisions of European competition law. Because tradable emissions allowances represent a new instrument of environmental policy, it is not surprising that this will require many adjustments and changes to the existing legal order.

Notes

1 "Directive 2003/87/EC of the European Parliament and of the Council of 13 October 2003 establishing a scheme for greenhouse gas emission allowance trading within the Community and amending Council Directive 96/61/EC," *Official Journal* L 275/32 (October 25, 2003). Regarding the evolution of this Directive and its main provisions, see Peeters (2003, pp. 82 et sqq.), Smith and Chaumeil (2002, pp. 207 et sqq.), and Gebers (2002, pp. 14 et sqq.).
2 Beginning with Dales (1968a, pp. 791 et seq.) and Dales (1968b, pp. 77 et sqq.); for a good overview of the debate, see Baumol and Oates (1988, pp. 177 et sqq.).
3 This step was first announced by the Commission in 1998 (Commission 1998), and was introduced to public discussion by a Green Paper (Green Paper 2000).
4 For an overview, see Nielsen and Jeppesen (2003, pp. 3 et sqq.). The efforts in individual member states are described in greater detail by Boots (2003, pp. 43 et sqq.) for the Netherlands; Minnesma (2003, pp. 53 et seq.), Netherlands; Pocklington (2002, pp. 217 et sqq.), Denmark and the United Kingdom.
5 On mixed agreements in the context of environmental policy, see, in general MacLeod *et al.* (1996, pp. 323 et sqq.) and Lavranos (2002, pp. 44 et sqq.).
6 On the Community authority to legislate the Directive, see Epiney (2001, pp. 213 et seq.).
7 For further references, see Epiney (2001, p. 214, note 27); according to a dissenting opinion, there is no comprehensive Community jurisdiction

regarding climate protection measures, as climate protection – being a cross-sectional task – reaches into other policy areas.

8 ECJ, case 300/89, *ECR* 1991 I-2867; ECJ, case 155/91, *ECR* 1993 I-939.

9 Thus the comment of Belgium regarding the Green Paper (2000); likewise the Economic and Social Committee, statement of September 20, 2000, *Official Journal* 2000, C 376, p. 22, no. 2.3.

10 In Germany, for instance, the Act on Trade in Greenhouse Gas Emission Allowances (Gesetz über den Handel mit Berechtigungen zur Emission von Treibhausgasen - TEHG) of July 8, 2004, *Federal Law Gazette (BGBl.)* I, p. 1578, regulates central features of the trading system, including the legal framework of allocation, sanctions, and the annual duty to surrender emission allowances; in paras. 15 and 16, it also addresses the applicability of financial provisions and details of the transaction process. This act came into force on July 15, 2004.

11 For a general discussion of the relationship between emissions trading and free trade, see Petsonk (1999, p. 185), and the articles collected in Chambers (2001).

12 See, for instance, the in-depth scoping paper prepared for the Commission by Werksman and Lefevere (1999, pp. 4 et seq.).

13 Werksman and Lefevere (1999, p. 9); Spieth (2002, pp. 63 et seq.), on the other hand, argues that this would only affect treaties of the EC with third-party states regarding mutual recognition of emissions allowances.

14 According to Art. 3 I it would be 5 percent, but for the EU and its member states 8 percent is fixed in Annex B; for an in-depth overview of the burden-sharing scheme, see CCAP (1999), passim.

15 While Council Decision (2002), Annex II, allows Portugal to increase its emissions by 27 percent, for instance, Luxembourg will be required to reduce its emissions by 28 percent.

16 The European Court of Justice developed fundamental rights at the EU level by case law, referring to common constitutional traditions of the member states, the European Convention of Human Rights, and general principles of law. The European Charter of Fundamental Rights was explicitly "welcomed" at the EU summit in Nice in December 2000, but not incorporated into the European treaties. It remains to be seen whether the ECJ will refer to the Charter in its case law.

17 See the treaty establishing a constitution for Europe, *Official Journal* C 310 (16 December 2004), pp. 0001–0474.

18 In the following text, this will be discussed with special reference to the legal debate in Germany; but the arguments, as a rule, can be applied equally to European law and other constitutions.

19 In Germany, for instance, para. 16 (2) of the aforementioned act implementing the Directive (note 10 above) specifies that an entry in the registry will be considered valid unless the recipient of allocated allowances is aware of an error at the time of allocation.

20 For the debate on the combination of instruments in environmental law, see, in general, Rodi (2000b, pp. 231 et seq.); according to Consideration no. 23 of the Directive, "emission allowance trading should form part of a

comprehensive and coherent package of policies and measures implemented at Member State and Community level."

21 The central regulatory instrument on energy efficiency in France mainly provides for wider planning measures; see Arts. 5–15 of Law No. 96–1236 on Air and Rational Use of Energy (Loi no. 96–1236 sur l'air et l'utilisation rationnelle de l'énergie) of 30 December 1996, *Journal Officiel* no. 1 of 1 January 1997, pp. 11 et sqq.

22 Skeptical: Spieth (2002, pp. 60 et seq.); existing emissions trading systems in the US (Clean Air Act, RECLAIM) are confronted with similar problems, see Rehbinder (2001, pp. 135 et seq., 145 et seq.).

23 Hirsch (1999, p. 392), explains how the issue of "hot spots" has not prevented the successful operation of emissions trading under the Clean Air Act.

24 See Giesberts and Hilf (2002, pp. 55 et seq.); on the other hand, Rehbinder and Schmalholz (2002, p. 9) also mention the possibility of unjustified advantages that might occur if enterprises benefit from tax exemptions or tax reliefs.

25 See Giesberts and Hilf (2002, pp. 55 et seq.). A regulation to this effect exists in the United Kingdom; see Krämer (2001, p. 31, note 69).

26 For an overview of the different promotion schemes for renewable energy in the member states, see Reiche and Bechberger (2004, pp. 843 et sqq.).

27 Commission (2001, Explanatory Memorandum no. 20); see also allocation criterion (4) in annex III: "In particular, no allowances should be allocated to cover emissions which would be reduced or eliminated as a consequence of Community legislation on renewable energy in electricity production . . ."

28 Bräuer *et al.* (2001, pp. 379 et seq.); this view is shared by the Commission (2001, Explanatory Memorandum no. 20).

29 See Spieth (2002, pp. 88 et seq.), invoking the principle of a consistent legal order and the principle of proportionality.

30 This was already recognized in DEFRA (2001); see also Spieth (2002, pp. 92 et seq., 102 et seq.) and Giesberts and Hilf (2002, pp. 85 et seq.).

References

Baumol, W. J., and Oates, W. E. 1988. *The Theory of Environmental Policy.* New York: Cambridge University Press.

BMU (German Federal Ministry for the Environment, Nature Conservation, and Nuclear Safety) 2000. *Germany's National Climate Protection Programme.* Berlin.

Boots, M. 2003. "Green certificates and carbon trading in the Netherlands," *Energy Policy* 31: 43–50.

Bräuer, W., Stronzik, M., and Michaelowa, A. 2001. "Die Koexistenz von Zertifikatemärkten für grünen Strom und CO_2-Emissionen – wer gewinnt und wer verliert?" *Zeitschrift für Umweltpolitik Und Umweltrecht* 3: 379–92.

CCAP (Center for Clean Air Policy) 1999. "Allocation of greenhouse gas reduction responsibilities among and within the countries of the European Union." Scoping Paper, Washington, DC.

Chambers, W. B. 2001 (ed.). *Inter-Linkages: The Kyoto Protocol and the International Trade and Investment Regimes*. Tokyo: UNU Press.

Commission 1996. "Communication from the Commission to the Council and the European Parliament on environmental agreements." COM (1996) 561, dated November 27, 1996.

   1998. "Communication from the Commission to the Council and the European Parliament: Climate change – towards an EU post-Kyoto strategy." Presented by the Commission of the European Communities, COM (1998) 353, final version dated June 3, 1998.

   2000. "Communication from the Commission to the Council and the European Parliament on EU policies and measures to reduce greenhouse gas emissions: Towards a European climate change programme (ECCP)." COM (2000) 88, final version dated March 8, 2000.

   2001. "Proposal for a Directive of the European Parliament and of the Council: Establishing a scheme for greenhouse gas emission allowance trading within the Community and amending Council Directive 96/61/EC." Presented by the Commission of the European Communities, COM (2001) 581, final version dated October 23, 2001.

   2004. "Communication from the Commission on guidance to assist member states in the implementation of the criteria listed in Annex III to Directive 2003/87/EC establishing a scheme for greenhouse gas emission allowance trading within the Community and amending Council Directive 96/61/EC, and on the circumstances under which *force majeure* is demonstrated." COM (2003) 830, final version dated January 7, 2004.

Commission Decision 2004a. "Commission Decision establishing guidelines for the monitoring and reporting of greenhouse Gas emissions pursuant to Directive 2003/87/EC of the European Parliament and of the Council." C (2004) 130, final version dated January 29, 2004.

   2004b. "Commission Decision concerning the temporary exclusion of certain installations by the United Kingdom from the Community emissions trading scheme pursuant to Article 27 of Directive 2003/87/EC of the European Parliament and of the Council." C(2004) 4240/2, final version dated October 29, 2004.

Council Decision 1993. "Council Decision 93/389/EEC of 24 June 1993 for a monitoring mechanism of Community CO_2 and other greenhouse gas emissions." *Official Journal* L 167 (July 9, 2003), pp. 0031–0033.

   2002. "Council Decision 2002/358/EC of 25 April 2002 concerning the approval, on behalf of the European Community, of the Kyoto Protocol to the United Nations Framework Convention on Climate Change and the joint fulfilment of commitments thereunder." *Official Journal* L 130, (May 15, 2002), pp. 0001–0020.

Council Directive 1996. "Council Directive 96/61/EC of 24 September 1996 concerning integrated pollution prevention and control." *Official Journal* L 257 (October 10, 1996), pp. 0026–0040.

   2001. "Directive 2001/77/EC of the European Parliament and of the Council of 27 September 2001 on the promotion of electricity produced from renewable energy sources in the internal electricity market." *Official Journal* L 283 (October 27, 2001), pp. 0033–0040.

2003. "Council Directive 2003/96/EC of 27 October 2003 restructuring the Community framework for the taxation of energy products and electricity." *Official Journal* L 283 (October 31, 2003), pp. 0051–0070.

2004. "Council Derivative 2004/101/EC of the European Parliament and of the Council of 27 October 2004 amending Directive 2003/87/EC establishing a scheme for greenhouse gas emission allowance trading within the Community, in respect of the Kyoto Protocol's project mechanisms." *Official Journal* L 338 (13 November 2004), pp. 0018–0023.

Dales, J. H. 1968a. "Land, water, and ownership," *Canadian Journal of Economics* 1: 791–804.

1968b. *Pollution, Property and Prices*. Toronto: University of Toronto Press.

DEFRA (UK Department for Environment, Food and Rural Affairs) 2001. *Framework for the UK Emissions Trading Scheme*. Wetherby.

Epiney, A. 2001. "Fragen des europäischen und deutschen Verfassungsrechts," in Rengeling (ed.), pp. 207–47.

Frenz, W. 2001. "Klimaschutz und Instrumentenwahl," *Natur und Recht* 23: 301–11.

Gebers, B. 2002. "Proposal for a Directive on greenhouse emissions trading within the European Community," *ELNI Review*, no. 1: 14–17.

Giesberts, L., and Hilf, J. 2002. *Handel mit Emissionszertifikaten: Regelungsrahmen für einen künftigen Markt*. Cologne: Heymann.

Green Paper 2000. "Green Paper on greenhouse gas emissions trading within the European Union." Presented by the Commission of the European Communities, COM (2000) 87, final version dated March 8, 2000.

Hirsch, J. M. 1999. "Emissions allowance trading under the Clean Air Act: a model for future regulations?" *New York University Environmental Law Journal* 7: 352–97.

Jans, J. H. 2003 (ed.). *The European Convention and the Future of European Environmental Law*. Groningen: Europa Law Publishing.

Kloepfer, M. 1998. *Umweltrecht*. Munich: Beck.

Krämer, L. 2000. *E. C. Environmental Law*. London: Sweet & Maxwell.

2001. "Rechtsfragen betreffend den Emissionshandel mit Treibhausgasen der Europäischen Gemeinschaft," in Rengeling (ed.), pp. 1–46.

Lavranos, N. 2002. "Multilateral environmental agreements: who makes the binding decisions?" *European Environmental Law Review* 11: 44–50.

MacLeod, I., Hendry, I. D., and Hyett, S. 1996. *The External Relations of the European Communities: A Manual of Law and Practice*. Oxford: Clarendon Press.

Michaelowa, A. 2003. "Germany – a pioneer on earthen feet?" *Climate Policy* 3: 31–43.

Minnesma, M. E. 2003. "Dutch climate policy: a victim of economic growth?" *Climate Policy* 3: 45–56.

Nielsen, L., and Jeppesen, T. 2003. "Tradable green certificates in selected European countries – overview and assessment," *Energy Policy* 31: 3–14.

Non-Paper 2002. "Non-paper of the European Commission – Directorate-General Environment, Directorate E: Global and International Affairs – on synergies between the EC emissions trading proposal." COM (2001)

198 *Michael Rodi*

581 and the IPPC Directive, final version dated January 22, 2002, (http://
europa.eu.int/comm/environment/climat/pdf/non-paper_ippc_and_et.pdf
[accessed April 2004]).

Peeters, M. 2003. "Emissions trading as a new dimension to European environmental law," *European Environmental Law Review* 12: 82–92.

Petsonk, A. 1999. "The Kyoto Protocol and the WTO: integrating greenhouse
gas emissions allowances trading into the global marketplace," *Duke Environmental Law and Policy Forum* 10: 185–220.

Pocklington, D. 2002. "European emissions trading: the business perspective,"
European Environmental Law Review 11: 209–18.

Rehbinder, E. 2001. "Erfahrungen in den USA," in Rengeling (ed.), pp. 127–64.

Rehbinder, E., and Schmalholz, M. 2002. "Handel mit Emissionsrechten für
Treibhausgase in der Europäischen Union," *Umwelt- und Planungsrecht* 22:
1–10.

Reiche, D., and Bechberger, M. 2004. "Policy differences in the promotion of
renewable energies in the EU member states," *Energy Policy* 32: 843–49.

Rengeling, H.-W. 2000. "Handel mit Treibhausgasemissionen," *Deutsches Ver-
waltungsblatt*, 115: 1725–34.

2001 (ed.). *Klimaschutz durch Emissionshandel.* Cologne: Heymann.

Richardson, B. J., and Chanwai, K. L. 2003. "The UK's climate change levy: is
it working?" *Journal of Environmental Law* 15: 39–58.

Rodi, M. 2000a. *Die Subventionsrechtsordnung: die Subvention als Instrument
öffentlicher Zweckverwirklichung nach Völkerrecht, Europarecht und deutschem
innerstaatlichen Recht.* Tübingen: Mohr Siebeck.

2000b. "Instrumentenvielfalt und Instrumentenverbund," *Zeitschrift für Ge-
setzgebung*, pp. 231–47.

Smith, M. J. H., and Chaumeil, T. 2002. "Greenhouse gas emissions trading
within the European Union: an overview of the proposed European directive," *Fordham Environmental Law Journal* 13: 207–24.

Spieth, W. F. 2002. *Europäischer Emissionshandel und deutsches Industrieanlagen-
recht.* Berlin: Schmidt.

Varma, A. 2003. "UK's climate change levy: cost effectiveness, competitiveness
and environmental impacts," *Energy Policy* 31: 51–61.

Voluntary Agreement 2000. "Agreement on climate protection between the
Government of the Federal Republic of Germany and German business
of 27.03.1996," further developed with agreement of 10.11.2000
(http://www.bmu.bund.de/en/1024/js/topics/climateprotection/agreement/
[accessed April 2004]).

Werksman, J., and Lefevere, J. 1999. "WTO issues raised by the design of an EU
Emissions Trading System." Scoping Paper, London.

Wolfrum, R. 2001. "Völkerrechtliche Beurteilung des Handels mit Emissionsrechten," in Rengeling (ed.), pp. 189–204.

Working Group 2002. "Report of the Working Group 'Emissionshandel
zur Bekämpfung des Treibhauseffektes'." (http://www.bmu.de/files/
emissionshandel_bericht_2001.pdf [accessed April 2004]).

13 Emissions trading schemes in Europe: linking the EU Emissions Trading Scheme with national programs

Sven Bode

Introduction

Emissions trading was first introduced in the United States during the mid-1970s. It was applied in several ways (e.g. to lead-free petrol and to ozone-depleting chemicals) among which the Acid Rain Program may have the closest similarity with potential national CO_2 trading schemes (UN 1995, pp. 19–23). In the context of the UN Framework Convention on Climate Change it first looked as if taxes could be the instruments of choice for countries to control the greenhouse gas emissions (NRP, 1995, p. 1). However, emissions trading at state level was finally formally introduced with the Kyoto Protocol, agreed in 1997. As parties to the Protocol lack information on abatement options and costs, the theoretical efficiency gains may never be realized by nation-to-nation trading. This may be one reason why the discussion on national trading schemes, i.e. involving sub-national entities, has intensified remarkably since then, and numerous reports by "industry/governmental" working groups have been published throughout the industrialized world. With national schemes emerging, the question of linkage arises. We analyze this aspect in general.

On the other hand, there are, already, two existing schemes in Europe. We describe these two systems and see how they can be linked with regard to technical feasibility, environmental integrity, and economic impacts. The latter aspect will be investigated with a focus on the linking national schemes in the context only of the Kyoto provisions, as it is generally understood that the linking of different schemes itself increases overall cost-efficiency.

Emissions trading

The concept of emissions trading

Compared to other economic instruments such as taxes, emissions trading has the advantage that the total quantity of emissions can be

199

determined prior to the introduction of the instrument by the quantity of emission rights/permits issued by the authorities. (In the following the terms *emission right* and *permit* are used equivalently). Furthermore, emissions trading allows for a cost-efficient meeting of emission targets as long as the market functions well. Initially, each participant has to be assigned a certain number of emission rights. At the end of the period, every participant has to hold at least the same quantity of emission rights as he released emissions into the atmosphere. Any surplus permits can be sold on the market (or possibly be banked). Buyers are those emitters whose marginal abatement costs are higher than the permit price in the market. In the long run, abatement costs are equalized.

However, before national schemes can start operation in real economies, several design features have to be decided.

Design of national emissions trading schemes

There follows, an overview on important features to be decided on when implementing emissions trading schemes. The detailed design affects economic efficiency, environmental integrity, and acceptability.[1] As the focus of this chapter is on linking of trading schemes, we discuss the features only briefly.

Absolute vs. specific targets   An absolute target for participants in a trading scheme helps to ensure the meeting of a national target. Meeting the target may require huge investments, especially when output is increased. With specific targets,[2] output can be increased as much as desired without the restrictions of absolute ones. This is why they are favored by industry. As permits are generated in comparison to business-as-usual scenarios (see Figure 13.1), increasing numbers of permits are generated with increasing output. This suggests additional environmental benefits.[3]

Stringency of the target   The more stringent the overall target, the higher the environmental effectiveness.[4] On the other hand, with increasing marginal abatement costs, the more stringent the target, the higher are total abatement costs.

Mandatory vs. voluntary participation   Depending on the detailed design, a mandatory scheme is likely to be more environmentally effective, as a greater number of participants than in a voluntary scheme can be expected. A voluntary system is likely to face a mismatch between supply and demand as only entities that expect themselves to be sellers may

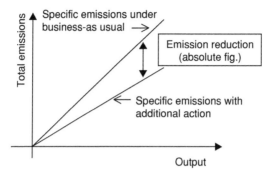

Figure 13.1. Absolute emission reductions with specific emission targets. *Source*: AGE, 2002b, p. 34.

want to joint the scheme. Thus, there might need to be some incentives to make more entities participate and accept an absolute cap (AGO, 1999a, p. 22). A mandatory scheme is likely to be more cost-efficient because of greater variance in abatement costs – depending on who has to participate.

Participants As for the mandatory scheme, a wide range of categories of participating emitters will reduce total costs.[5] On the other hand, transaction costs may increase if small and/or mobile sources are to be part of the scheme. Compelling upstream sources[6] to participate is one way to solve this problem. (For a detailed discussion, see CCAP, 1999.) Furthermore, producers of indirect emissions (e.g. emissions resulting from electricity consumption) can be obliged to surrender certificates.

Coverage of gases As abatement costs vary for different gases, the inclusion of as many gases as possible increases efficiency. On the other hand, transaction costs can increase when sources cannot be administered adequately (NZME, 1998, p. 22). For example, it might be impossible to calculate emissions by means of standardized emission factors and input (in the way it is possible for fossil fuels, for example), so that continuous measurement would be necessary.

Mode of allocation Permits may either be allocated for free or be charged. If we neglect transaction costs and assume competitive markets, the efficiency of the system does not depend on the initial allocation. It has "only" distributional effects (AGO, 1999a, pp. 26–50).

Monitoring, verification, and reporting (MVP)   MVP provisions have to be set against the background of the trade-off between completeness and costs (WBCSD, 2001, p. 8).

Banking and borrowing   Banking and borrowing between different commitment periods allow an intertemporal optimization and thus can reduce costs. Borrowing, however, is generally badly regarded by environmental NGOs as it is perceived to violate environmental integrity.

Non-compliance provisions   Law enforcement is an important aspect of all environmental legislation. There are no special requirements for emissions trading.

Market access   The question of whether only entities with targets or every legal/natural person has the right to purchase emission rights has to be answered. The latter option may result in higher prices when, for example, environmental NGOs buy rights in order to redeem them.[7]

Compatibility with existing instruments   Compatibility with existing regulation is important both in regard to accordance with a constitution and in regard to the acceptance of emissions trading in a political economy.[8]

Register   A register is necessary to administer the permits and to allow checks of authenticity. As long as it is assured that each permit exists only once and that it is cancelled after being surrendered by an indebted participant, there are no specific requirements for a national register (AGE, 2002b, pp. 107–12).

Use of project-based credits   The use of credits from emissions reduction projects either in the non-participating sector in the home country or abroad can be an appropriate tool for increasing cost-efficiency even though a higher order of problems may occur. Environmental integrity strongly depends on the rules for calculating the project-based emissions reductions.

Treatment of new sources and plant shut-down   New sources could simply be obliged to buy permits on the secondary market, just as existing growing participants have to do. Equity considerations may, on the other hand, call for an initial allocation equal to the one for the early participants. Plant shut-down should also be considered in order to avoid incentives for shut-downs by "eternal rent-seekers". (For a similar discussion, see Pedersen, 2000.)

Compliance period   The length of the compliance periods can be set as desired. Following the Kyoto provisions, it might be five years from 2008 onward. However, annual compliance seems reasonable as (Haites and Aslam, 2000, p. 31):

- it is the standard for many reporting requirements (e.g. other emissions reporting, taxes)
- it would help governments with the annual reporting obligation under the UNFCCC
- it may help to facilitate the treatment of plant shut-down.

Liability   Two kinds of liability can be distinguished: seller and buyer liability.[9] Seller liability puts the responsibility in the case of non-compliance on the participant who has sold some of its permits. Buyer liability, on the other hand, would result in a cancellation of trades in case the seller is non-compliant. There are different criteria for assessing liability rules – for example, environmental effectiveness, cost to participants, or market confidence (IEA, 1999, p. 17). Kerr (1998, p. 9) believes that seller liability is the better option as long as serious sanctions in case of non-compliance are imposed. This should not cause any problems within national legislation.

Existing greenhouse gas emissions trading schemes in Europe

Even though there is an intensive discussion on the implementation of greenhouse gas emissions trading schemes at entity level in several Annex B countries (see, for example, AGO, 1999b, Commission, 1999, Hauf, 2000, MIES, 2000, AGE, 2002a, and Council, 2002) there are only two existing public[10] systems in Europe: in Denmark and the United Kingdom.[11]

The Danish system

In 1999 the Danish parliament approved a bill on CO_2 quotas for electricity production as part of a legislative reform of the electricity sector (DEA, 1999). Absolute targets for emissions from electricity generation are set to 23 million tonnes of CO_2 in 2000 being reduced by 1 million tonnes per year until 2003.[12] The 2003 target is only about 66 percent of historical emissions from 1994 to 1998 and thus can be considered as a stringent one.[13] Emission rights are not allocated to companies with historical emissions smaller than 100,000 tonnes of CO_2 per year from combined heat and power production.[14] As a consequence of this rule, only eight companies actually have to participate in the trading scheme, two of which hold about 93 percent of the permits allocated. Thus, it cannot be considered as a competitive market. Nevertheless, more than 90 percent of CO_2 emissions from power generation are covered.

The permits were allocated free of charge based on historical emissions in the period 1994–1998. Emissions are calculated on the basis of fuel input and standardized emission factors. Companies have to report all relevant data once a year to the Minister of Environment and Energy who decides on compliance. Detailed rules for penalties in the event of suppressing or submitting incorrect or misleading information are given. In the case of non-compliance a penalty of 40 DKr has to be paid for each tonne of CO_2 emitted which is not covered by a permit. Any income from penalties is spent on achieving additional energy savings. Banking is possible with certain restrictions. A "saving limit" has been introduced according to which banking is only possible if emissions are lower than the limit.[15]

Transfer of permits has to be reported to the Minister of Environment and Energy within four weeks of an agreement being reached. So far the use of emission certificates from the project-based mechanism is not foreseen. However, the Minister is authorized by the bill to specify such rules. Last but not least, the Minister can withhold a portion of the total permits in order to allocate them to new sources. The allocation is relative to the new producer's estimated CO_2 emissions. In the event that there are no new producers, which could indeed have been expected for the period until 2003, the permits withheld are redistributed to the existing electricity producers. (For details, see Queen, 1999, and Pedersen, 2000.)

The UK system

The UK system was developed by the Emissions Trading Group, which was led by industry and included the UK government. A scheme involving voluntary participation was developed, with different ways of entry being offered, as discussed in the following paragraphs.

1 Participation through a target set by a Climate Change Levy Agreement is possible. Companies in such an agreement have to meet specific or absolute targets to obtain an 80 percent discount on the Climate Change Levy. By participating in emissions trading they can increase flexibility on the way to compliance. In order not to inflate

the overall market with "virtual" reductions (recall Figure 13.1) and thus undermining stringency, permits from the "specific sector" can only be sold to the "absolute sector" as long as the former is overall a net buyer.[16] Otherwise, the so-called "gateway" will close. Companies that opt in only have to carry out additional reporting and verification measures over the agreement requirements if they want to sell permits. The compliance period is on a biennial basis after the introductory period from January 1, 2002 to December 31, 2002. Permits are only generated at the end of these years (so-called "milestone years"). Companies failing to meet the target lose at least the 80 percent discount for the following two-year period.

2 Any company with direct or indirect[17] greenhouse gas emissions within the UK can also ask to participate in the scheme with sources not covered by an existing agreement.[18] Companies bid in an auction for absolute emissions reductions calculated against a baseline that describes what would have happened without the reductions induced by the auction. The baseline is the average emissions for the three years from 1998 to 2000. The auction is designed as an *descending clock auction* and a total amount of £ 215 million is spent.[19] Each participant who wins in the auction has set itself a linear emission reduction path with five annual targets until 2006. For these so-called "direct participants," guidelines for measurement and reporting of emissions are provided. Non-compliance results in non-payment of the incentive for the year the target has not been met as well as a reduction of permits allocated in the next year amounting to the shortfall multiplied by a penalty factor. Finally, detailed rules for divestments and investments are given.

3 UK-based projects can earn credits if they lead to quantified emissions reductions. Rules are still under discussion, but it is clear that projects will have to be approved by government.

In contrast to the Danish scheme all greenhouse gases, not simply CO_2, are considered.[20] Unlimited banking is allowed until 2007. Banking into the first Kyoto commitment period is possible only for participants with absolute targets. The quantity is restricted to the extent that they have exceeded their targets.

Generally, anyone who wants to enter the scheme is free to do so. However, it goes without saying that anyone who wants to hold, buy, or sell permits has to have an account in the registry.[21] The UK government intends to allow the use of credits from the project-based mechanisms under the Kyoto Protocol but point out that a decision will only be taken after the rules have been decided. (All information in this section comes from DEFRA.)

Linking schemes

General considerations

As long as the abatement costs in separate trading schemes are different, the linkage of two schemes can result in increased overall cost-efficiency. However, given that on the balance one country is either a net importer or a net exporter, the permit price will go down in the former and up in the latter. Consequently, selling entities in the importing country will lose whereas buyers will win. The contrary goes for the exporting country. This in turn may raise resistance from potentially losing participants to the linking of schemes (Haites and Mullins, 2001, p. viii).

The impacts of a particular choice on different features have been discussed above. These impacts are a general concern in the design of a national system. Differences may, however, prevent linkage for technical reasons or affect environmental integrity when schemes are linked. Table 13.1 shows in what ways these two aspects are affected.

On the compatibility of the UK and Danish schemes

After the general analysis presented in Table 13.1 the UK and Danish schemes are specifically considered in Table 13.2.

To sum up, the two schemes could probably be linked with little technical effort (depending on the registries), but such linking could at the same time affect environmental integrity owing to the differing non-compliance provisions.

In this context it is worth mentioning the first permit swap between the two systems. In summer 2002, Royal Dutch Shell and Elsam swapped carbon allowances (Buchan, 2002). However, mere international trade in permits is different from the linking of schemes as discussed in this chapter. The use of foreign permits for compliance requires approval by national authorities. The acquisition of UK permits by Elsam – which has no operation in the UK – has to be considered as a simple investment, the same as for any share.

Linking national schemes in the context of the Kyoto Protocol

After discussing the linkage of national schemes from technical and environmental points of view, we analyze the economic impact in the context of the Kyoto provisions in this section.

Table 13.1. *Linking national trading schemes: technical feasibility and environmental integrity*

Design feature	Effect of differences in design features
Absolute vs. specific target	Linkage technically feasible as long as some units are defined (e.g. tonnes of CO_2) but risks weakening environmental integrity if there is a net sale of permits from the specific to the absolute system by increasing output (see also Figure 13.1).
Stringency of target	Linkage technically feasible; overall stringency remains unaffected by linking (for different incentives to manipulate stringency prior to the linkage, see discussions in the section on economic compatibility).
Mandatory vs. voluntary participation	Linkage technically feasible; as permit price will go up in one system and down in the other, incentives to join may also be increased. If the allocation of permits is generous ("hot air") in the system where prices go up, a greater number may volunteer because of linkage and thus environmental integrity may be weakened.
Participants	Linkage technically feasible; environmental integrity may be endangered especially if systems with direct and indirect emissions from the same product are linked.
Coverage of gases	Technical feasibility and environmental integrity are unproblematic with regard to linking schemes with different coverage of gases as long as reasonable conversion factors are applied in both systems.[a]
Mode of allocation	The method of allocation does not affect the technical feasibility of linkage nor environmental integrity.
Monitoring, verification and reporting (MVR)	Technical feasibility unaffected by MVR; higher prices due to linking and lax MVR provisions may give incentives to cheat and thus affect environmental integrity.
Banking and borrowing	No impact on technical feasibility or environmental integrity from banking. For borrowing, difference does not cause technical problems but can undermine environmental integrity.
Non-compliance provisions	Linkage technically feasible; but difference in penalties and enforcement can weaken environmental effectiveness as the lowest penalty determines the place of non-compliance.
Market access	Unproblematic from both technical and environmental points of view.
Register	Can *a priori* prevent linkage as well as negatively affect environmental integrity. However, structures can be adopted causing higher costs.
Use of project-based credits	Linkage technically feasible; environmental integrity might be affected if quality of standards is different.
Treatment of new sources/plant shut down	Technically unproblematic; environmental integrity may be affected in the event that perverse incentives are given to create new sources due to generous allocation.

Table 13.1. (*cont.*)

Design feature	Effect of differences in design features
Compliance period	Unproblematic from both technical and environmental points of view.
Liability	With different liability provisions, trading would have to be limited to surplus permits on the seller's account after compliance has been established.

Note: [a] Global Warming Potentials (GWP), contained in the Kyoto Protocol, have been adopted by a political decision. Other conversion factors for different gases are also conceivable (see, for example, IPCC, 2001, pp. 388–90).
Source: The basic argumentation follows Haites and Mullins (2001, pp. 38–64).

The Kyoto provisions

The Kyoto Protocol – agreed during the 3rd Conference of Parties to the UNFCCC in Kyoto in 1997 – defines absolute emission targets (so-called Assigned Amounts) for countries listed in Annex B for the first commitment period, 2008–2012. The targets are defined as a percent-age figure compared to GHG emissions in 1990. In order to enable a cost-efficient meeting of these targets, some so-called flexible mechan-isms have been introduced, among which is emissions trading. Parties listed in Annex B to the Protocol are (under certain conditions) allowed to trade the underlying emission rights, the so-called Assigned Amount Units (AAUs). Emissions without any flexible mechanisms would have to decline sooner or later in all countries according to the national targets. With trading the emissions path will change – maybe even before 2008 (see Figure 13.2).[22] However, as the system only starts in 2008, one has to ask how international pre-2008 trading interacts with the Kyoto provisions.

It is interesting to note that there are no concrete mandatory emissions paths for reaching the Kyoto targets. Article 3(2) of the Kyoto Protocol says that "Each Party included in Annex I shall, by 2005, have made demonstrable progress in achieving its commitments under this Proto-col" but it will be interesting to see how the term *demonstrable progress* is interpreted in 2005. As there is, furthermore, no penalty mentioned if a Party does not make demonstrable progress, the emissions path can be assumed to be completely undetermined.

Table 13.2. *Linking national trading schemes: technical feasibility and environmental integrity – the case of Denmark and the UK*

Design feature	Effect of differences in design features
Absolute vs. specific target	The specific targets in the UK scheme do not cause any problems for linking the two schemes as this aspect is already satisfactorily considered by the gateway in the British scheme.
Stringency of target	Stringency remains unaffected by linking; incentive to inflate total quantity of permits by net-selling country not realized as both have a clear reduction target, given their Kyoto obligations.
Mandatory vs. voluntary participation	Marginal costs are so far unknown for the two systems. With the price valve of 40 DKr/tonne of CO_2 it is, however, unlikely that many (if any at all) companies in the UK will opt in because of higher prices. Furthermore, the British allocation mode cannot be judged to be generous ("hot air").
Participants	As the UK is a net importer and Denmark a net exporter of electricity (UCTE, 2000), problems with double counting in environmental integrity due to different approaches (indirect vs. direct) are not expected to occur.
Coverage of gases	No problems due to consideration of different gases.
Mode of allocation	The method of allocation is not affecting technical feasibility of linkage nor environmental integrity.
Monitoring, verification and reporting (MVR)	Unclear if MVR are more lax in net-selling country; thus uncertain whether undesirable incentives are given.
Banking and borrowing	Only banking is allowed in the two schemes; thus no problems with technical feasibility or environmental integrity for banking.
Non-compliance provisions	Fixed penalty in Denmark whereas company-specific penalty in the UK (e.g. dependent on payment received in the auction). However, the Danish penalty can be judged to be very soft and thus the Danish safety valve could be expected to be used by participants in British scheme.
Market access	Unproblematic from both technical and environmental points of view.
Register	Unclear whether structures are similar or additional efforts are necessary.
Use of project-based credits	Detailed rules have not yet been specified in either of the countries.
Treatment of new sources/ plant shut-down	Perverse incentives are not apparent.
Compliance period	Unproblematic from both technical and environmental points of view.
Liability	Unproblematic, as same liability provisions in both systems.

210   *Sven Bode*

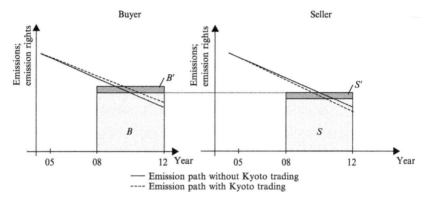

Figure 13.2. Change of emission path considering emissions trading under the Kyoto provisions for a simple two-country case.

International trading prior to the first commitment period

As mentioned above, linking trading schemes can result in increased overall cost-efficiency on the global scale. However, apart from efficiency on a global scale the incidence of costs has also to be discussed.

International emissions trading prior to 2008 may either be based on the exchange of AAUs or not. For analyzing this interaction let us consider a two-country, two-period model and consider first the situation without any international trading prior to the first commitment period.

Kyoto trading only   We assume that – with regard to the Kyoto target – one country will be a net buyer whereas the other will be a net seller. (Note that the model discussed below has been highly simplified for illustrative purposes. A general version is presented in annex 1.) The two countries have the same reduction obligation in each period (that changes, however, over time). Banking is not allowed. The cost functions of the countries are quadratic.[23] The lifetime of an investment in emissions reduction is one period.[24]

Without loss of generality, let a denote the buying and b the selling country. Indices 1 and 2 denote the two periods. The two countries face the optimization problem:

$$\min_{R_{a1},R_{a2},P_2} C_a = \alpha_a R_{a1}^2 + \alpha_a R_{a2}^2 + \pi_2 P_2;$$
$$\min_{R_{b1},R_{b2},P_2} C_b = \alpha_b R_{b1}^2 + \alpha_b R_{b2}^2 - \pi_2 P_2 \tag{1}$$

s.t.

$$R_{a1} \geq T_1; \ R_{b1} \geq T_1; \ R_{a2} + P_2 \geq T_2; \ R_{b2} - P_2 \geq T_2$$

where $C =$ cost, α is a parameter, $R =$ emissions reduced internally, $\pi =$ permit price (assuming a perfect market where each participant faces the same price), $P =$ quantity of permits bought or sold, and $T =$ reduction obligation.

Whereas T_2 should be based on the Kyoto target, there is more freedom when defining T_1.

First-order conditions are given in annex 2. Problem (1) solves as:

$$R_{a1} = T_1; R_{b1} = T_1; \lambda_{a1} = 2\alpha_a T_1; \lambda_{b1} = 2\alpha_b T_1$$
$$R_{a2} = \frac{2\alpha_b}{\alpha_a + \alpha_b} T_2; \ R_{b2} = \frac{2\alpha_a}{\alpha_a + \alpha_b} T_2; \ \pi_2 = \lambda_{a2} = \lambda_{b2} = \frac{4\alpha_a\alpha_b}{\alpha_a + \alpha_b} T_2;$$
$$P_2 = \frac{(\alpha_a - \alpha_b)}{\alpha_a + \alpha_b} T_2 \tag{2}$$

where $\lambda =$ Lagrange multiplier.

We can see that, by introducing trading in the second period, marginal abatement costs (λ_{i2}) become the same for both countries.

Non AAU-based international emissions trading before 2008 In the event that no AAUs are used in the linked schemes another "commodity"[25] has to be transferred. Let us denote the commodity as the *pre-Kyoto unit* (PKU). Generally, a government can issue as many PKUs as desired. The selling country has an incentive to increase the number of permits as it is beneficial to its industry. As this is at the expense of the environment, a pro-environment buying country may look for instruments to reduce the importation of "worthless" permits. Rehdanz and Tol (2002) analyze the different impacts of a discount factor, a tariff, and a quantity limit. In the following analysis we assume, however, that the PKU allocation prior to the first commitment period is based on the Assigned Amount and that arbitrary flooding of the market does not occur. For a linear compliance path the situation can be depicted as in Figure 13.3.

Extending (1) with trading in both periods gives:

$$\min_{R_{a1},R_{a2},P_1,P_2} C_a = \alpha_a R_{a1}^2 + \pi_1 P_1 + \alpha_a R_{a2}^2 + \pi_2 P_2;$$
$$\min_{R_{b1},R_{b2},P_1,P_2} C_b = \alpha_b R_{b1}^2 - \pi_1 P_1 + \alpha_b R_{b2}^2 - \pi_2 P_2 \tag{3}$$

s.t.

$$R_{a1} + P_1 \geq T_1; \ R_{b1} - P_1 \geq T_1; \ R_{a2} + P_2 \geq T_2; \ R_{b2} - P_2 \geq T_2$$

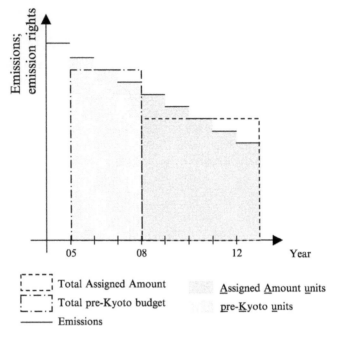

Figure 13.3. Permit budget prior and during the first commitment period.

First-order conditions are given in annex 3. Problem (3) solves as:

$$R_{a1} = \frac{2\alpha_b}{\alpha_a + \alpha_b} T_1; \quad R_{b1} = \frac{2\alpha_a}{\alpha_a + \alpha_b} T_1; \quad \pi_1 = \lambda_{a1} = \lambda_{b1} = \frac{4\alpha_a\alpha_b}{\alpha_a + \alpha_b} T_1;$$

$$P_1 = \frac{(\alpha_a - \alpha_b)}{\alpha_a + \alpha_b} T_1$$

$$R_{a2} = \frac{2\alpha_b}{\alpha_a + \alpha_b} T_2; \quad R_{b2} = \frac{2\alpha_a}{\alpha_a + \alpha_b} T_2; \quad \pi_2 = \lambda_{a2} = \lambda_{b2} = \frac{4\alpha_a\alpha_b}{\alpha_a + \alpha_b} T_2;$$

$$P_2 = \frac{(\alpha_a - \alpha_b)}{\alpha_a + \alpha_b} T_2$$

(4)

where λ = Lagrange multiplier.

As we can see, the quantity of PKUs purchased by country a depends on the reduction obligations and the abatements costs in the two countries. Even though being in compliance with the pre-Kyoto target, emissions are less reduced in the buying country in the pre-Kyoto period than without any linkage of the trading schemes. As permits are bought, country a ultimately finances the emissions reduction in country b without obtaining anything in return. It could not even state that it had made *demonstrable progress* in emissions reductions. Consequently, government a may argue for weak reduction obligations in the pre-Kyoto period or insist on a transfer of AAUs in order to benefit in some way. This point is analyzed in the next section. Note, however, that this system would be cost-efficient from a global climate policy perspective.

AAU-based international emissions trading before 2008   We still assume that the national total budgets are consistent with the Kyoto targets.

As a consequence of the aforementioned "subsidy effect" we now assume that the buying country demands a transfer of an equal quantity of AAUs with each PKU bought from the other country. As emissions must only be "backed up" by AAUs from 2008 on, they can be used for any trading scheme prior to the start of the Kyoto scheme. They do not have to be redeemed at the end of 2007, for instance. Thus, the total quantity of AAUs will not change as a result of their use in early trading schemes. However, ownership will change.

We consider the aforementioned by changing the budget constraints in (2). Any permit bought (sold) in period 1 is added (subtracted) in the second period. (Note that this is not banking in the traditional sense). The amended constraints are:

$$R_{a1} + P_1 \geq T_1; \ R_{b1} - P_1 \geq T_1; \ R_{a2} + P_2 + P_1 \geq T_2; \\ R_{b2} - P_2 - P_1 \geq T_2 \tag{5}$$

See annex 4 for first-order conditions. The problem with constraints (5) solves as:

$$R_{a1} = \frac{2\alpha_b}{\alpha_a + \alpha_b} T_1; \ R_{b1} = \frac{2\alpha_a}{\alpha_a + \alpha_b} T_1; \ \pi_1 = \lambda_{a1} = \lambda_{b1} = \frac{4\alpha_a\alpha_b}{\alpha_a + \alpha_b} T_1;$$

$$P_1 = \frac{(\alpha_a - \alpha_b)}{\alpha_a + \alpha_b} T_1$$

$$R_{a2} = \frac{2\alpha_b}{\alpha_a + \alpha_b} T_2; \ R_{b2} = \frac{2\alpha_a}{\alpha_a + \alpha_b} T_2; \ \pi_2 = \lambda_{a2} = \lambda_{b2} = \frac{4\alpha_a\alpha_b}{\alpha_a + \alpha_b} T_2; \tag{6}$$

$$P_2 = \frac{(\alpha_a - \alpha_b)}{\alpha_a + a_b} T_2 + \frac{(\alpha_b - \alpha_a)}{\alpha_a + \alpha_b} T_1$$

Comparing (6) with (4) we can see that the quantity traded in period 2 (P_2) changes. As $\alpha_b - \alpha_a < 0$ by definition (abatement costs in country a are higher) the second term becomes negative and thus fewer permits are traded. Thus, with all other unknowns being unchanged the transfer of AAUs along with PKUs reduces the total cost in the buying country. The latter should argue for strong reduction obligations in the pre-Kyoto period (second term in P_2). On the other hand, total cost is increasing for the selling country which in turn should prefer the approach presented first (no AAU transfer).

Discussion and conclusion

If we take the results in (2), (4), and (6) and substitute them in the cost functions, we get the compliance costs for both countries (see annex 5).

We find that the buying country prefers the AAU-transfer to the no-AAU-transfer scenario. However, it prefers both approaches to the Kyoto-trading-only scheme as long as we assume that the government is interested in cost-efficient international climate policy instruments prior to the start of the first commitment period. It may, however, be reluctant to "subsidize" reductions in the other country without getting anything (but the *pre-Kyoto units*) in return.

The situation is different for the selling country: it prefers the no-AAU-transfer scenario to all other options. Furthermore, it favors the Kyoto-only approach over the AAU-transfer approach as additional costs from forgoing benefits from trading in the first period are over-compensated by reduced costs in the second period (see annex 5). Apart from this, the two countries have differing interests with regard to the stringency of the reduction obligation in period 1 (see Table 13.3).

One can see that there is an inherent conflict of interests between seller and buyer with regard to the transfer of AAUs in international emissions trading prior to 2008. Against this background, one may question whether governments will voluntarily decide to link their trading schemes prior to 2008.

Unfortunately, there is no information available on the marginal abatement costs for the targets set for Denmark or the UK. Thus, no recommendation to the two governments of a preferred approach is possible.

In October 2001 the European Commission presented a proposal for a mandatory emissions trading scheme within the EU (Commission, 2001).[26] Keeping the results given in Table 13.3 in mind, an obligation to participate will inevitably entail winners and losers among member states with regard to the compliance costs of Kyoto commitments and might even provoke resistance in the event that governments are aware of their positions.

Table 13.3. *Preferences for different approaches and stringency of reduction obligation under different design options for international emissions trading*

	Lifetime of investment: one period	
	Net buyer	Net seller
Support of different approaches		
Kyoto-only-trading	Low[a]	Medium
No-AAU-transfer	Medium[a]	High
AAU-transfer	High	Low
Preferred stringency of reduction obligation in period 1 for different approaches		
Kyoto-only-trading	Indifferent	Indifferent
No-AAU-transfer	Indifferent	Indifferent
AAU-transfer	Strong	Weak

Note: [a] Only if country is interested in cost-efficient international climate policy prior to 2008.

Summary

Before greenhouse gas emissions trading can start at the entity level, several design features have to be decided. Linking of these national schemes can result in increased cost-efficiency. But, as in sovereign nation-states these decisions may differ, the linkage may be prevented for technical reasons. Environmental integrity may also be affected depending on the design chosen.

The analysis reveals that potential technical obstacles can probably be overcome by incurring additional costs. This goes, for example, for differences in registry structures. Environmental integrity may easily be affected. If this is to be avoided, systems would have to be adapted, or linkage would not be possible.

For the only two existing schemes in Europe (Denmark and the UK), it is likely that linkage would be possible without causing any problems with regard to the two aforementioned aspects. The situation is, however, different from the economic point of view. Even though the overall cost-efficiency can be increased, the incidence of costs in the context of the Kyoto regime, which may start in 2008, suggests that governments could refrain from linking their schemes voluntarily prior to 2008: net buyers and net sellers do have opposing interests with respect to the transfer of AAUs. This also means that a mandatory linkage is likely to produce winners and losers among member states.

Annexes

Annex 1

General version of (2):

$$\min_{R_{i1},R_{i2},P_{i1},P_{i2}} C_i = \alpha_{i1} R_{i1}^2 + \pi_1 P_{i1} + \frac{\alpha_{i2} R_{i2}^2}{1+\delta} + \frac{\pi_2 P_{i2}}{1+\delta}$$

s.t.

$$R_{i1} + P_{i1} \geq E_{i0} + A_{i1}; R_{i2} + P_{i2} \geq E_{i0} + A_{i2}$$

where δ = discount rate, E = emissions, and A = permits allocated.

Annex 2

First-order conditions for (1), Kyoto trading only:

$$2\alpha_a R_{a1} - \lambda_{a1} = 0 \qquad 2\alpha_b R_{b1} - \lambda_{b1} = 0$$
$$2\alpha_a R_{a2} - \lambda_{a2} = 0 \qquad 2\alpha_b R_{b2} - \lambda_{b2} = 0$$
$$\pi_2 - \lambda_{a2} = 0 \qquad -\pi_2 + \lambda_{b2} = 0$$
$$R_{a1} - T_1 = 0 \qquad R_{b1} - T_1 = 0$$
$$R_{a2} + P_2 - T_2 = 0 \qquad R_{b2} - P_2 - T_2 = 0$$

Annex 3

First-order conditions for (2), Non-AAU-based PKU trading:

$$2\alpha_a R_{a1} - \lambda_{a1} = 0 \qquad 2\alpha_b R_{b1} - \lambda_{b1} = 0$$
$$\pi_1 - \lambda_{a1} = 0 \qquad -\pi_1 + \lambda_{b1} = 0$$
$$2\alpha_a R_{a2} - \lambda_{a2} = 0 \qquad 2\alpha_b R_{b2} - \lambda_{b2} = 0$$
$$\pi_2 - \lambda_{a2} = 0 \qquad -\pi_2 + \lambda_{b2} = 0$$
$$R_{a1} + P_1 - T_1 = 0 \qquad R_{b1} - P_1 - T_1 = 0$$
$$R_{a2} + P_2 - T_2 = 0 \qquad R_{b2} - P_2 - T_2 = 0$$

Annex 4

First-order conditions for (4), AAU-based PKU trading:

$$2\alpha_a R_{a1} - \lambda_{a1} = 0 \qquad 2\alpha_b R_{b1} - \lambda_{b1} = 0$$
$$\pi_1 - \lambda_{a1} = 0 \qquad -\pi_1 + \lambda_{b1} = 0$$
$$2\alpha_a R_{a2} - \lambda_{a2} = 0 \qquad 2\alpha_b R_{b2} - \lambda_{b2} = 0$$
$$\pi_2 - \lambda_{a2} = 0 \qquad -\pi_2 + \lambda_{b2} = 0$$
$$R_{a1} + P_1 - T_1 = 0 \qquad R_{b1} - P_1 - T_1 = 0$$
$$R_{a2} + P_2 + P_1 - T_2 = 0 \qquad R_{b2} - P_2 - P_1 - T_2 = 0$$

Annex 5

Country a (net buyer): Kyoto-only-trading:

$$C_a^{(1)} = \alpha_a T_1^2 + \alpha_a \left(\frac{2\alpha_b}{\alpha_a + \alpha_b} T_2 \right)^2 + \frac{4\alpha_a\alpha_b}{\alpha_a + \alpha_b} T_2 \frac{(\alpha_a - \alpha_b)}{\alpha_a + \alpha_b} T_2$$

No-AAU-transfer:

$$C_a^{(2)} = \alpha_a \left(\frac{2\alpha_b}{\alpha_a + \alpha_b} T_1 \right)^2 + \frac{4\alpha_a\alpha_b}{\alpha_a + \alpha_b} T_1 \frac{(\alpha_a - \alpha_b)}{\alpha_a + \alpha_b} T_1 + \alpha_a \left(\frac{2\alpha_b}{\alpha_a + \alpha_b} T_2 \right)^2$$
$$+ \frac{4\alpha_a\alpha_b}{\alpha_a + \alpha_b} T_2 \frac{(\alpha_a - \alpha_b)}{\alpha_a + \alpha_b} T_2$$

AAU-transfer:

$$C_a^{(3)} = \alpha_a \left(\frac{2\alpha_b}{\alpha_a + \alpha_b} T_1 \right)^2 + \frac{4\alpha_a\alpha_b}{\alpha_a + \alpha_b} T_1 \frac{(\alpha_a - \alpha_b)}{\alpha_a + \alpha_b} T_1 + \alpha_a \left(\frac{2\alpha_b}{\alpha_a + \alpha_b} T_2 \right)^2$$
$$+ \frac{4\alpha_a\alpha_b}{\alpha_a + \alpha_b} T_2 \left[\frac{(\alpha_a - \alpha_b)}{\alpha_a + \alpha_b} T_2 + \frac{(\alpha_b - \alpha_a)}{\alpha_a + \alpha_b} T_1 \right]$$

$$C_a^{(1)} > C_a^{(2)} > C_a^{(3)}$$

Country b (net seller): Kyoto-only-trading:

$$C_a^{(1)} = \alpha_a T_1^2 + \alpha_a \left(\frac{2\alpha_b}{\alpha_a + \alpha_b} T_2 \right)^2 \frac{4\alpha_a\alpha_b}{\alpha_a + \alpha_b} T_2 \frac{(\alpha_a - \alpha_b)}{\alpha_a + \alpha_b} T_2$$

No-AAU-transfer:

$$C_b^{(2)} = \alpha_b \left(\frac{2\alpha_a}{\alpha_a + \alpha_b} T_1 \right)^2 - \frac{4\alpha_a\alpha_b}{\alpha_a + \alpha_b} T_1 \frac{(\alpha_a - \alpha_b)}{\alpha_a + \alpha_b} T_1 + \alpha_b \left(\frac{2\alpha_a}{\alpha_a + \alpha_b} T_2 \right)^2$$
$$- \frac{4\alpha_a\alpha_b}{\alpha_a + \alpha_b} T_2 \frac{(\alpha_a - \alpha_b)}{\alpha_a + \alpha_b} T_2$$

AAU-transfer:

$$C_b^{(3)} = \alpha_b \left(\frac{2\alpha_a}{\alpha_a + \alpha_b} T_1 \right)^2 - \frac{4\alpha_a\alpha_b}{\alpha_a + \alpha_b} T_1 \frac{(\alpha_a - \alpha_b)}{\alpha_a + \alpha_b} T_1 + \alpha_b \left(\frac{2\alpha_a}{\alpha_a + \alpha_b} T_2 \right)^2$$

$$- \frac{4\alpha_a\alpha_b}{\alpha_a + \alpha_b} T_2 \left[\frac{(\alpha_a - \alpha_b)}{\alpha_a + \alpha_b} T_2 + \frac{(\alpha_b - \alpha_a)}{\alpha_a + \alpha_b} T_1 \right]$$

$$C_b^{(3)} > C_b^{(1)} > C_b^{(2)}$$

Notes

1 Including compatibility with existing regulation, equity, and competitiveness issues.
2 I.e. emissions per reference figure (e.g. tonnes of CO_2 per kWh).
3 This is indeed true, but only compared to the business-as-usual scenarios. Absolute emissions may, however, increase.
4 Bearing in mind the Kyoto targets for Annex B countries, these targets are already fixed. Governments now have to allocate targets to the participating and non-participating emitters.
5 "Participating," in this chapter, is understood as being obliged to surrender permits at the end of a compliance period. The question of who is allocated the permits at the beginning is – at least from a theoretical point – another issue.
6 For example, fuel producers/importers or fuel wholesalers.
7 However, even if purchase by non-participants is not allowed, they may find participating entities that will redeem permits for them.
8 For example, major parts of German industry oppose emissions trading as proposed by the EU Commission, while pointing out the successful voluntary agreement (BDI, VDEW, BGW, VIK 2002).
9 Combinations of these two basic options are also possible. For a detailed discussion, see IEA (1999).
10 Private systems exist, for example, within the companies BP and Shell.
11 The Dutch Erupt/Cerupt program (see http://www.carboncredits.nl/) cannot be considered as a trading scheme at entity level, even though it has been successfully implemented, with business being involved.
12 The system became operational only in 2001, as the European Commission raised a number of questions before approving the system in April 2000.
13 Total emissions from electricity production in Denmark strongly depend on exports to other Scandinavian countries that regularly face energy shortages in dry summers when the yield from hydro power stations is low.
14 I.e. low emitters (<100,000 tonnes of CO_2 per year) that only produce electricity are allocated permits.

15 The saving limit was set to 20 Mio. t CO_2 for each year until 2003.
16 This will be the case as long as the abatement costs are lower in the absolute sector.
17 Indirect emissions result from energy consumption (e.g. electricity) during the production of which GHG emissions were released. An emission factor of 0.43 g CO_2/kWh was laid down. Power generators are to restrict their involvement as direct participants to self-consumption or by taking on responsibility for other parties' emissions.
18 Government will decide on a case-by-case basis about entry into the scheme.
19 Thirty-four participants won the auction in March 2002. Emission reductions totalled about 4 million tonnes CO_2 equivalent.
20 There are some exemptions as, for example, the CH_4 emissions from landfill activities that are already covered by the Landfill Directive.
21 There are four kinds of accounts: compliance, trading, retirement, and cancellation accounts.
22 The Netherlands can be given as an example. Since they realized that meeting the Kyoto target at home would be quite expensive, they prepared the purchase of emission rights under the Kyoto provisions. This allows for increased emissions according to the no-Kyoto-trading case even before 2008. (See http://www.carboncredits.nl/ for further information.)
23 They represent the aggregated abatement cost functions of the participants in the national trading schemes.
24 The underlying model is taken from Rehdanz and Tol (2002) who study a one-period problem.
25 It is still not clear what legal status the permits will have (commodity, commercial paper, etc.).
26 As it is only now being implemented, we do not want to discuss the different design features.

References

AGE [Arbeits Gemeinschaft Emissionshandel] 2002a. "Bericht des Vorsitzenden der AGE über die Ergebnisse der Phase I, Arbeitsgruppe Emissionshandel zur Bekämpfung des Treihauseffektes (German Emissions Trading Group)." (http://www.bmu.de/download/dateien/emissionshandel_bericht_2001.pdf [accessed July 3, 2002]).
    2002b. "Materialienband zum Zwischenbericht 2001, Arbeitsgruppe Emissionshandel zur Bekämpfung des Treibhauseffektes (German Emissions Trading Group)." (http://www.ag-emissionshandel.de [accessed July 3, 2002]).
AGO 1999a. "National Emission Trading, Issuing the Permit." Discussion paper 2, Canberra: Australian Greenhouse Office, Canberra.
    1999b. "National Emission Trading." Discussion Paper 1–4, Australian Greenhouse Office, Canberra.
BDI, VDEW, BGW, VIK 2002. "Stellungnahme der deutschen Wirtschaft zum Richtlinien-Vorschlag für einen europaweiten Handel mit Treibhausgas-Emissionsberechtigungen." Berlin.

Buchan, D. 2002. "Companies agree first pollution permit swap," *Financial Times*, May 7, 2002.

CCAP 1999. *Identifying the Proper Incidence of Regulation in a European Union Greenhouse Gas Emissions Allowance System*. Washington, DC: Center for Clean Air Policy.

Commission [The Quota Commission, Norway] 1999. "Summary and Recommendations to the Ministry of Environment for the national trading for greenhouse gases." (http://odin.dep.no/md/engelsk/publ/rapporter/022021-020006/index-dok000-b-n-a.html [accessed February 5, 2002]).

Commission [European Commission] 2001. "Proposal for a Directive of the European Parliament and of the Council establishing a scheme for greenhouse gas emissions allowance trading within the European Community and amending Council Directive 96/61/EC." COM(2001) 581, final version dated October 23, 2001.

Council 2002. "Proposal for a Directive of the European Parliament and of the Council establishing a scheme for greenhouse gas emissions allowance trading within the Community and amending Council Directive 96/61/EC." Working Document ENV/02/08, Brussels: Council of the European Union.

DEA 1999. *The Electricity Reform – Agreement between the Danish Government, the Liberal Party, the Conservative Party, the Socialist People's Party and the Christian People's Party on a Legislative Reform of the Electricity Sector*. Copenhagen: Danish Energy Agency.

DEFRA [UK Department for Environment, Food and Rural Affairs]. http://www.defra.gov.uk/environment/climatechange/trading/index.htm.

Haites, E., and Aslam, M. A. 2000. *The Kyoto Mechanisms and Global Climate Change – Coordination Issues and Domestic Policies*. Arlington, VA: Pew center on Global Climate Change.

Haites, E., and Mullins, F. 2001. "Linking domestic and industry greenhouse gas emissions trading systems." Prepared for Electric Power Research Institute (EPRI), International Energy Agency (IEA), and International Emissions Trading Association (IETA).

Hauf, J. 2000. *The Feasibility of Domestic CO_2 Emission Trading in Poland*. Risø, R-1203(EN), Roskilde, Denmark: Risø National Laboratory.

IEA 1999. "An assessment of liability rules for international GHG emissions trading." Information Paper, International Energy Agency, Paris.

IPCC 2001. *Climate Change 2001 – The Scientific Basis*. Cambridge: Cambridge University Press.

Kerr, S. 1998. *The Allocation of Liability in International GHG Emissions Trading and the Clean Development Mechanism*. Resources for the Future (http://www.rff.org/).

MIES 2000. "Implementing an emissions credits trading system in France to optimize industry's contribution to reducing greenhouse gases." Final, MIES – Industry Working Group.

NRP 1995. "Tradable carbon permits: feasibility, experiences, bottlenecks." Dutch National Research Programme on Global Air Pollution and Climate Change, Bilthoven.

NZME 1998. "Technical design issues for a domestic emissions trading regime for greenhouse gases: a working paper." Ministry for the Environment (New Zealand) (http://www.mfe.govt.nz/about/publications/climate/climatechange.htm [accessed January 17, 2002]).

Queen 1999. "Act on CO_2 quotas for electricity production." (http://www.ens.dk/graphics/publikationer/laws/actonco2quotaforelectricityproduction.pdf [accessed September 2, 2002]).

Pedersen, S. L. 2000. "The Danish CO_2 emissions trading system," *RECIEL* 9: 223–31.

Rehdanz, K., and Tol, R. 2002. "On national and international trade in greenhouse gas emission permits." Discussion Paper (February 19, 2002), (http://www.uni-hamburg.de/Wiss//FB/15/Sustainability/Working%20Papers.htm [accessed February 25, 2002]).

UCTE (Union for the Co-ordination of Transmission of Electricity) 2000. "Physical electricity exchanges 2000." (http://www.ucte.org/Statistik/English/Default_Stat_E.htm[accessed August 24, 2001]).

UN 1995. "Controlling carbon dioxide emissions: the tradable permit system." United Nations Conference on Trade and Development (UNCTAD), Geneva.

WBCSD 2001. "The greenhouse gas protocol – a corporate accounting and reporting standard." World Business Council for Sustainable Development, Conches-Geneva.

14   Concluding observations

Bernd Hansjürgens

The Kyoto Protocol of 1997 brought climate policy onto the national and international agenda. To reach the Kyoto greenhouse gas emissions target of an overall reduction of 5 percent (from 1990 levels) among developed countries is, however, only a first step toward stabilizing the climate at a non-deleterious level. In the long term a much larger reduction of global emissions will be needed. Economists doubt that the goals of climate protection can be achieved in the frame of a "win-win" scenario, i.e. with gains for the economy *and* the environment, or without additional costs for society. As climate policy rarely provides a free lunch, the control of greenhouse gases is associated with costs and, thus, is likely to be a quite expensive task. It is therefore crucial to search for cost-effective policies for climate protection.

The analysis in this book indicates that tradable permits are the most suitable instrument for climate protection. Emissions trading has the potential to control greenhouse gas emissions at the lowest economic costs. The emission cap safeguards the environmental goals, while trading is a highly flexible and dynamic solution. It is also easily enforceable at the firm level: the monitoring and enforcement of an emissions trading scheme guarantees 100 percent compliance. This is almost impossible through command-and-control regulations, which still dominate in most fields of environmental policy. Emissions trading also changes the relationship between the regulator and the emitting firm. While in existing command-and-control policies the final responsibility for pollution control lies with the regulator, emissions trading schemes make business firms decide upon the how, where, and when of abatement. The regulatory influence of the government is limited to setting the emissions cap, and to monitoring and enforcement.

The chapters in this book analyzed emissions trading as a regulatory instrument for climate policy from various angles. Thus, emissions

The author would like to thank Reimund Schwarze and Frank Wätzold for valuable comments on an earlier draft of this chapter.

trading was compared with other regulatory instruments for the control of greenhouse gases. The US experiences in emissions trading and their implications for climate policy were discussed, as were the potential of relative targets and how a domestic carbon trading scheme in the United States should be designed. Finally, several chapters addressed various aspects of the emerging European market for CO_2.

Emissions trading works. There is plenty of experience with diverse existing emissions trading schemes, particularly in the USA (chapters 5 and 6).[1] For the newly introduced EU Emissions Trading System (ETS) (European Union, 2003a) it is too early to evaluate whether it will be successful or not. The centrally chosen design options, however, fulfill all prerequisites for a successful trading program (Kruger and Pizer, 2004). So there are reasons for being optimistic that this trading market will also work. The basis for this optimism lies in the following three arguments:

1 The comparison of instruments for climate protection reveals that, for a number of reasons, climate policy is a natural case for emissions trading.
2 With regard to the chosen design options for the European emissions trading market, important lessons from the US experience have been adopted. There is little reason to think that these design options would not work with regard to the ETS.
3 The European emissions trading scheme is an open, flexible, and simple solution. It is flexible in allowing for corrections of potential shortcomings of the program, and it is open to be extended to other greenhouse gases, sectors, and countries. It can (and should) be linked with other trading schemes, both on the European national level, and on the international (global) level.

As it is not possible to repeat all the arguments of the preceding chapters, the focus in the remainder of this conclusion will be on the analysis of the three above-mentioned arguments. They mark the most important general lessons of this book.

Climate policy as a natural case for emissions trading

In the field of climate policy there are several instruments on the political agenda, ranging from command-and-control measures and taxes to tradable permits. As chapter 2 pointed out, climate change could be tackled by a variety of instruments. However, climate policy is characterized by features which indicate that adoption of the instrument of emissions trading under real-world conditions is feasible and favorable.

The arguments in favor of this instrument are mentioned in several chapters of this book. They include the following.

Great differences in abatement costs. Textbook analysis tells us that market-oriented instruments such as taxes and tradable permits should be preferred. If abatement costs among the emitting sources vary considerably, then efficiency demands that taxes or tradable permits should be used to equalize marginal abatement costs. Global climate change is an excellent case for this. The marginal cost of abating greenhouse gases varies enormously within and between the sectors of the economy as well as between different regions (countries) of the world. This holds especially between industrialized countries on the one hand and economies in transition ("transformation countries") and developing countries on the other. However, it can also be seen within industrialized countries like the member states of the European Union where great differences in marginal abatement costs exist.

Absence of existing regulation. Emissions trading is thought to have great potential if polluters are given complete flexibility regarding the choice of cost-effective strategies for reducing emissions, i.e. if the pollutants of concern are not subject to existing regulations.[2] As far as climate protection is concerned, emissions trading is regarded as a favorable option because alternative regulatory measures to reduce greenhouse gases do not yet exist to a significant extent, and in those countries where such measures are already in place, they have mainly been implemented as voluntary agreements or taxes which, at least in principle, allow inclusion.

Uncertainty in damage costs. In the case of full information about the marginal costs and marginal benefits of abatement, prices (taxes) and quantities (tradable permits) lead to similar results. However, if uncertainty about marginal abatement costs is significant, and if expected marginal abatement costs are quite flat and marginal benefits of abatement fall relatively quickly, then a quantity instrument will be more efficient than a price instrument (Weitzman, 1974). In the climate change case, the damage functions are very hard to assess and highly controversial. On the one hand, some authors have pointed out that marginal benefits are relatively flat for a long-lived stock pollutant like CO_2 and marginal costs are relatively steep (Pizer, 2002, Newell and Pizer, 2003). In this case, price-based mechanisms should be preferred. On the other hand, there is some evidence for potentially major changes in the climate system when emissions increase, i.e. threshold effects, that are highly politically and economically relevant. In cases where such a threshold exists, a policy that sets a limit to emissions at "secure" levels can be justified.[3] An absolute standard is then needed (such as a capping of global greenhouse emissions). Thus, if emission goals are politically very important to fulfill, a tradable permit system has obvious advantages.

Measurability. Measurability of pollutants is a decisive precondition for the implementation of tradable permits. Measurability of greenhouse gases can be measured either directly as emissions or by using input factors (i.e. heat inputs) as proxies for the emissions quantities. CO_2, for example, is a pollutant which is relatively easy to measure because the CO_2 emissions of fossil fuels can be expressed via input–output ratios. Therefore, a carbon emissions trading scheme is easy to implement. The other greenhouse gases can be expressed in carbon equivalents. They are, however, not as easy to measure. In particular, the role of sources and sinks for greenhouse gases is difficult to determine. An extension of a CO_2 emissions trading market to other greenhouse gases is therefore faced with some difficulties. The choice between upstream and downstream systems is also determined by the complex balancing of incentives at the firm level and enforceability. As was determined in chapters 2 and 8, demanding that all carbon emissions from fossil fuel burning should be capped is very attractive from an environmental viewpoint. From a transaction-cost perspective, however, capping of all emissions could hardly be achieved by a downstream design. An upstream design, however, is more prone to distorted abatement incentives at the firm level (market failure).

Political feasibility. Emissions trading can also be seen as an adequate instrument for climate protection because the free allocation of permits (grandfathering) is a vehicle to reduce both the burden of emissions trading schemes for the participating firms and the political resistance of interest groups to the introduction of such an instrument.[4] Thus, although an auctioning of permits is favored in textbook economics (because of its higher economic effectiveness), grandfathering is the mechanism for the allocation of permits which is *politically* feasible.

Effects on innovation. With respect to innovation, the question of whether a tradable permit system is superior to emissions regulation or taxes is rather undecided. The reason is that we have only limited knowledge about the factors determining innovation. It can be expected that there is a multitude of factors that are decisive for the innovation activities of firms in an economy, among which regulation is only one factor (Porter and van der Linde, 1995, Jaffe and Palmer, 1997). Therefore, any conclusions about the innovation effect of emissions trading have to be drawn with care. While individual firms have stronger incentives for developing new technologies if market-based instruments such as taxes or tradable permits are used, the picture becomes somewhat puzzling if the potential gains from abatement for adopters are taken into account. As was demonstrated in chapters 3 and 4, emissions standards and emissions taxes provide stronger incentives for the diffusion of new abatement technologies than tradable permits. The latter instrument, however, whether auctioned or grandfathered, is dynamically efficient with regard to the underlying approach of standards and prices.

Uniformly mixed pollutants. The theory of emissions trading and the twenty years' experience of different forms of emissions trading reveal that this instrument is rather successful if the pollutant is uniformly mixed (i.e. if it is a homogenous good) and as long as environmental problems are not characterized by "hot spots" (i.e. if the environmental damage is not influenced by the regional distribution of emissions) (Tietenberg, 1985, Tietenberg, 1998). Because CO_2 is a uniformly mixed pollutant and the contribution of greenhouse gases to global warming does not depend on their location, climate protection is considered to be a most suitable candidate for emissions trading. This has a consequence for the design options of an emissions trading scheme: The existence of uniform mixed pollutants means that there is no reason to limit banking or borrowing.

In summary, these arguments lead to the conclusion that emissions trading is an excellent instrument for environmental policy and a natural case for climate policy. As was stated in chapter 6 by Denny Ellerman, "If ever there were an environmental problem designed to emissions trading, global warming is it."

Experiences from the United States and design options for Europe

Important lessons for emissions trading as an instrument for climate policy can be derived from recent experiences with existing emissions trading markets. The lessons from previous schemes can be applied to greenhouse gas emissions trading as a new field of application. Indeed, many design features of the newly emerging European emissions trading markets can be traced back to the US cap-and-trade systems, particularly the SO_2 Allowance Trading Program.

Important design features of the three US emissions trading cap-and-trade systems (the SO_2 Allowance Trading Program, the RECLAIM program, and the OTC NO_X Budget Program) and the EU trading schemes (Denmark, the UK, and the EU ETS) are summarized in Table 14.1.[5]

The table indicates that many design features of the US schemes have been adopted in the European trading schemes, particularly in the ETS (clear definition of rights, grandfathering as the allocation method,

Table 14.1. *Comparison of US and European emissions trading cap-and-trade systems*

	SO$_2$ Acid Rain	RECLAIM	OTC NO$_x$ Budget	Denmark	UK ETS	EU
Sectors covered	Electricity generators >25 MW	All fixed sources with emissions >4 tons	Electricity generators >15 MW	Electricity producers >100,000 tonnes CO$_2$/a	• "Direct Participants": emitters from various sectors; • "Climate Change Agreement Participants": industrial power consumers	Electricity producers and other combustion installations >20 MW; refineries, pig iron/steel, lime, cement clinker, glass, ceramics, paper/cardboard, pulp.
Gases covered	SO$_2$	SO$_x$, NO$_x$	NO$_x$	CO$_2$	CO$_2$, CH$_4$	2005–2007: CO$_2$; from 2008: all Kyoto gases
Duration	1995–2010	1994–2010	1999–2003	2001–03	2002–06 (to be replaced progressively by the EU scheme)	From 2005 on
Phased nature?	Phase I (until 1999) Phase II (from 2000)	No phases	No phases	No	No	More sectors and gases can be included after 2007

Table 14.1. (*cont.*)

	SO$_2$ Acid Rain	RECLAIM	OTC NO$_x$ Budget	Denmark	UK ETS	EU
Reduction Target	−50% (vs. 1980 by 2000, then constant)	−75% (NO$_x$), −60% (SO$_x$) (vs. 1994 by 2003, then constant)	−75% (vs. 1990 by 2003)	−27.1% (2001); −30.7% (2002); −34.0% (2003);	−13% for "direct participants"	−8%
Mandatory? Opt-outs?	Yes No	Yes No	Yes No	Yes No	No Not applicable	Yes For installations from 2005–07
Opt-ins?	Yes; in Phase I, early entry by Phase II units allowed (including re-exit)	Yes, for units <4 tons and public installations such as hospitals, but no re-exit allowed	Yes, in some states	No	Yes (via the auction for the direct participants)	Yes, for installation below the size thresholds from 2005–07
Number of covered units	Phase I: 263; Phase II: ca. 2000	40 (SO$_x$), 352 (NO$_x$)	>1000	8	32 ("Direct Participants"); ca. 5000 ("Agreement Participants")	ca. 10,000–12,000
Primary allocation	Grandfathering	Grandfathering	Grandfathering	Grandfathering	Grandfathering	Grandfathering (at least 95% in 2005–2007 and at least 90% from 2008)

Allocation metric	Benchmarking with heat input, one benchmark for all participants	Benchmarking based on fuel input or production output	Partly absolute emissions, partly (input- or output-) benchmarking	Absolute emissions 1994–98	In general, historic emissions; absolute emissions ("Direct Participants"), relative emissions with updating ("Agreement Participants")	Decided by each member state; state aid supervision by the European Commission
Extra allowances for new entrants?	Yes	Yes	Yes (in some states)	Yes	Not, in general, applicable (voluntary scheme)	Decided by each member state
Temporal flexibility	Banking, no borrowing	Neither banking nor borrowing	Banking with devaluation in cases of high banking rates; no borrowing	Nearly unlimited banking; no borrowing	Full banking; no borrowing	Full banking; no formal borrowing, but in effect possible from one year to the next

Table 14.1. (cont.)

	SO$_2$ Acid Rain	RECLAIM	OTC NO$_x$ Budget	Denmark	UK ETS	EU
Penalty for non-compliance	$2000 plus deduction from next year's allocation	Max. $500 for each non-compliance day, plus deduction from next year's allocation	Three times the current allowance price	40 DKK (ca. €5.4) per excess ton; no deduction from next year's allocation	• "Direct Participants": withdrawal of the incentive payments plus deduction from next year's allocation with a 30% surcharge • "Agreement Participants": withdrawal of the tax relief	€40 (2005–07), €100 (from 2008) per excess ton plus deduction from next year's allocation
Monitoring	Measuring and continuous reporting	Measuring and continuous reporting for main emitters; otherwise, calculation from emission factor and fuel consumption	Measuring and continuous reporting for acid rain units; for others, calculation from emission factors and fuel consumption	Calculation	Calculation or measurement	Calculation or measurement

voluntary provisions for opt-in and opt-out, banking and borrowing, and monitoring and enforcement) (see also Kruger and Pizer, 2004). Some of the US experience for carbon emissions trading should be reiterated in this final chapter, drawing particularly upon the detailed analysis in chapters 6, 8, 11, and 12.

Clear definition of rights. The right to emit must be clearly defined and not be based on a case-by-case approval. This is the big difference between the credit-based systems of the early 1970s and the cap-and-trade systems of today. The credit-based systems have not worked well, particularly because of the high transaction costs which were associated with the strong influence of the regulator. Clearly defined rights are the basis of all US emissions trading schemes as well as of the EU systems.

Grandfathering as the allocation method. With respect to the allocation method, experiences with existing trading markets reinforce what is acknowledged in the economic analysis of environmental policy instruments: the reduction of political resistance and the lowering of the burdens of an emissions trading scheme for the firms clearly indicates that grandfathering should be given priority over auctioning in practice. It is therefore not surprising that all existing cap-and-trade markets in the USA and Europe are dominated by grandfathering as the allocation method. The Directive for the EU ETS leaves the member states the opportunity to allocate "at least 95% of the permits (for the first trading period beginning in 2005) respective 90% (for the second trading period from 2008 on) via grandfathering to the emitting firms" (European Union 2003a). As the companies in the EU are in competitive markets, it is very unlikely that the member states will make use of the option to auction permits. Thus, a 100 percent grandfathering can be expected.

Provisions for voluntary opt-ins and opt-outs. Because the extension of the European Emissions Trading System is a prerequisite for increasing the number of participants, provisions offering additional options for voluntary participation can be a decisive element for such a system. Voluntary opt-ins generally improve the market performance. However, at least two conditions must be fulfilled. First, the transaction costs of integrating additional firms into the system should not be too high. For the US Allowance Trading program it was reported that the division of the market into two phases had led to a significant increase of administrative costs at the Environmental Protection Agency. According to McLean (1996, p. 148) 75 percent of total costs were caused by the division into two phases (see also Rico, 1995, p. 121). Second, because the potential of a later phase-in can have effects on a firm's decisions to abate, adverse selection must be taken into account. In addition, there might be an influence on the market price if opt-in or opt-out options are allowed.

Banking and borrowing. In order to achieve maximum cost savings, firms in an emissions trading scheme should be given the highest possible flexibility. No prescription should be made either with respect to the choice of abatement technology, or with respect to the time-scale of emissions reduction. Because the greenhouse gases accumulate in the atmosphere over decades or even centuries, the time-scale of reduction measures is not very significant. This implies that banking and borrowing should be allowed in greenhouse gas emissions trading. Banking, in particular, offers diverse benefits: it can dampen price fluctuations and serve as an accelerator of emissions reductions (see chapter 6).

Monitoring and enforcement. Compliance in a trading market is much more important than in a framework which is based on command-and-control measures. While the latter instrument may only fail in achieving the environmental objective, in a trading system the whole emissions trading market may collapse. Against this background, the important role of emissions monitoring and sanctions have been acknowledged both in the USA and the ETS. In an emissions trading market, 100 percent compliance with environmental goals can be achieved. This is a clear advantage of such a scheme compared to traditional command-and-control measures, which in many cases are characterized by undercompliance.

Politics do matter, but only in the design phase. The US experience indicates that politics matter, primarily in the phase of designing a tradable permit system. In particular, the initial allocation of permits is always the subject of intense political discussions and rent-seeking by interest groups. The experiences in the USA with the free allocation of allowances to firms show the deeply political nature of these processes (Kruger and Pizer, 2004). This could also be observed in the EU ETS where the national allocation plans of the fifteen member states had to be submitted to the European Commission by the end of March 2004 and where intensive rent-seeking by the affected industrial groups took place. However, once implemented, the influence of government authorities in an emissions trading scheme is quite limited. This represents a fundamental difference between emissions trading cap-and-trade systems and other regulatory instruments in environmental policy. Whereas in command-and-control systems (and still in credit-based emissions trading systems) the governmental authorities have a rather far-reaching responsibility for the whether, when, and how of emissions abatement, in a cap-and-trade system the entire responsibility is given to the affected firms. Thus, newly adopted emissions trading schemes will in the long run also change the role of regulators and regulated firms.

In addition to the US experience, there are at least two general lessons for carbon emissions trading which are influenced by the characteristics of the pollutants.

Sectors covered. Because reductions in the overall costs of emissions abatement depend on the number of participants and the differences in abatement costs among the emitting sources, it is obvious from an economic perspective that an emissions trading scheme should cover as many emitting sectors of the economy as possible. A broad approach is also supported by the models of cost savings which were published on behalf of the European Commission before the EU ETS was introduced. The cost savings are considerably higher if the trading market is not restricted to certain sectors.[6] However, the aim for a broad range of sectors to be covered by an emissions trading scheme has hardly been fulfilled in the design of the European ETS. Instead, an approach has been chosen which has a focus on power plants in the electricity sector (and some closely related sectors). Only about 45 percent of the CO_2 emissions and roughly one–third of the greenhouse gases of the fifteen (prior to May 2004) European member states are covered by this program. It has become clear that, in the long run, a CO_2 emissions trading system for the power sector alone cannot be the final answer (Svendsen and Vesterdal, 2003, p. 305) and that the scope of the program must be extended.

Upstream or downstream? The decision about the sectors to be involved in a CO_2 emissions trading scheme stands in close relation to the question of whether an upstream or a downstream system should be employed. As was shown in chapter 8, an economy-wide upstream system, which is applied not at the point of emission but at the point where fossil fuel enters the economy, has clear advantages from an economic perspective. Since all sectors of the economy could be included in this system, the price incentive could work across the entire economy. In addition, the requirements for monitoring the emissions seem easier to manage. However, in the EU another option was chosen. The EU decision for a downstream carbon emissions trading system was motivated by the idea of including emissions which emerge in industrial processes and leaving the system open for other greenhouse gases. The processes and also the other greenhouse gases would be difficult to measure; they are easier to monitor in a downstream system. This design feature can thus be explained as a consequence of the higher transaction costs which would emerge in an upstream system. In addition, the Kyoto Protocol follows the territoriality principle concerning emissions accounting, i.e. the emissions are attributed to the national inventory of the country where the fuel is combusted (chapter 11). This does not fit in with an upstream scheme.

In sum, it can be said that emissions trading is a highly promising policy instrument for climate protection. Many of the design features of the US emissions trading schemes have been adopted in the European Union and a lot of lessons have been learnt from the US schemes. The EU ETS will most probably lead to considerable cost savings. Against this background the new EU ETS is destined to be a success.

Prospects for emissions trading

In the United States, the development of climate policy in general and the role of emissions trading in particular can hardly be predicted. The USA is not willing to adhere to the absolute limits which are the basis of the Kyoto commitment. Instead, there is a much stronger focus on intensity targets (chapter 7). This can be explained by the higher rates of GDP growth in the USA than in the EU in the 1990s and at the beginning of the new century.

Nevertheless, it can be expected that the role of emissions trading as an instrument of climate policy will increase in the future, particularly in Europe. In this context, it is important to judge the ETS against the motivation to set the ground and take a first step towards a global greenhouse gas emissions trading scheme (chapter 11). A functioning European carbon emissions trading scheme will serve as a blueprint for company-based international emissions trading way beyond the European continent (e.g. Japan).

An important feature of the European ETS is that it is oriented toward a gradual extension over time to more sectors and to other gases. Such extensions are directed not only toward other geographical regions within and outside Europe, but also toward synergy with other emissions trading systems, and with project-based mechanisms such as Joint Implementation and the Clean Development Mechanism.

- With respect to its broader application, the ETS allows new member states and other states to take part in the EU trading.
- With respect to the linking of trading systems, the design options chosen must allow for a combination of different schemes. So far, this linkage is technically possible between the EU ETS and the national schemes in Denmark and the UK. It causes, however, additional

costs and produces winners and losers among the member states. (chapter 13).

- With respect to project-based mechanisms, the European Commission is currently developing a proposal for the linking of project-based credits from JI and CDM to the EU emissions trading system credits, with the aim of full exchangeability of these credits (DEFRA, 2003, European Union, 2003b).

These extensions indicate that the current EU trading system is the starting point which can lead to much wider applications. Such extensions must be implemented with caution. With every extension we enter a new field where our knowledge is limited. It is therefore important critically to analyze the extensions in detail.

Notes

1 For a deeper analysis, see Burtraw (1996), Ellerman *et al.* (2000), and Ellerman *et al.* (2003).

2 This is one of the reasons why, in the USA, some authors, at least at the beginning of the 1990s, had doubts whether the SO_2 allowance trading market would work properly. It was expected that owing to utility regulation in the energy sector, firms would not have enough flexibility to react according to abatement costs and allowance prices. See Bohi and Burtraw (1992) and Bohi (1994). Regulation in the utility sector may also have a negative influence on the transaction costs of emissions trading schemes (Stavins 1995).

3 It should be noted, however, that this view is only partly shared in the USA. As climate change is expected to affect the USA comparably modestly, the USA would be a loser from domestic mitigation policies. Therefore, adaptation to climate policy is possibly cheaper in the USA than mitigation (Steurer, 2003, p. 355).

4 The influence of rent-seeking by special interest groups on the US SO_2 program was described by Kete (1993). It was also demonstrated, on the basis of a political economy approach, by Joskow and Schmalensee (1998). In chapter 10 of this book this approach is applied in analyzing lobbying in the European ETS.

5 Table 14.1 is taken, in a slightly modified form, from Hansjürgens and Gagelmann (2003). The detailed explanation of the design factors and the sources for the table can be found there.

6 See the results of the PRIMES model in the study by Capros and Mantzos (1999). This study was, *inter alia*, the basis for the European Commission's decision to propose the EU ETS. On the basis of the PRIMES model, Svendsen and Vesterdal (2003) have shown that the cost savings of a EU-wide tradable permit system with a comprehensive coverage of emissions would be 32 percent (compared to a system with no trading between the member states), while the savings of a system containing only the electricity and steam sector would be 13 percent.

References

Bohi, D. 1994. "Utilities and state regulators are failing to take advantage of emissions allowance trading," *Electricity Journal* 7: 20–27.

Bohi, D., and Burtraw, D. 1992. "Utility investment behavior and the emissions trading market," *Resources and Energy* 14: 129–53.

Burtraw, D. 1996. "The SO_2 emissions trading program: cost savings without allowance trades," *Contemporary Economic Policy* 14: 79–94.

Capros, P., and Mantzos, L. 1999. *Energy System Implications of Reducing CO_2 Emissions – Analysis for EU Sectors and Member States by Using the PRIMES Ver. 2 Energy System Model*. Institute of Computers, Communications and Systems, National Technical University of Athens.

DEFRA (UK Department of Environment, Food and Rural Affairs) 2003. "Amendment to EU Emissions Trading Scheme – Linking the Kyoto Project Based Mechanisms with the European Union Emissions Trading Scheme." Unpublished manuscript, London.

Ellerman, A. D., Joskow, P. L., and Harrison, D. Jr. 2003. *Emissions Trading in the US. Experience, Lessons and Considerations for Greenhouse Gases*. Washington, DC: Pew Center on Global Climate Change.

Ellerman, A. D., Joskow, P. L., Schmalensee, R., Montero, J.-P., and Bailey, E. 2000. *Markets for Clean Air. The US Acid Rain Program*. Cambridge: Cambridge University Press.

European Union 2003a. "Directive 2003/87/EC of the European Parliament and of the Council of 13. October 2003 establishing a system for greenhouse gas emissions trading within the European Community and amending Council Directive 96/61/EC." *Official Journal*, L 275, October 25, 2003.

2003b. "Proposal for a Directive of the European Parliament and of the Council amending the Directive establishing a scheme for greenhouse gas emission allowance trading within the Community, in respect of the Kyoto Protocol's project mechanisms." COM (2003) 403 final, Brussels.

Hansjürgens, B., and Gagelmann, F. 2003. "CO_2-Emissionshandel – Ein umweltpolitisches Instrument auf dem Vormarsch" ("CO_2 emissions trading – an instrument in environmental policy on the advance"), *UmweltWirtschaftsForum* (Special Issue on Emissions Trading) 11: 4–8.

Jaffe, A. B., and Palmer, K. 1997. "Environmental regulation and innovation: a panel data study," *Review of Economics and Statistics* 79: 610–19.

Joskow, P. L., and Schmalensee, R. 1998. "The political economy of market-based environmental policy: the US acid rain program," *Journal of Law and Economics* 41: 37–83.

Kete, N. 1993. "*The politics of markets: the acid rain control policy in the 1990 Air Act amendments.*" Unpublished Ph.D. dissertation, Johns Hopkins University.

Kruger, J., and Pizer, W. A. 2004. *The EU Emissions Trading Directive: Opportunities and Potential Pitfalls*. RFF Discussion Paper 04-24, Washington, DC: Resources for the Future.

Concluding observations 237

Concluding observations 237

McLean, B. J. 1996. "*Evolution of marketable permits. The US experience with sulphur dioxide allowance trading.*" Unpublished paper, Environmental Protection Agency, Washington, DC.

Newell, R., and Pizer, W. A. 2003. "Regulating stock externalities under uncertainty," *Journal of Environmental Economics and Management* 45: 416–32.

Pizer, W. A. 2002. "Combining price and quantity control to mitigate global climate change," *Journal of Public Economics* 85: 409–34.

Porter, M., and van der Linde, C. 1995. "Green and competitive: ending the stalemate," *Harvard Business Review* 73: 120–34.

Rico, R. 1995. "The US allowance trading system for sulfur dioxide: an update on market experience," *Environmental and Resource Economics* 5: 115–29.

Stavins, R. N. 1995. "Transaction costs and tradable permits," *Journal of Environmental Economics and Management* 29: 133–48.

Steurer, R. 2003. "The US's retreat from the Kyoto Protocol: account of a policy change and its implications for future climate policy," *European Environment* 13: 344–60.

Svendsen, G. T., and Vesterdal, M. 2003. "Potential gains from CO_2 trading in the EU," *European Environment* 13: 303–13.

Tietenberg, T. 1985. *Emissions Trading: An Exercise in Reforming Pollution Policy.* Washington, DC: Resources for the Future.

1998. "Tradable permits and the control of air pollution," in H. Bonus (ed.), *Umweltzertifikate – Der steinige Weg zur Marktwirtschaft.* Berlin: Analytica, pp. 11–31.

Weitzman, M. 1974. "Prices vs. quantities," *Review of Economic Studies* 41: 477–91.

Index

For EU product safety concerns, contact us at Calle de José Abascal, 56–1°, 28003 Madrid, Spain or eugpsr@cambridge.org.

www.ingramcontent.com/pod-product-compliance
Ingram Content Group UK Ltd.
Pitfield, Milton Keynes, MK11 3LW, UK
UKHW042212180425
457623UK00011B/180